FAMILY COURT SOLUTIONS

DEFEAT NARCISSISTS, BULLIES, AND LIARS IN DIVORCE AND CUSTODY BATTLES

Winning the Battle for Your Future from
the Emotional High Ground

By Carl Knickerbocker, JD

@unapologeticparenting

FAMILY COURT SOLUTIONS
by Carl Knickerbocker, JD

Copyright © 2024 Carl Knickerbocker, JD

DEDICATION

To Leandra, my best friend and confidante,
who has traveled every step of this journey with me.

"Do the best you can until you know better.
Then when you know better, do better."

– Maya Angelou

TABLE OF CONTENTS

INTRODUCTION

"If you tell the truth, you don't have to remember anything."
– Mark Twain

Navigating family court is no walk in the park under normal circumstances, and it becomes an uphill battle when you're dealing with a high-conflict co-parent who thrives on chaos and manipulation. Or, as the saying goes, if it's a walk in the park, it's like Jurassic Park. Instead of raptors, you're facing high-conflict narcissists, false allegations, financial strain, manipulative legal tactics, and bullying. That's likely why you picked up this book.

Maybe you're tired of feeling one step behind in a twisted game you never signed up for. Maybe you'd rather be dealing with raptors than the drama, lies, and relentless underhanded tactics. Or maybe your primary concern is shielding your children from the brunt of this toxic conflict. Very likely, you're experiencing all of the above, and you're feeling exhausted from it all.

Whatever your reasons, you're in the right place.

In this book, *Family Court Solutions*, we will dive deep into a variety of strategies you can lean on as you face a high-conflict personality (HCP) in family court – particularly the charming yet frustrating subset of HCPs known as narcissists. You'll learn not just to survive but to thrive and emerge victorious from what may feel like the most mentally taxing, confusing, and emotionally exhausting battle of your life.

First, a disclaimer: While the goal of defeating a narcissist, bully, or liar – as promised in the subtitle – might suggest a fierce, no-holds-barred attack, the real promise of this book is to teach you smart, strategic warfare where your greatest weapon is your integrity. This guidebook offers a far more organized and targeted approach than what you see in the chaos of the typical family court circus. Your aim is to stay cool and collected, using logic over emotion (as tough as that may be), and consistently playing by the rules – even when your adversary and their allies do not.

Think of your position as defending your family's honor in a duel, where your primary weapons are matters of character and patterns of behavior. It's not just about throwing mud or winning by force; it's about leveraging your integrity to achieve victory.

Why focus on integrity? Because in the eye of the legal storm – the center ring of the circus – your behavior, both past and present, is under the microscope. Judges are keenly observant folks who can smell shenanigans and detect deceit from a mile away, and they don't like it. By ensuring your hands are clean, you elevate your standing in court, especially when the other party is stuck in the mud.

It's about being the bigger person, the adult in the dynamic, even when you feel the urge to kick and scream against taking the high road. Why take the higher path and focus on integrity when the other party is doing anything but behaving? Why stick to the rules when they seem to get away with flouting them? It's not easy, but as you'll see throughout this book, it's unequivocally worth it on every level.

In the chapters to follow, we'll cover how to document every sneaky move and blatant lie your HCP ex makes – not for the drama, but for the dossier. You'll become a pro at collecting compelling evidence, from text messages that scream "I'm unreasonable!" to subtler signs of manipulative behavior. You'll learn how to compile a stack of evidentiary bricks that can be assembled into the solid structure for your case.

And because we all know that family court isn't a quick sprint but a taxing marathon, I'll share strategies designed to help you keep your energy up and your spirit intact throughout the ordeal. After all, this isn't just a fight for your rights but for your sanity and peace of mind, too.

To this end, the book will cover three primary strategies that will ensure you are putting your best foot forward in family court:

- **Counter Tactics:** Get ready to learn the ins and outs of the narcissistic and high-conflict games, because understanding the playbook of an HCP puts you ten steps ahead. We'll dissect common manipulative tactics (brace yourself: It's almost like they all read the same manual!). More importantly, I'll share best practices for countering these tactics, helping you control the narrative and keep the truth front and center.

- **Evidence is King:** This isn't just about telling your side of the story; it's about effectively proving it. So often, people show up thinking they have a compelling case when all they really have are emotions and a stack of inadmissible and low-quality evidence. In the courtroom, well-documented evidence speaks louder than words (even if those words are dramatically delivered by your ex). We'll go through how to gather, organize, and present your evidence so clearly and convincingly that even the most skeptical judge will take notice.

- **Support Systems and Self-Care:** Lastly, but perhaps most crucially, we'll talk about taking care of yourself through this process. Dealing with an HCP can be draining, both emotionally and mentally. I'll guide you on how to build a support system and maintain your mental health. After all, what's the point of winning if you're too spent to enjoy the victory with your loved ones?

By the end of this book, you'll not only be more knowledgeable about the workings of family court and HCPs, but you'll also be armed with practical, actionable strategies to handle your case with confidence and skill. You'll be ready to face the court, backed by a clear conscience and a solid case.

So buckle up; it's going to be quite the ride – but I promise, you won't be riding alone. Let's get you prepped and ready to face the courtroom with something even better than a winning smile – a winning strategy.

Purpose of the Book

When you're caught in the emotional whirlwind of a family court dispute, especially one involving an HCP, it can feel like you've been thrust into a dramatic soap opera that you didn't even audition for. Family court litigation often feels like a grim episode of life that will never improve and never end.

The plot twists? Unpredictable and often illogical. The antagonist? Over-the-top and as deceitful as they are malicious. And the stakes? Higher than ever, particularly when the wellbeing of your children hangs in the balance.

That's where this book comes in: Consider it your opportunity to transform what feels like a downward spiral into a story of growth and personal triumph.

Family Court Solutions is crafted with a singular purpose: to equip you with the knowledge, strategies, and tools needed to navigate the treacherous waters of family court against an HCP, particularly one with significant narcissistic tendencies. It's designed to move you from helpless spectator to confident protagonist in your own courtroom drama, ensuring that you're actively managing and strategizing your legal journey, rather than merely reacting to events.

To further support your journey, I encourage you to explore the official companion guide, a comprehensive Mastery Workbook containing 100 powerful exercises designed to help parents build their case in family court. This guide complements the strategies discussed in this book, providing you with practical tools to reinforce your understanding and actions as you navigate this complex landscape.

At the heart of every strategy is not only knowing but understanding and accepting the reality of your opposing party. Here, that opposition is not just the familiar face of your ex-partner but the complex and often baffling behaviors typical of HCPs.

That's why the book begins with a clear overview of the problematic and highly narcissistic personality traits you can expect to encounter throughout the process. Chances are, the patterns you observe during litigation are the same behaviors you have seen them display for years and years. By understanding how HCPs consistently operate, what motivates them, and how they manipulate and play games, you can anticipate their actions and prepare effective responses, keeping yourself several moves ahead in this legal chess game.

Beyond understanding and acceptance, the purpose of this book is to equip you with practical tools for dealing with high-conflict and narcissistic opponents. From documenting communications to collecting tangible evidence, you'll learn how to build a case that is not only strong but also irrefutable. The aim is to build a case that's driven by facts and evidence, bullet-proof against impeachment, and compellingly clear.

Keep in mind that when dealing with HCPs in the courtroom, it's easy to feel overwhelmed by theatrics and lies. While the HCP may rely on loud outbursts and crocodile tears to win, the legal victory is often served to the party who exhibits the ability to think and demonstrate factual evidence most effectively.

That's why this book emphasizes strategic planning over emotional reactions. It's about making calculated moves that align with your long-term goals, securing the best outcome for you and your children rather than seeking temporary victories that merely feed ego and short-term desires.

Family court battles can be draining, not just financially but emotionally, physically, mentally, and spiritually. These conflicts can lead to illness and mental breakdowns, and too often leave parents traumatized and drained of resources. An essential aim of this book is to help you navigate these challenges while maintaining your integrity and mental health. Staying true to your highest values and maintaining a clear conscience are paramount, providing you with the moral high ground that can sway court opinions in your favor.

Ultimately, the purpose of this book is empowerment. Knowledge is power, and by the last page, you'll not only understand the legal battlefield – you will also feel equipped to assert your rights effectively and protect your interests vigorously.

So, as you turn these pages, think of each chapter as a step towards empowerment, a guide to dismantling the daunting façade of the HCP and reclaiming control of your narrative. You know the other party will do everything possible to mislead the court into believing a false narrative that serves their self-centered interests. The way to counteract that inevitability is to clearly and accurately present the realities of the situation and your proper behavior through facts and evidence.

This isn't just about surviving the ordeal of family court; it's about emerging victoriously, with your head held high and a brighter future ahead.

Mapping the Road Less Traveled

The recommendations in this book were developed after years of research, my almost two decades of professional experience as a litigator, and my own painstaking experience with a high-conflict divorce and custody battle, which taught me how to protect my family's future during and after a contentious court fight.

After experiencing firsthand how courts and legal professionals are often woefully unequipped to handle the unique challenges posed by HCPs, I created a community called Unapologetic Parenting, which offers a unique take on how to approach family court litigation as well as a new way of looking at co-parenting.

Unfortunately, the current model of trendy-trendy co-parenting does little to protect and heal families going through high-conflict divorce and custody battles. Instead, it leads to more conflict and enmeshment that benefits the financial vultures of the divorce industry: ill-intentioned attorneys, therapists, and mediators who can be found circling divorce courts and profiting from the drama that HCPs inflict on vulnerable families.

Likewise, the conventional approach to family court litigation often causes more harm than good. The family law field is populated by many lawyers and professionals who hardly seem to have their clients' best interests at heart and often lack a clear understanding of ethical, procedural, or personal responsibilities.

When my first book, *The Parallel Parenting Solution*, was released in 2021, it provided an alternative path for families dealing with HCPs in the courtroom, and readers flocked to my Instagram page (@UnapologeticParenting) in droves. The book has remained a #1 bestseller in multiple categories on Amazon for over three years. *The Parallel Parenting Solution* discusses HCPs in depth and offers what I consider the most effective model of co-parenting, based on individual accountability, autonomy, and well-defined boundaries.

This book, *Family Court Solutions*, builds on the lessons I learned in navigating the road less traveled – characterized by fewer conflicts and reduced litigation – and takes it one step further by addressing your family's specific needs in the courtroom. By following these recommendations, you will not only protect yourself and your family from the manipulations of HCPs but also improve your chances of success when your day in court arrives. Ultimately, you will gain greater peace of mind after your legal victory, knowing you acted with integrity.

Common High-Conflict Behaviors in Family Court

Dealing with a high-conflict personality (HCP) in the high-pressure environment of family court can be one of life's most daunting challenges. It's hands-down one of the worst experiences someone can ever go through. The entire process is essentially a traumatic event and can sometimes last for years.

Individuals with HCP traits often employ a range of predictable and common manipulative tactics that can leave even the most prepared individuals feeling confused, overwhelmed, and emotionally drained. Facing a true HCP opponent can feel like having your mind and reality undermined at every turn. They lie straight-faced to the court and seem to sincerely believe their own delusions. They falsely accuse. They say one thing, do another, and then blame you for everything. This book will explore these dysfunctional dynamics in greater detail, highlighting the specific challenges they pose within the legal system while equipping you with strategies to navigate these turbulent waters.

Among the manipulative tactics employed by HCPs, high-conflict behaviors typically manifest as contentious, manipulative, and destructive interactions. HCPs may exhibit rigidity, emotional volatility, and a refusal to acknowledge differing viewpoints, leading to persistent blame-shifting and a complete lack of accountability for their actions. These traits can significantly derail legal proceedings and create emotional distress.

Among their manipulative strategies, HCPs often twist facts to suit their narrative, employing tactics such as lies, omissions, and misrepresentations to present themselves favorably or discredit others. They may also exaggerate or fabricate information to bolster their claims, sending child protective services and law enforcement on wild goose chases based on callous and outlandish false allegations.

Victim positioning is another common tactic, wherein HCPs cast themselves as the wronged party to elicit sympathy and sway legal decisions in their favor. By feigning victimhood, they can justify unreasonable demands and manipulate perceptions within the courtroom.

Gaslighting is yet another psychological manipulation frequently used by HCPs to destabilize their opponents. In a family court context, this involves making others doubt their memories or perceptions, insisting that events occurred differently than remembered, thereby creating confusion and uncertainty. They often turn this tactic on their own legal counsel, mental health professionals, and the court itself, making everyone question what reality truly means after hearing so many shifting stories.

Additionally, HCPs love to exploit emotional reactions to gain an advantage in disputes. By provoking feelings of anger or distress in their opponents, they can trigger emotional outbursts that undermine credibility, especially in the eyes of judges and mediators who value composure. They antagonize and provoke until they elicit an emotional reaction, then immediately switch to the victim role, using your reaction as evidence that you are the one with all the problems.

As we delve into each of these tactics throughout the book, we will provide insights and recommendations for countering these manipulative behaviors, empowering you to advocate effectively for yourself and your children.

Strategies for Managing High-Conflict Behaviors

Navigating family court with an HCP requires mental and emotional endurance as well as a clear, rational strategy. This book is designed to equip you with effective methods to counteract the disruptive tactics employed by these challenging and toxic personalities.

From maintaining a composed demeanor to utilizing legal and psychological resources, these strategies are vital for managing the practical aspects of your case while mitigating the emotional toll of a family court battle. Here, you will learn how to stay two steps ahead, ensuring that your responses are rational and calculated, your evidence is meticulously prepared, and your emotional well-being is protected and supported.

You will learn to transform your approach from reactive to proactive, empowering you to handle high-conflict situations with confidence and integrity, ultimately steering your legal journey toward a more favorable outcome. Dealing with an HCP opponent means engaging with someone who consistently displays patterns of dysfunctional behaviors and lacks accountability for their actions. You, on the other hand, will be the party who stands in front of the court with clean hands and a clear sense of personal accountability.

I will discuss the importance of maintaining thorough records of all interactions, including saving texts, emails, and voicemails, and documenting verbal communications. Proper documentation can help expose the reality of the situation in court, countering the manipulations of a high-conflict ex. For every lie they tell, there's often a screenshot to contradict it. This strategy serves as your foundational defense against manipulation and falsehoods. Effectively managed documentation not only strengthens your case but also boosts your confidence and readiness in handling the legal challenges posed by HCPs.

A point worth repeating is that tangible and direct evidence is key. The HCP operates in the realm of subjectivity and distortion; therefore, the strongest attack is one based on objective evidence, direct testimony, and blazing clarity.

Moreover, I will review a two-pronged approach that includes both legal and psychological preparation – the twin pillars essential for successfully navigating family court against a high-conflict individual.

Legally, it is imperative to work with an attorney who specializes in high-conflict cases and understands the nuances of family law. Sadly, this is often easier said than done, and finding an attorney who understands both family law intricacies and HCPs often feels like searching for a unicorn. However, such a lawyer can provide wise and rational guidance on legal strategies, help interpret complex legal principles, and prepare you for the potential deceptive maneuvers of the opposing party. High-quality preparation includes rehearsing your testimony, understanding the likely legal arguments of the other side, refining your impeccable communications and behaviors, and connecting you with mental health support.

Psychologically, preparing yourself involves building resilience and managing stress. It requires education about and radical acceptance of what you're dealing with in the form of an HCP opponent and co-parent. Engaging with a therapist or coach who has significant and credible experience in dealing with high-conflict situations can be immensely beneficial. A specialized coach or therapist can offer coping strategies to handle emotional provocations, help maintain your mental health, train communication and response skills, define boundaries, and provide a supportive space to process the intense emotions that often accompany these court battles.

Together, both forms of preparation empower you to approach your case with a clear, focused mind and a robust emotional foundation.

Staying above the fray is also critical when dealing with HCPs in family court. It means not stooping to the other party's level and keeping your hands clean. As difficult as it might be, maintaining a calm and composed demeanor in all interactions related to the case – and demonstrating impeccable behavior –

is paramount to your success. In my experience, when clients tank their own cases, this is precisely where they fail: They refuse to follow the orders, can't control their reactions, and lash out. In other words, they act like out-of-control HCPs and are often treated as such.

The moral of the story? Control yourself. This is especially true in the courtroom or under the scrutiny of a court-professional such as a custody evaluator, Guardian ad Litem, or minor's counsel. Demonstrating impeccable long-term behavior is the key to presenting yourself as reasonable and reliable, contrasting sharply with the characteristic erratic and impulsive behaviors of the HCP.

Remember, HCPs often seek to elicit emotional responses that they can use against you in court to undermine your credibility. They provoke to drag you down to their level or lower. By remaining calm and composed, you present yourself as a rational and stable individual, which can significantly influence the court's perception in your favor.

Practically, this means carefully considering your reactions and responses in all interactions, whether in person, on the phone, or through written communications. Avoid engaging in arguments or responding impulsively to accusations or inflammatory remarks. Instead, take a measured approach by pausing to reflect before responding, sticking to facts, and avoiding emotional language. Set rules for yourself that define your standards for whether, when, and how you communicate.

Employing this level of self-discipline not only strengthens your position in the eyes of the court but also protects your mental well-being during the stressful legal process. By clearly defining your rules and standards for communication with the other parent, you can avoid reacting to every message that comes in. Instead, you apply your rules and leave it at that.

Furthermore, educating yourself on legal rights and processes is essential when navigating family court, particularly to set realistic expectations about potential outcomes. It is easy to find a lawyer who will tell you what you want to hear and promise you the sun, moon, and stars... after you hand over a hefty retainer, of course. Having unrealistic expectations is one of the most common and damaging driving factors in high-conflict custody litigation. In reality, the vast majority of family court cases should not exist – not because everyone should hold hands and be happy-happy co-parents, but because they lack a factual or legal basis to exist in the court system. However, few have the ethics or awareness to shut down pointless litigation before it begins.

Understanding the legal landscape can empower you to make informed decisions and anticipate possible moves by the opposing side. Knowledge truly is power in these situations, allowing you to discern what battles are worth fighting and which are likely to be futile based on legal precedents and the typical inclinations of judges.

It's important to recognize that family courts prioritize the best interests of children and aim for fair resolutions, but the outcomes may not always align with your initial hopes and desires. Generally, the courts will prioritize public policy, which typically promotes consistent parent-child contact with both parents. In other words, most family courts lean toward equalizing parenting time rather than tipping the scales hard in one direction or another. The public policy of most states aims for balanced time, either in a 50/50 schedule or something close to it. The parent who stands before the court wanting to increase their parenting time has a much lower burden than the parent trying to take away time from the other side.

By becoming informed about your legal rights and the common procedures in family court, you can make strategic decisions based on probable outcomes. For example, demanding full custody with no visitation for the other parent might be unrealistic unless there's substantial evidence of harm or neglect. Demanding extreme custody outcomes that contradict state policy and the court's typical inclinations – absent compelling evidence – only serves to make you appear as the high-conflict party who does not have the children's best interests in mind. Making demands that are misaligned with state policy, probable outcomes, and factual evidence is often a recipe for failure on multiple fronts.

The book also emphasizes leaning on a support system of friends, family, and professionals in order to provide the emotional sustenance needed to navigate this challenging journey, especially when facing an HCP. Each plays a crucial role in providing emotional sustenance and practical assistance.

Family and friends can offer a listening ear and a comforting presence, helping to alleviate the isolation that often accompanies legal disputes. They can also assist with logistical needs, such as childcare or transportation, which can be particularly helpful during court dates or meetings with your attorney. Find those around you who are grounding, supportive, and rational, and lean on them for guidance and support.

Support groups provide a platform to connect with others who are in similar situations, allowing for the sharing of experiences and strategies that can be both enlightening and empowering. A word of caution: There are innumerable online support groups and social media pages rife with terrible advice and harmful strategies. Professional coaches, counselors, or therapists – especially those experienced in dealing with high-conflict personalities and scenarios – can help you manage stress and emotional upheaval, ensuring you maintain your psychological health throughout the process. A combination of high-quality family and professional support is often the best medicine.

Together, these support networks reinforce your resilience and enable you to navigate your legal journey with greater confidence and stability.

Importance of Personal Accountability and Impeccable Behavior

In the emotionally charged arena of family court, particularly when entangled in disputes with HCPs, the importance of personal accountability and impeccable behavior cannot be overstated. For a highly narcissistic individual, accountability is like garlic to a vampire; true HCPs are repulsed by it. To them, they have done no wrong, can do no wrong, and any faults are always your responsibility. From the court's perspective, it is rare to encounter someone who has their act together and presents themselves professionally and with integrity. You – who you are and how you conduct yourself, both inside and outside the courtroom – serve as the first and most compelling exhibit in your case.

This extended focus on character and conduct is vital not only because it influences the perceptions of judges and opposing counsel but also because it fundamentally shapes the course and outcome of your legal battle, your mental health, and your family's future.

Why Personal Accountability Matters

Personal accountability refers to your ability to take responsibility for your actions and their outcomes, as well as your willingness to abide by legal and ethical standards. In family court, this is especially important, as the court's primary mandate is to make decisions that best serve the interests of children, which includes ensuring they are placed in a stable, responsible, and nurturing environment.

Judges often view each parent's behavior as a reflection of their parenting style and their capacity to provide a supportive home life. If you engage in actions that could be perceived as irresponsible or antagonistic – such as violating court orders, engaging in verbal altercations, or demonstrating unreliability in visitation schedules – it can significantly tarnish your credibility and hurt your case.

Conversely, showing a consistent pattern of responsible, composed behavior can significantly boost your standing in any legal proceeding. This may sound deceptively simple, like beating a dead horse, but the encouragement to focus intensely on impeccable behaviors and accountability goes far deeper than simply being a good person.

Consider it from the court's perspective: What does the judge see day in and day out? They see people who generally can't get their acts together, people who hurt their kids, people who don't know how to conduct themselves professionally (sometimes including the lawyers), and people who deserve to go to jail. They observe people who are dysregulated and traumatized, who appear unable to function healthily without the court's intervention.

Into this scenario then steps a person who is on-point, striving to comply with the court orders by acting rationally, owning their errors, and demonstrating zero concern for the court. This person instantly stands out to the court, because they are aligned with everything the court ultimately wants to see.

The Power of Impeccable Behavior

In this context, impeccable behavior serves as a breath of fresh air for the court; however, it demands more than simply avoiding wrongdoing – it requires actively cultivating a persona that exudes integrity, respectfulness, and maturity. In legal disputes, particularly those involving custody, demeanor can often speak louder than testimonies. For instance, if you consistently demonstrate patience and respect during court proceedings, even in the face of provocation, you signal to the court your capability to handle parenting under stress.

Keep in mind that impeccable behavior extends to all forms of communication related to the case, including written, verbal, and digital interactions. Avoid disparaging the other party publicly or privately, as these actions can be presented in court as examples of your character and potentially used against you.

In an era where emails, texts, and social media posts can be subpoenaed as evidence, maintaining professionalism and decorum in every exchange is crucial. In today's society, there is essentially no such thing as privacy, especially online. Posts and comments shared in a private group often make their way onto the exhibit list. That one scathing message you decide to send late at night to the other parent is almost guaranteed to be waved in front of the judge.

Adopting a strategy of impeccable behavior is a tactical advantage. You are your first and most compelling exhibit. Your lived experience serves as your best offense and defense, while the HCP's lived experience often becomes their greatest risk and liability.

Demonstrating Personal Accountability and Impeccable Behavior

In court, your demeanor and conduct are under constant scrutiny, which makes "who you are and how you present yourself" the initial and most critical Exhibit A in any court proceeding.

Prioritizing personal accountability and maintaining impeccable behavior not only positions you favorably in the eyes of the court during the current conflict but also lays a robust foundation for all future interactions and relationships once the courtroom battles have subsided. This strategic focus extends beyond merely navigating legal hurdles; it aims to cultivate an environment of respect and trust that fosters healthier post-court dynamics.

Throughout this book, we will explore numerous ways you can demonstrate personal accountability and impeccable behavior, which are the essence of integrity:

1. **Follow Legal Advice and Court Orders**: Always adhere to the guidance of high-quality legal counsel and comply with any directives and orders from the court. Taking a disciplined approach to compliance can significantly influence the outcome of your case. I've seen too many people scuttle an otherwise strong case by their failures in this area. When your HCP opponent consistently fails to comply with orders and behaves poorly, your own failure to follow the court's directives essentially gives

them a get-out-of-jail free card. Non-compliance not only harms your case but also strengthens theirs.

2. **Document Your Actions**: Keeping meticulous records of your compliance and interactions is crucial when navigating the complexities of family court, particularly in high-conflict scenarios. Thorough documentation can significantly bolster your credibility and support your claims, showcasing your commitment to acting in the best interests of your children. Here, the emphasis is on preparing to clearly demonstrate facts and reality through data points and evidence.

3. **Engage Constructively**: Engaging constructively, whether in mediation or in family court, especially amid a high-conflict dispute, requires a focused effort to contribute positively to discussions and negotiations, regardless of the provocations you face. Demonstrating a commitment to fairness and respect during legal proceedings can help set a tone for future interactions, particularly in co-parenting arrangements. This not only benefits your legal standing but also fosters a more stable and supportive environment for your children.

4. **Seek Support**: Managing your behavior in stressful situations can be challenging. Seeking support during the stressful and often overwhelming process of navigating family court is essential for maintaining your emotional and psychological well-being. This support can come from various sources, each providing unique benefits

to help you manage stress, anger, or frustration. Many clients find it beneficial to work directly with a coach who is well-versed in effective co-parenting and communication skills.

5. **Reflect Well Publicly and Privately**: Consistency in your public and private persona is key. Ensure that your social media profiles and public behaviors reflect the same values and maturity you profess in court. This includes interactions with your children, ex-partner, and even mutual acquaintances. Consistency in your demeanor and ethics, regardless of the audience, reinforces your credibility and demonstrates your genuine commitment to high standards of conduct. When embroiled in a family court battle, your entire life is under the microscope. What you say at church can end up being repeated in court. What you post as a joke online may come to haunt you later as a character assassination attempt.

Demonstrating personal accountability and impeccable behavior not only has immediate benefits in court but also yields long-term advantages for your relationships, particularly with your children. It sets a strong example for them in handling adversity with grace and integrity, as well as managing emotions under pressure. When dealing with an unyielding HCP, even one parent who acts reasonably and amicably can have a long-term positive effect, contributing to the development of children into well-adjusted, resilient individuals.

Focusing on integrity is not just about winning a case in the traditional sense; it's about winning the fight for your family's future from the emotional high ground, which is a far more profound and sustainable victory over the long run. By adhering to high standards of personal conduct, you demonstrate to the court – and more importantly, to your children! – that you are committed to principles of fairness, respect, and integrity. This commitment influences not only legal outcomes but also the personal and interpersonal aftermath of the proceedings.

In essence, by embodying accountability and impeccable behavior, you aim to win not just a case, but also respect and trust, paving the way for a better outcome for everyone, especially the children, whose lives are most affected by the results of family court proceedings.

Achieving such a holistic victory is far more rewarding and enduring, setting a precedent for all your future personal and interpersonal engagements.

And it's all possible when you focus on winning with integrity!

Yours very truly,

Carl Knickerbocker, JD

2024

1

UNDERSTANDING HIGH-CONFLICT PERSONALITIES

Stepping into a family court scenario with a high-conflict personality (or HCP) can feel akin to walking into a storm: unpredictable, confusing, and often overwhelming. And in this storm, there may be sharks – sharks in suits. Before you can effectively navigate this storm, it's crucial to understand the elements you're facing. This chapter aims to unpack the complex psychological landscape of HCPs, particularly those with narcissistic traits commonly encountered in contentious family law disputes.

HCPs are not just difficult people or simply disagreeable co-parents. They are individuals who consistently exhibit patterns of specific, disordered behaviors that routinely and needlessly escalate conflicts rather than resolve them. Typically, these personalities demonstrate excessive emotional responses, a distorted sense of their own importance, and an inability to consider others' perspectives. They often lack accountability for their actions and seem to sincerely believe in events and realities that contradict the evidence. Understanding these traits is not about labeling or diagnosing your opponent in court – that is a job for professionals – but about preparing yourself to interact with them effectively, anticipating potential challenges, and strategizing accordingly.

At the heart of many high-conflict personalities and interactions are traits that are consistent with narcissistic personality disorder (NPD) and other Cluster B personality disorders. NPD is characterized by an inflated sense of self-importance, a deep need for excessive attention and admiration, troubled relationships, and a lack of empathy for others, among other traits. While not all high-conflict individuals have NPD, many exhibit enough narcissistic traits to complicate legal interactions significantly. Whether or not your ex has narcissist traits or some other flavor of contentious tendencies, family courts are packed with HCPs, and they tend to manipulate facts, project their own shortcomings onto others, and use communication as a weapon rather than a means of understanding.

It's important to emphasize that the focus is on consistent patterns of behavior. All people act in self-centered ways from time to time. We have all experienced periods of attention seeking and troubled relationships. We have all been dishonest at times, and we have all broken rules. However, this discussion centers on those individuals who seem to make a career out of these traits. They consistently and predictably exhibit these behaviors, and their patterns do not change. They may manage to clean up their profiles for a few months to put on a good show, but it's only a matter of time before their masks fall and the patterns emerge again in full force.

HCPs are identified by their long-standing and consistent patterns of combative, disordered, and damaging behaviors.

Definition and Characteristics of an HCP

Understanding the characteristics of an HCP is essential for anyone entering a legal battle or dealing with high-conflict situations. To effectively manage these interactions, you need to recognize and understand what's broken in order to know which tools to use. For the purposes of this book, we will emphasize the traits of narcissists, as these traits are nearly universal in HCPs, and because narcissistic personality traits tend to wreak the most havoc in family courts. Simply put, HCPs are not always diagnosable narcissists, but individuals with significant narcissistic traits are always high conflict.

It doesn't matter whether your ex is a narcissist, a bully, a liar, or some combination of these. A thorny rose by any other name is still a pain. It also doesn't matter whether they have been formally diagnosed with a personality disorder or mental illness. What matters is whether your ex exhibits high-conflict traits that cause significant amounts of conflict and chaos. If the answer is "yes" – even if you simply *suspect* it is – then you're in the right place.

Not all individuals who exhibit high-conflict traits meet the full criteria for a personality disorder; however, understanding the following core characteristics of HCPs is crucial for anticipating and mitigating their impact in family court settings.

Grandiosity

Grandiosity is the hallmark of HCPs and narcissism and is one of the most identifiable and impactful characteristics in family court disputes. Individuals display an exaggerated sense of self-importance and believe they are superior to others. They see themselves as the only ones who know the best interests of the children and often exaggerate their achievements and talents, expecting to be recognized as superior even without corresponding accomplishments.

Those exhibiting this trait sincerely think they are the most brilliant people in the room, especially in the courtroom. They believe they know better than doctors, lawyers, judges, and anyone else who disagrees with them. Grandiosity may manifest as seemingly boundless self-confidence, but it is often fragile under criticism. This inflated self-perception is not merely confidence; it represents a pervasive overestimation of one's capabilities and status.

In legal settings, grandiosity can lead to several problematic behaviors. An HCP might make outrageous claims about their financial contributions to the family or their role in the upbringing and welfare of the children, often overshadowing or completely disregarding the contributions of the other parent.

The grandiose parent sees themselves as the sole contributor, while the other parent is chopped liver.

Their grandiose view of themselves can also make them more likely to dismiss legal advice or feedback that doesn't align with their self-image. In trials of serial killers and sociopaths, a consistent observation is that they often believe they understand the legal system better than anyone else, going against their legal counsel. They may even believe they understand the legal process better than their attorneys or that the judge will naturally favor them once their "obvious" merits are presented. It's not uncommon for them to fire their legal representation close to the trial, believing they alone know what to do.

Delusional Fantasies

HCPs often indulge in delusional fantasies about unlimited success, power, brilliance, beauty, or ideal love. They may believe they are unique or special and can only associate with other high-status individuals or institutions, revealing a profound disconnection from reality that shapes their interactions and expectations. They often engage in grand daydreams about their future, envisioning themselves with unparalleled success, influence, and control – whether it's vast wealth, supreme authority, or unmatched achievements.

In family court, such fantasies can lead to unrealistic and rigid positions in legal negotiations. An HCP might insist on full custody, convinced that they are uniquely equipped to guide and nurture the child to a successful future while dismissing the other parent's contributions and capabilities. Similarly, they might anticipate a divorce settlement that heavily favors them, based on an inflated belief in their financial entitlements or contributions. They feel entitled to everything and persuading them to consider otherwise is usually futile. They are not only delusional but also entrenched in their beliefs.

HCPs may hold delusional beliefs about the other parent, including unwavering beliefs in their own false accusations. No amount of evidence can disprove their claims; they cling to "their truth" regardless of the facts. They are convinced that their delusions are reality and that it is more likely for objective facts to be wrong than for their perceptions to be flawed.

These delusional expectations complicate legal proceedings, as they are often unwilling to consider reasonable solutions that don't align with their grandiose vision. They refuse to agree to anything that doesn't severely punish the other parent for being the villain they falsely imagine. Understanding this trait helps in strategizing how to bring them closer to a more grounded perspective, often requiring clear evidence and firm legal guidance to counter their fantastical beliefs in court.

Need for Excessive Admiration

The need for excessive admiration is a critical aspect of high-conflict behavior, reflecting a deep dependency on external validation to bolster self-esteem. HCPs derive their sense of self-worth from external validation and praise, often fishing for compliments or manipulating situations to center themselves in the spotlight. They can become significantly distressed, or even angry when such admiration is absent. This craving influences their behavior in overt and subtle ways, particularly in family court, where they may portray themselves in an excessively favorable light.

In legal contexts, this incessant demand for admiration can manifest as an unrelenting portrayal of themselves as the ideal parent or the more committed partner, often exaggerating their contributions while downplaying or negating those of the other party. For the HCP seeking admiration and validation, the family court setting is the ultimate stage for their performance. They not only receive attention but also seek validation backed by the authority of the state.

This need drives HCPs to seek validation from their social circles and legal authorities, including judges and mediators. Their arguments and submissions may be peppered with mentions of their achievements and sacrifices, aimed at winning the court's favor.

Understanding this need is crucial, as it often underpins their motivations and actions in court, influencing how they misrepresent their case and respond misleadingly.

Sense of Entitlement

HCPs often possess an unreasonable expectation of especially favorable treatment or automatic compliance with their demands. They expect others to cater to their needs without being considerate in return, leading to impatience or anger when these expectations are unmet. They feel entitled to anything they want simply by virtue of their existence.

This trait can be particularly disruptive in family court settings, where fair and equitable resolutions are sought. HCPs often approach legal disputes with a firm belief that they inherently deserve more favorable outcomes, whether regarding asset division, custody arrangements, or support payments. To them, their entitlement means they deserve everything, while the other parent deserves nothing. In their view, there's only room for one entitled party at the table.

Such entitlement can lead to unreasonable demands during negotiations, such as insisting on larger shares of marital assets or more favorable custody terms without regard for legal standards or the other party's rights. Their arguments often lack evidentiary support or rational basis. They may react with indignation or anger when decisions don't favor them, perceiving such outcomes as personal attacks rather than reasoned judgments.

Interpersonally Exploitative Behavior

HCPs often take advantage of others to achieve their own ends, exhibiting parasitic tendencies. This may involve manipulating or exploiting others without regard for their feelings or interests. This trait is deeply ingrained in their interactions, particularly evident in how they manipulate relationships for personal gain.

In family court, this can manifest in detrimental ways. An HCP might exploit the other parent's weaknesses or emotional states to gain an upper hand in custody disputes or financial negotiations. They may leverage shared children as tools in their strategy, using them to garner sympathy or manipulate outcomes in their favor. Additionally, they might extract information or concessions from the other party during seemingly benign interactions or joint therapy sessions, only to use it against them in court.

Recognizing and addressing this exploitative behavior is crucial. It requires vigilance and a strategic approach to interactions, ensuring that communications are documented and that any agreements made are formally recorded to prevent misuse.

Lack of Empathy

Lack of empathy is a defining trait of HCPs, characterized by an inability to recognize or relate to the feelings and needs of others. This deficiency profoundly affects interpersonal relationships and can significantly impact legal disputes, especially in family court, where children's emotional and psychological welfare is paramount.

By nature, HCPs feel like the center of the universe and struggle to identify with others' feelings and needs. They tend to be dismissive and insensitive to the sufferings and needs of others, especially when it conflicts with their own interests or desires. This lack of empathy drives their ability to engage in heartless and damaging behaviors, as they will do whatever it takes to achieve their goals, indifferent to the harm caused to others. The capacity to empathize is a fundamental human characteristic that highly narcissistic and psychopathic individuals often lack.

In family law cases, lack of empathy might manifest as a disregard for the emotional impact of their actions on their children or the other parent. For example, in custody disputes, they may focus solely on winning or punishing the other party rather than considering what arrangement genuinely serves their children's best interests. They may be indifferent to the pain their strategies inflict on the family, viewing the court case as a competition to win rather than a problem to solve cooperatively. They may advance financial scorched-earth campaigns or make false accusations of abuse without batting an eye. To them, the ends justify the means, and the collateral damage is of no concern.

This trait complicates negotiations, as HCPs often cannot appreciate the other party's perspective or the compromises needed for a fair resolution. It also prevents them from recognizing their own faults or taking accountability. Understanding this emotional blind spot is crucial for legal professionals and opposing parties, helping them set realistic expectations for the HCP's behavior in negotiations and court proceedings.

Unbridled Envy (or Suspicion of Envy)

HCPs often either envy others or believe others are envious of them. This perception feeds into their sense of superiority, making them feel they possess attributes others covet. This characteristic significantly colors their interactions and decision-making processes, particularly in high-stress environments like family court.

HCPs frequently perceive others as having more or achieving more, which fuels their sense of entitlement and competitive nature. An HCP who believes others enjoy what they alone deserve can become a relentless adversary. This envy may drive them to engage in legal battles to equal or surpass what they perceive others have, rather than focusing on what is equitable for all parties involved, including their own children.

Conversely, their belief that others are envious of them contributes to a grandiose self-image that is out of touch with reality. They may interpret reasonable requests or legitimate criticisms from the other party as manifestations of jealousy, dismissing them without consideration.

This distorted perception complicates negotiations and legal proceedings, as HCPs driven by envy may refuse to settle for anything that seems like a concession, perpetuating conflict and complicating resolution efforts.

Arrogant and Haughty Behaviors or Attitudes

Arrogant and haughty behaviors are common manifestations of a personality disorder, characterized by an air of superiority and disdain for others perceived as inferior. This is often observed in the patronizing or contemptuous behaviors displayed by individuals with narcissism, who may come across as snobbish, disdainful, or patronizing.

Such attitudes can significantly impact interpersonal interactions, particularly in high-stakes environments like family court. Such HCPs may exhibit contemptuous or patronizing behavior towards the other party, legal professionals, and even the court itself, believing they understand the legal process better and deserve a more favorable outcome due to their perceived superiority. This attitude underlies their disregard of court orders and rules, as they see themselves above such constraints.

Arrogance may manifest as dismissive comments, rolling eyes, smirking, or a condescending tone when addressing the court or opposing counsel. Such behavior strains communication, complicates negotiation, and negatively influences how judges and mediators perceive their character and intentions.

It's crucial for those dealing with HCPs in legal settings to recognize these behaviors as part of a broader mental disorder, whether diagnosable or not. This understanding helps prevent taking such behaviors personally and encourages a professional, strategic approach to the case. Addressing these traits can help mitigate their negative impact, fostering a more respectful and productive legal environment.

Psychological Underpinnings of High-Conflict Behaviors in Legal Conflicts

The psychological underpinnings of high-conflict behaviors in legal conflicts are complex and rooted in the deeper aspects of personality and behavioral patterns that define narcissism and other personality disorders. Understanding these foundations can provide valuable insights into why HCPs act the way they do in legal settings, particularly in high-stakes environments like family court.

1. Fragile Self-Esteem

    Despite their outward appearance of confidence and superiority, HCPs often have very fragile self-esteem. This vulnerability is central to understanding their behavior in legal conflicts. When an HCP's self-view is challenged or threatened – such as through a divorce or custody battle – their reaction is often disproportionate and aggressive. They may use litigation as a way to bolster their ego and regain a sense of control or superiority.

2. Need for Control and Dominance

    HCPs have a compulsive need for control and often view relationships and interactions through the lens of a power dynamic in which they must emerge as the dominant party. In legal conflicts, this need translates into efforts to manipulate proceedings, outcomes, and even people, including legal professionals and judges. They may use various tactics like lying, gaslighting, or financial manipulation to maintain or regain control.

3. Hypersensitivity to Criticism

    HCPs are acutely sensitive to criticism and can perceive even neutral actions as personal attacks. In legal settings, routine proceedings or necessary negotiations can be misconstrued as affronts to their person. This hypersensitivity can lead to explosive reactions or an escalation in conflict, as HCPs attempt to "defend" themselves against perceived slights.

1. Projection

HCPs frequently employ projection, attributing their own negative characteristics or intentions to others. This mechanism can be particularly pronounced in legal disputes where they may accuse the opposing party of behaviors that they themselves are guilty of, such as selfishness, dishonesty, or even abuse. This not only deflects attention from their actions but also confuses the legal issues at hand.

4. Reaction Formation and Denial

HCPs frequently use reaction formation – expressing the opposite of what they feel or believe – and denial to cope with situations where they cannot accept reality. For instance, if facing potential loss in court, an HCP might publicly bolster their confidence or degrade the significance of the court's decisions, while internally they might be struggling with fear of failure.

Impact of High-Conflict Traits in Legal and Family Conflicts

The impact of high-conflict traits on legal and family conflicts can be profound and far-reaching, often complicating proceedings and exacerbating tensions. In the setting of family court, where emotions already run high, the behaviors associated with HCPs can lead to protracted disputes and a breakdown in communication that makes resolution more difficult.

HCP's grandiosity and need for admiration can drive them to unrealistic demands regarding custody or property division, expecting outcomes that align with their inflated self-image. Their lack of empathy makes it difficult for them to consider the emotional and psychological needs of their children or the impact of their demands on the family. This can result in legal strategies that are aggressive and punitive rather than conciliatory or aimed at mutual benefit.

Furthermore, the manipulative behaviors typical of high-conflict individuals, such as lying and gaslighting, can erode trust to the point where cooperative negotiation becomes impossible. These tactics often aim to confuse and destabilize the other party, making it challenging to establish a factual basis for discussions. This can lead to significant delays in proceedings, increased legal costs, and a greater emotional toll on all involved, particularly the children.

HCPs may also react with anger or retaliation when they feel slighted or when decisions do not favor them, leading to further legal challenges and appeals that extend the conflict. The court's ability to discern these traits and their impact is crucial in managing these cases effectively. Recognizing the influence of high-conflict behavior can help in formulating approaches that mitigate its negative effects, focusing on strategies that promote fairness and the well-being of children above the desires or demands of any individual party.

Common Manipulative Tactics Used by HCPs in Family Disputes

In family disputes, particularly those that escalate to the courtroom, HCPs often deploy a series of manipulative tactics designed to confuse, control, and skew the narrative in their favor. In practice, we see these tactics and behaviors all the time. All... the... time. These tactics can be profoundly disruptive, complicating proceedings and causing emotional turmoil for all parties involved. Recognizing these tactics is the first step toward developing effective counterstrategies.

Gaslighting

Gaslighting is a psychological manipulation tactic frequently employed by HCPs to destabilize the other parent. By deliberately causing them to doubt their own memory, perceptions, and even sanity, the gas lighter aims to weaken their confidence and credibility. This tactic is especially damaging in custody battles, where the ability to clearly advocate for oneself and one's children is critical. Over time, the victim may become confused, second-guess their actions, or even withdraw entirely, making it easier for the narcissist to control the narrative and influence court decisions to their advantage.

Projection

Projection is a psychological defense mechanism commonly used by HCPs. By attributing their own negative traits, intentions, or harmful behaviors onto the other parent, the HCP shifts focus away from their own actions and creates confusion and mistrust. This tactic can distort reality, making it difficult for the other parent to defend themselves, as they are often accused of behaviors they did not commit. The confusion created by projection not only damages the accused parent's credibility but can also influence custody decisions, as it may paint them in an unfairly negative light, giving the HCP an advantage in the court's eyes.

Triangulation

Triangulation is a tactic frequently employed by HCPs in family court disputes to destabilize relationships and shift power dynamics. In this strategy, the HCP recruits a third party – often a child, relative, or even a professional like a therapist – to align against the other parent. This tactic creates emotional wedges and loyalty conflicts, placing the child or third party in a difficult position where they feel compelled to choose sides. The resulting emotional strain disrupts healthy parent-child dynamics, erodes trust, and often complicates custody arrangements, as the child may become confused, alienated, or manipulated into favoring the triangulating parent.

Exploiting Emotional Vulnerabilities

Exploiting emotional vulnerabilities is a tactic used by HCPs in family court disputes to target the other parent's insecurities – such as fear and guilt – to gain an advantage in negotiations and undermine their confidence, complicating custody arrangements and diverting attention from the child's best interests.

Victim Positioning

Victim positioning is a powerful manipulation tactic frequently used by HCPs in divorce and custody disputes to control the narrative and gain sympathy. By portraying themselves as the victim, the HCP shifts attention away from their own harmful behaviors, painting a picture where they are the ones being unfairly treated. This tactic is especially effective in court settings, where emotions run high and parties are often inclined to side with the person appearing to suffer. The false victim narrative can cloud the court's judgment, distorting perceptions of both parents. In doing so, the HCP can manipulate the legal system, skewing custody outcomes in their favor and leading to unjust decisions that do not accurately reflect the true dynamics of the family conflict.

Smear Campaigns

Smear campaigns are a damaging tactic commonly used by HCPs to undermine the other parent's reputation and credibility. By spreading false information, rumors, or exaggerated claims, the HCP seeks to paint the other parent in a negative light, portraying them as unfit or irresponsible. This tactic not only creates confusion and mistrust among those involved, but it can also influence legal professionals, such as judges or custody evaluators, who may be swayed by the negative narrative. By damaging the other parent's standing, the HCP positions themselves as the more suitable caregiver, potentially swaying custody decisions in their favor.

Love Bombing and Devaluation

Love bombing and devaluation are manipulative tactics often employed by HCPs to control and destabilize the other parent. The process begins with love bombing, where the HCP overwhelms the targeted parent with excessive affection, praise, and attention. This creates an illusion of harmony and emotional closeness, leading the other parent to believe that the relationship is positive and stable. However, this phase is soon followed by sudden devaluation, characterized by harsh criticism, emotional withdrawal, and rejection. This abrupt shift leaves the targeted parent confused, emotionally destabilized, and questioning their own worth, which can weaken their confidence and affect their ability to effectively navigate the court process.

Utilizing Legal Systems as a Weapon

Utilizing legal systems as a weapon is a manipulative strategy often used by HCPs in family court disputes to gain control and exert pressure on the other parent. In this tactic, the HCP exploits legal processes – such as filing excessive motions, making false accusations, or dragging out court proceedings – not with the goal of resolution, but to harass, intimidate, and financially burden the other parent. This method can prolong disputes, causing significant emotional and financial strain, while diverting attention away from the children's well-being. By weaponizing the legal system, the HCP seeks to wear down the other parent and gain an unfair advantage in custody or visitation arrangements.

Parental Alienation

Parental alienation occurs when one parent unjustly influences a child to reject or distance themselves from the other parent, creating deep emotional divides. However, HCPs often weaponize this concept by falsely accusing the other parent of alienation, using it as a smokescreen to divert attention from their own harmful behaviors. By fabricating claims of alienation, the HCP can create confusion, manipulate perceptions in court, and paint themselves as the victim, even when they are the ones undermining the child-parent relationship. To counter these false accusations, the targeted parent must diligently document their positive interactions with the child and seek professional assessments, such as family therapy or custody evaluations, to clarify the true family dynamics and expose the manipulative tactics at play.

Using Children as Messengers

Using children as messengers between parents in high-conflict situations places an unnecessary and harmful emotional burden on them. When a child is asked to relay messages or negotiate between their parents, they are pulled into adult conflicts they are neither emotionally equipped nor mature enough to handle. This can lead to anxiety, guilt, and confusion, as they may feel responsible for the outcome of these interactions. Additionally, the risk of misunderstandings increases, as the child may misinterpret or miscommunicate important information, further escalating tensions between parents. This practice undermines the child's sense of security and can damage their emotional well-being.

False Accusations

In custody proceedings, it is not uncommon for one parent to falsely accuse the other of neglect or abuse to gain a strategic advantage. These accusations are often made to influence court decisions regarding custody or visitation, painting the accused parent in an unfavorable light. Such false claims can have devastating consequences, leading to significant emotional and financial strain for the parent being targeted. They may face reputational damage, experience heightened stress, and incur costly legal fees in their efforts to defend themselves. The emotional toll can also affect their ability to focus on maintaining a healthy relationship with their child during the dispute.

Withholding Information

Withholding information is a manipulative strategy frequently employed by HCPs in legal disputes to gain control and sway outcomes in their favor. By deliberately concealing or misrepresenting critical details – such as financial information, schedules, or important decisions regarding the child – the HCP creates an uneven playing field, making it difficult for the other party to make informed decisions. This tactic obstructs fair negotiations, as it prevents transparency and hinders the court's ability to assess the full situation accurately. The result is often skewed decision-making that benefits the HCP, leaving the other party at a disadvantage and potentially leading to unjust outcomes in custody or financial arrangements.

Financial Manipulation

Financial manipulation is a control tactic often employed by one parent in family disputes to gain an unfair advantage by leveraging economic resources. This may involve actions such as withholding child support payments, underreporting income, or misrepresenting financial assets during court proceedings. The goal is to destabilize the other parent's financial stability, making it more difficult for them to provide for the child's needs or maintain their own legal representation. By limiting the other parent's financial resources, the manipulative parent can exert control over custody or visitation arrangements, all while creating additional stress and uncertainty that further disrupts the child's well-being and the targeted parent's ability to advocate for themselves.

Sudden Compliance or Agreement Reversals

A manipulative parent may use the tactic of feigning agreement during negotiations, giving the impression of cooperation and willingness to settle disputes amicably. However, once the discussions progress or agreements are close to being finalized, they may deliberately backtrack or change their stance. This tactic prolongs the legal process, forcing the other parent to restart negotiations or take additional legal action, which increases costs and delays resolution. By doing so, the manipulative parent creates additional emotional and financial strain, further complicating custody arrangements and dragging out the legal proceedings.

Excessive Litigation

HCPs often engage in excessive litigation as a deliberate tactic to emotionally and financially wear down their opponents. By filing relentless motions, appeals, and other legal actions, they aim to prolong the legal process and create ongoing stress for the other party. This strategy forces the opponent to continuously respond to legal demands, driving up legal costs and depleting emotional resources. The ultimate goal is to exhaust the other parent into submission or disadvantage, making them more likely to settle on unfavorable terms. This approach also distracts from the core issues, such as the child's well-being, by keeping the conflict focused on endless legal maneuvers.

Navigating High-Conflict Traits in Legal Settings

Understanding common high-conflict and narcissistic traits and tactics and anticipating how they might manifest during legal disputes is crucial for effective strategy planning in family court. When dealing with an HCP, it's not a matter of *whether* these traits and tactics will emerge – it's a matter of when, how often, and how severe the behaviors will present themselves.

Knowing that deception and distortion of reality are central tactics for HCPs, it's important to maintain meticulous documentation and gather evidence from the outset in order to counter false narratives or delusional claims. Additionally, preparing emotionally to handle such turbulent personalities – by depersonalizing their behaviors, staying calm, avoiding reactions to provocations, and keeping interactions strictly professional – can mitigate significant emotional tolls and help maintain focus on the legal issues.

To further enhance your preparation, I highly recommend utilizing the official *Mastery Workbook*, a companion guide to *Family Court Solutions*. This powerful resource provides structured exercises and tools designed to help you systematically build your case in family court. With its comprehensive guidance, you can effectively apply the strategies discussed in this book, ensuring you're thoroughly prepared to document your experiences and present a compelling narrative in court.

By employing the following strategies, you can navigate the legal challenges posed by an HCP more effectively, minimizing their ability to manipulate the proceedings and increasing your chances of a favorable outcome.

Preparation and Documentation

Dealing with an HCP in court requires intentional, proactive, detailed, and organized preparation. It's essential to document all interactions, keep detailed records of communications, and gather concrete evidence to counteract the distortions and fabrications presented by the HCP. Given their tendency to manipulate facts, a robust collection of documented evidence helps maintain the integrity of your case and safeguard your peace of mind.

Tips for preparation and documentation:

- Keep a record of emails, texts, and phone calls. If possible, avoid phone calls and in-person meetings all together and require all communications to be in writing. If in writing, try to have all correspondences condensed into a co-parenting communications app.

- Write summaries of conversations and note dates, times, and witnesses. Using a devoted weekly calendar for his task is often helpful.

- Collect photos, videos, or other relevant documentation to support your case. Save them to a secure location and keep duplicate copies in case of data loss.

- Develop a chronological account of events related to your case and cross reference specific pieces of evidence that you believe are important for major events and conflicts on the chronology.

- Ensure everything is clearly labeled and easily accessible. As an attorney, I always appreciate it when clients can hand me a clear, concise, and easy-to-navigate collection of exhibits as opposed to a disorganized pile.

Legal Representation

Working with an attorney who has experience handling high-conflict scenarios is crucial. Such professionals are better equipped to navigate the manipulative tactics employed by HCPs and can advocate effectively on your behalf, ensuring that the legal strategy is both proactive and reactive where necessary. They can also serve as a buffer, reducing direct interactions that might escalate conflict.

If hiring such an attorney for active representation is not possible in your area or is not supported by your finances, a highly effective (and often better) alternative is hiring a skilled attorney in a consulting-only capacity. Doing so often keeps legal expenses to a minimum while providing access to knowledge and support.

Tips for legal representation:

- Research potential attorneys with significant experience in high-conflict cases.

- Schedule consultations with at least two attorneys to discuss your case.

- Choose an attorney who understands high-conflict behaviors and manipulation tactics, and who can articulate their strategies for handling such personalities.

- Select an attorney willing to set realistic expectations, even if it means potentially losing your business.

- Share all relevant information and concerns with your attorney in an organized manner.

- Ensure your legal strategy includes both proactive and defensive elements.

Setting Boundaries

It's important to establish and maintain clear boundaries with a high-conflict opponent, especially when you are required to co-parent with them throughout the active litigation process. This means limiting communication to necessary and formal channels and avoiding engagement in their attempts at provocation. Boundaries help in managing the emotional toll and keeping interactions strictly professional.

Tips for setting boundaries:

- Decide on formal communications channels (e.g., email or co-parenting apps only) and stick to them.

- Practice responses to potential provocations to remain calm. It is often helpful to workshop your responses with a coach who is experienced with honing communications with antagonistic co-parents.

- Track any instances of boundary violations and enforce them consistently.

- Inform your opponent of your boundaries and communication preferences and stick to your standards.

- Discuss boundary-setting strategies with your attorney to make sure your practices are aligned with the preferences and leanings of your local judge.

Psychological Resilience

Building psychological resilience is key when dealing with a high-conflict co-parent, as the situation can involve long-term stress and re-traumatization. Consulting a coach or therapist familiar with high-conflict behavior, interpersonal trauma, and vagus nerve dysregulation can provide support and coping strategies, helping you stay emotionally grounded despite the challenges.

Tips for psychological resilience:

- Find a coach or therapist specifically experienced in dealing with high-conflict and narcissistic behavior.

- Work with your therapist on specific techniques to manage stress and promote healthy vagus nerve function.

- Work with your therapist to define boundaries and develop a compelling vision for the life you want to create for yourself and your loved ones.

- Schedule regular time for activities that promote your well-being, especially physical exercise.

- Use mindfulness or grounding exercises to maintain emotional stability.

- Connect with friends, family, or support groups for additional social support. When you spend time with friends and family, do your best to talk about and bond over things other than just your court-related issues.

Courtroom Strategy

In the courtroom, maintaining a calm, composed demeanor is crucial. HCPs often attempt to provoke emotional reactions by creating drama and escalating tension. By resisting emotional responses, you can avoid falling into their trap and keep the focus on the issues at hand. Demonstrating reliability, stability, and a clear, factual approach will contrast sharply with the erratic behavior often exhibited by HCPs, positively influencing the court's perception and strengthening your credibility.

Tips for courtroom strategy:

- Adopt a calm and collected presentation style for court dates.

- Prepare statements and responses that are strictly factual and supported by direct evidence.

- Role-play potential courtroom scenarios with your attorney or a trusted friend.

- Focus on providing clear, evidence-backed examples for the judge rather than making unsupported claims.

- Identify triggers and rehearse your reactions, remaining composed under provocation. Practice grounding techniques to keep you focused and calm in the moment.

- Keep notes on courtroom proceedings and any comments made by the judge that give you a glimpse into their thinking.

Conclusion: Navigating Legal Conflicts with HCPs

Engaging in a legal dispute with a high-conflict individual requires patience, strategy, and resilience. The distortions and challenges posed by such personalities can be overwhelming, but with the right tools and support, they can be effectively managed. The goal is to equip those facing these disputes with the understanding and strategies necessary to protect their interests and achieve the healthiest, most equitable outcomes possible.

Understanding the nature of HCPs, anticipating the potential complications their behavior brings, and preparing accordingly can help secure favorable legal outcomes while also maintaining your own mental health and well-being throughout what can often be a grueling process. Ultimately, the aim in any legal dispute, especially those involving family matters, should be to resolve issues in a way that promotes healing and allows parties capable of growth to move forward productively and positively.

With knowledge and effective strategies, you can face these challenges with greater confidence and clarity.

Key Takeaways:

- **Recognize the Signs:** Awareness of high-conflict traits such as grandiosity, lack of empathy, need for admiration, and hypersensitivity to criticism is crucial. Recognizing these traits early on in legal proceedings can help in formulating a strategic approach that anticipates potential manipulations and disruptions.

- **Preparation is Key:** Dealing with an HCP in court requires meticulous preparation. This includes gathering comprehensive documentation, maintaining clear and organized records, and preparing emotionally for the tactics an HCP might employ. Forensic accounting may be necessary in cases where financial manipulation is suspected.

- **Educate Yourself and Your Team:** Understanding the nature of high-conflict behavior not only prepares you but can also inform your legal team about the specific challenges of your case. Educating others involved can improve the coordinated response and effectiveness of your legal strategy.

- **Professional Guidance:** Engaging with legal professionals who have experience in dealing with HCPs can make a critical difference. These professionals are not only familiar with the law but understand how to apply it in ways that mitigate the fallout from the HCP's behavior. Psychological support for both the parties and their children is also crucial to help them cope with the emotional toll.

- **Maintain Clear Boundaries:** Setting and maintaining clear boundaries is essential. This can include limiting direct communication with your HCP ex and using formal channels for all necessary interactions to avoid personal confrontations and manipulations.

- **Strategic Communication:** When dealing with an HCP, keep all communication to the point and evidence based. Avoid emotional engagement and responses to provocations. This helps in keeping the legal process focused and reduces the emotional strain on yourself.

- **Expect the Unexpected:** HCPs often react unpredictably, especially when they feel their position is threatened. Being prepared for a range of possible behaviors – including surprising moments of compliance, aggressive litigation, or unexpected concessions – can help you stay one step ahead.

- **Focus on the Big Picture:** It's easy to get caught up in the minutiae of battles with an HCP. Keeping an eye on the overall goals – such as the best interests of children in custody cases or fair asset distribution in divorce proceedings – can help maintain a clear direction and avoid unnecessary conflicts.

- **Legal and Ethical Considerations:** Always adhere to legal and ethical standards. HCPs may push or break boundaries, but maintaining your integrity is crucial not only for your case but for your long-term well-being.

- **Support Systems Are Vital:** Don't go it alone. A support system, whether made up of friends, family, support groups, or mental health professionals, can provide the emotional backing and reassurance needed to navigate this challenging time.

2

PREPARING YOUR CASE
WITH INTEGRITY

Participating in a contentious divorce or custody battle can be one of the most challenging, demoralizing, and traumatizing experiences a person ever faces. Referring to family court cases as traumatizing experiences is not an exaggeration or understatement. Those who go through custody disputes with a high-conflict opponent often carry the emotional, mental, physical, and financial wounds for years.

For those entangled in high-conflict family disputes, especially where narcissistic behaviors and high-conflict tactics are involved, the manner in which one prepares and presents their case can significantly influence the outcome. When going to war in the family court system, it is not only about what you fight for but how you fight for it.

The importance of personal integrity and accountability throughout the legal process cannot be underestimated. These qualities are critical elements that often define both the course and resolution of legal disputes and shape your entire psychological and physical experiences during and after the ordeal.

Defining Integrity in High-Conflict Cases

Integrity in high-conflict cases transcends mere honesty. It encompasses much more than just expressing "your truth." Integrity and accountability involve adhering to a code of ethical behavior that respects not only the judicial process but also the rights of all parties involved, including the opposing party. In the context of family court, this means engaging in practices that uphold the law, maintaining respect for everyone involved, and striving for resolutions that prioritize the well-being of children and fairness in outcomes. Integrity ensures that your actions, both inside and outside the courtroom, align with a principled stance that supports the judicial system's goal of equitable resolutions.

Legally speaking, integrity means engaging in practices that promote transparent and equitable proceedings. It involves following court orders and consistently appearing when, where, and how you are required. It requires avoiding deceitful tactics that undermine the spirit of the law, such as hiding assets, making false accusations, or manipulating evidence.

Importantly, acting with integrity also means adhering strictly to court orders and legal directives, demonstrating respect not just for the letter of the law but for its intent as well.

By upholding these standards, individuals can show the court that they are contributing to a more just legal system, supporting the court's mission to ensure that outcomes are based on merit and fairness rather than deceit or coercion. Integrity and accountability align you with the highest goals and functions of the court itself.

Integrity as a Strategic Advantage

In the heat of a legal battle, particularly in family law cases, it's easy to focus solely on winning. It can be tempting to concentrate on defeating the other party and doing whatever it takes to avoid losing. However, trying to win at the cost of personal integrity not only jeopardizes your chances of success but can also profoundly impact your post-trial reality on multiple levels. Acting without integrity is a high-risk tactic that may yield short-term gains at the expense of long-term credibility, peace, and stability.

Believe it or not, judges and mediators are often adept at recognizing when parties are acting out of spite or deception. Such behaviors can severely backfire, resulting in legal decisions that are unfavorable to the party lacking integrity. Conversely, exhibiting integrity throughout court proceedings creates a positive impression on judges and increases the likelihood of gaining their favor.

While it may seem counterintuitive in a situation charged with emotion and intense personal stakes, maintaining high levels of integrity offers a significant strategic advantage. Approaching your case with a clear ethical stance can streamline proceedings by reducing conflicts and complications that arise from underhanded tactics. The overall level of conflict decreases significantly and quickly when one party refuses to compromise their integrity and commits to impeccable behavior. Embodying integrity can expedite the resolution process, lower legal costs, and improve the chances of a favorable outcome.

Additionally, acting with clarity, integrity, and radical accountability often discourages the other side from using deceitful tactics, as they know such behavior will not easily manipulate or destabilize an ethically solid opponent. It's easy for HCPs to get away with manipulative tactics and games when the other party is wallowing with them in the mud. It's easy for HCPs to fight dirty when the other party fails to stand in front of the court with clean hands. Taking an accountability-focused approach claims the moral high ground and strategically positions one to potentially secure the most favorable legal outcomes possible.

Perhaps most importantly, the example you set through your actions during this time can leave a lasting impression on your children. Court success is one thing, but your legacy is another. Our children are often more aware of what's happening than we realize, and how you conduct yourself throughout the custody battle will teach them how to deal with adversity and conflict in their own lives. Acting with integrity ensures that you model behaviors reflecting maturity, respect, and ethical responsibility, which your children will see and remember.

Navigating the Legal Landscape with Integrity

A critical component of preparing your case with integrity involves understanding the legal landscape. This includes familiarizing yourself with the specific laws and regulations governing your case, as well as the procedural rules of the court in which you are litigating. An informed party is an empowered party, capable of making decisions and strategies that are both effective and justifiable in the eyes of the law.

Family court is rarely, if ever, anything like what is portrayed in movies and television shows. Almost every client who retains my firm arrives on our doorstep with many misconceptions about family court, how it functions, and what is realistically possible. The interwebs is full of inaccurate and unhelpful information regarding family court, including fictitious posts made by questionable online personalities, advertising pages for law firms that are essentially sales pitches, and mass-produced filler content that is not state-specific and often flat-out wrong. The moral of the story: Be very careful with and critical of online information sources, as they are often outdated, irrelevant, and incorrect.

To aid in growing your understanding, it is advisable to invest time in learning about family law through available resources such as legal books, educational seminars, online courses, and consultations with legal professionals. Get to know the family code for your state. Invest in several hours of consultation time with a local attorney to have candid conversations about the local court system, judges, and typical outcomes. Knowledge is a powerful tool that not only enhances your ability to navigate the legal system effectively but also increases your confidence through the process.

As you prepare for your case, physically go to the courthouse several times to see how the courts operate. When possible, sit in on hearings and watch how hearings are conducted and how judges respond in different situations. Familiarize yourself with the routines and jargon of the courtroom. Spending time observing the courthouse and proceedings often has a significant calming effect on your nervous system and can help you show up at your own hearing feeling calmer and more collected.

Navigating the legal landscape in family court requires a realistic understanding of what can be reasonably expected based on precedent and common judicial decisions in similar cases. Family courts aim to make decisions that are in the best interests of the children and fair to all parties, often prioritizing equitable solutions over one-sided victories. Therefore, it's crucial to temper expectations and approach your case with a grounded perspective on likely outcomes.

Again, it is easy to go on social media and read countless stories about extreme family court decisions, both positive and negative, most of which are highly inaccurate and misleading. All-or-nothing outcomes rarely exist in the absence of extreme and terrible facts, yet you can easily find influencers and online personalities who are ready to sell you the secret to winning "full custody," whatever that means. The point is to invest in quality education and wise counsel rather than building your expectations around someone's sales pitch or unverifiable claims.

Educating yourself about the typical rulings and standards in family law within your jurisdiction can prevent the disillusionment that might come from overly optimistic or unrealistic promises made by some attorneys or portrayed by online personalities.

For instance, it's relatively easy to find a money-hungry attorney or random influencer who throws around "full custody" and "sole custody" terms like they are easily attainable goals: *You want full custody? You should have it because you don't like the way the other parent packs lunches. Pay my retainer and let's have some hearings!*

And then after the client has spent a large portion of their savings and gone into credit card debt, the judge enters a middle-ground decision aligned with the policies of the state.

Understanding these nuances and preparing accordingly can help in formulating a more effective legal strategy. Engaging with experienced legal professionals who provide a balanced view rather than pie-in-the-sky scenarios is essential. Such realism not only prepares you for potential challenges but also strategically positions you to advocate effectively for your interests within the bounds of what is realistically achievable.

As we delve deeper into the specifics of preparing your case with integrity, remember that the choices you make now will resonate far beyond the courtroom. They will impact your personal relationships, your standing in the community, and most importantly, the well-being of your family.

This point is worth repeating: The choices you make now will resonate. Now means starting right away! If there are things you need to change, change them. If there are things you need to do or stop doing to align yourself with the court orders, do or stop doing those things right now. If you think about your co-parenting messages and cringe, start working with a coach to help you develop better communication skills today.

If you anticipate that litigation could be coming down the line, start laying your foundation of impeccable behavior today. Whatever you are doing that helps the other side build their case, stop doing it. Take away their toys. Give them nothing to play with or use against you.

With a foundation built on integrity, you equip yourself not just to face the challenges of today but to emerge with your dignity and conscience intact, ready to begin the next chapter of your life regardless of the outcome. This brings us back to the concept of legacy. The strategies in this book are about far more than simply going to family court and increasing your odds of success. They also help you build a healthier foundation and legacy for your family, which is crucial when one parent exhibits high-conflict behaviors. Your example of integrity and accountable living will guide and protect your children from the negative and chaotic influences of the other parent's behaviors.

Understanding four areas of concern in the sections to follow can help you act with greater integrity as you prepare for and navigate through the family court system. These involve: legal procedure, legal documentation, legal compliance, and legal planning.

Section I – Legal Procedure: Understanding the Legal Landscape

Navigating family court requires a comprehensive understanding of the legal framework that governs these disputes. This knowledge is crucial not only for making informed decisions but also for setting realistic expectations about the outcomes of your case.

Family law varies significantly state by state and jurisdiction by jurisdiction, but there are common principles and procedures that universally apply. Familiarizing yourself with the basics of legal proceedings in family court can demystify the process and prepare you for the complexities ahead.

Basic Principles of Family Law

Family law is primarily concerned with matters involving family relationships, such as marriage, divorce, child custody, and support. The overriding principle in custody cases is the best interests of the child, which compels judges to prioritize children's health, safety, and welfare when making decisions.

In divorce cases, the guiding principle is fair treatment for all parties involved, which means that the division of assets and debts must be equitable (though not necessarily equal). Fair treatment in spousal support is based on the financial circumstances of each party.

Best interests of the child: This is the cornerstone of decisions regarding child custody and visitation. Courts consider a range of factors, such as the child's age, health, emotional ties to each parent, and each parent's ability to provide care and stability. The goal is to support the child's health, safety, welfare, and happiness.

Equitable treatment in divorce: Family law seeks to ensure fair and equitable treatment of both parties in a divorce. This includes equitable distribution of assets and debts, which means that property acquired during the marriage must be divided fairly, though not necessarily equally, based on each party's contribution and future needs.

Support obligations: Family law governs the determination and enforcement of support obligations, including child support and alimony. Child support is usually decided based on standardized guidelines that consider the income of both parents, the needs of the children, and other relevant factors. Alimony considerations might include the duration of the marriage, the standard of living established during the marriage, and each spouse's financial resources and needs.

These basic principles aim to balance fairness, justice, and the welfare of children, guiding the courts in resolving the complex and often sensitive issues that arise in family law cases. In addition to these principles, there is a public policy and legislative intent shared by all states that presumes parents and children should have consistent and routine time together to promote the parent-child relationship, unless compelling evidence rebuts this presumption. More states are creating statutory presumptions that state that, in the absence of convincing evidence of significant abuse or neglect, equal parenting time is what's best for families. Asking the court to depart from this public policy and legislative value is often a challenging uphill battle.

It is helpful to think of this last principle as a strong river that flows toward equalized parenting time, consistent parent-child interactions, and routine schedules. The party aligned with the flow of the river has a much easier job than the party fighting against the currents. Altering the course of the river is often a major undertaking that requires the presentation of significant evidence to override the policies and values of the state. If your case is built around aligning yourself with public policy, then your evidence should be crafted to showcase your alignment. If your case requires the court to depart from public policy, then your evidence needs to be carefully considered and organized to overcome the currents.

Family Court Versus Criminal Court

Family courts differ significantly from criminal courts in both purpose and the nature of the proceedings. Understanding these differences is crucial for setting realistic expectations about what can be achieved in family court.

While criminal courts focus on adjudicating crimes against the state and imposing penalties, family courts address legal issues arising within families, such as divorce, custody, and support. Their primary emphasis is on mediation and finding solutions that prioritize the best interests of all family members, especially children.

Family courts tend to be less formal than criminal courts and encourage negotiation and settlement rather than adversarial battles. This approach aims to preserve family relationships, a goal often absent in criminal proceedings.

In family court, the focus is on equitable resolutions that support the restructuring of families, rather than on winning or losing. It's important to understand that family courts are generally not punitive; instead, they aim to address the needs of the family without assigning blame or punishment. They also strive to resolve issues with minimal intrusion on the parental rights of the parties. This perspective helps manage expectations about the court's role and highlights the importance of compromise and collaboration in family law cases.

Key Concepts in Family Law

The following key concepts are foundational to the family court system. Most decisions made by a judge or mediator will revolve around these three areas of concern:

1. **Custody and visitation:** Understanding the difference between physical and legal custody is vital. Physical custody determines where the child lives, while legal custody involves decision-making rights regarding the child's upbringing, including education, healthcare, and religious instruction.

   Custody can be sole (granted to one parent) or joint (shared between both). Visitation, or parenting time, refers to how parents will share time with their children. Even if one parent has sole physical custody, the non-custodial parent typically retains the right to regular visitation. This schedule can be flexible or fixed, depending on what the court deems in the best interests of the child, considering factors such as the child's routine, the parents' locations, and their relationship with the child. Effective custody and visitation arrangements aim to foster a stable, loving environment that supports the child's well-being and development despite changes in family structure.

2. **Support obligations:** Child support and spousal support (alimony) are significant issues in family law, crucial for ensuring financial stability post-separation or divorce.

   Child support is determined based on guidelines that consider the parents' income, the number of children, and necessary expenses related to their care. The intent is to equitably share financial responsibilities to maintain the children's standard of living.

   Spousal support, or alimony, is less formulaic and depends on factors such as the duration of the marriage, each spouse's earning capacity, age, health, and contributions to the marriage, including childcare and career sacrifices. The goal of alimony is to offset any unfair economic effects of divorce by providing continuing income to the non-wage-earning or lower-wage-earning spouse. Laws and standards for spousal support can vary widely by state.

3. **Asset division:** In divorce cases, understanding whether your state follows equitable distribution or community property laws is essential.

   Equitable distribution states divide marital assets based on fairness rather than equality. Factors considered include each spouse's economic circumstances, the duration of the marriage, and each party's contributions (both financial and non-financial) to the marriage. This does not necessarily mean a 50/50 split but rather what is considered equitable or fair.

   Community property states, on the other hand, generally view all assets acquired during the marriage as jointly owned and typically divide them equally upon divorce, regardless of who earned or spent more during the marriage. Understanding the principles governing asset division in your jurisdiction is essential for preparing for the financial outcomes of your divorce.

Local Laws and Regulations

Each state or region has unique statutes and case law that influence family law proceedings. For instance, some states are "no-fault" divorce jurisdictions, meaning you do not need to prove wrongdoing to obtain a divorce, while others require established grounds for divorce. Familiarity with your jurisdiction's specifics can significantly impact your legal strategy. Different states calculate child support in different ways. Some states have 50/50 presumptions and others do not. Some states have generous alimony laws and others are highly restrictive.

Understanding local laws is essential when navigating family court, as they shape the proceedings and outcomes of family law cases. Family law is governed at the state level in the United States, leading to significant variation in specific laws and procedures. Being well-informed about these variations is crucial for anyone involved in a family law dispute.

Divorce laws: States differ in their grounds for divorce, with both "fault" and "no-fault" bases. In "fault" states, you must prove wrongdoing, such as adultery or abandonment. In "no-fault" states, irreconcilable differences are sufficient. Some states require a separation period before filing for divorce, while others do not.

Property division: States vary in how marital property is divided. Community property states (like California and Texas) generally divide all marital property equally, while equitable distribution states (such as New York and Florida) divide property equitably, which may not mean equal. Factors considered include each spouse's financial situation, contributions to the marriage, and future needs.

Child custody and support: Local laws dictate child custody decisions, guided by the best interests of the child. What constitutes "best interests" can vary, with factors including the child's age, the parents' caregiving abilities, and the child's wishes. Child support guidelines – based on models like income shares or percentage of income (and in some states, the Melson formula) – aim for fairness and consistency, but implementation can differ significantly between states.

Alimony: Eligibility for spousal support and the factors determining its amount and duration can vary widely. Some states consider the standard of living established during the marriage, the duration of the marriage, and each spouse's earning capacity. Others may have more modern approaches that also consider the immediate employability and necessary time for the supported spouse to become financially independent.

Enforcement and modification of orders: The procedures for enforcing and modifying family law orders – such as those for child support, custody, and alimony – also vary. Some states may have more stringent measures for enforcement, including wage garnishment and seizing of assets, while others might focus more on mediation and reconciliation efforts before enforcing orders.

Importance of understanding local regulations: Navigating family court effectively requires an understanding of these local laws not only to prepare one's case accordingly but also to set realistic expectations about outcomes. For example, knowing whether your state is a no-fault state can help you understand that marital misconduct will generally not sway property division or alimony decisions.

Furthermore, each jurisdiction may have different procedural rules that could affect your case, such as specific forms, deadlines for submission, and even particular courtroom etiquette. Most jurisdictions have their own unique set of local rules and many courts have rules that are specific for each particular judge. Misunderstanding these rules can lead to delays in your case or even sanctions from the court.

By understanding the local legal landscape, you can better navigate the complexities of family law and increase your chances of achieving a favorable outcome.

Best Practices for Navigating Local Laws and Regulations

1. **Consult a local attorney:** An experienced family law attorney can offer valuable guidance on how local laws may affect your case.

2. **Educate yourself:** Attend local seminars, read about your state's family laws, and consider joining support groups to learn from others who have faced similar situations.

3. **Stay updated:** Laws and regulations can change, so it's important to stay informed about any updates or reforms in family law in your jurisdiction.

Procedural Rules

Family courts have specific rules regarding the filing of documents, court appearances, and evidence presentation. Understanding these rules can prevent procedural errors that might delay your case or impact its outcome. For instance, knowing the deadlines for submitting financial affidavits or how to properly request a modification to child support can be pivotal.

Understanding and adhering to the procedural rules of family court is essential for any party involved in a family law dispute. These rules, which can vary significantly between jurisdictions, govern everything from how documents should be filed to how hearings are conducted. Navigating these rules effectively can prevent unnecessary delays, avoid procedural errors, and help present a case in the best possible light.

Filing legal documents: The process begins with submitting necessary legal documents, such as petitions for divorce, custody, or support, as well as responses to these petitions. Each court has specific requirements for what must be included, how the documents should be formatted, and deadlines for filing. Failure to adhere to these requirements can result in a delay in proceedings or, in some cases, dismissal of the case.

Service of process: After filing, documents must be legally served to the other party. This notifies them of the legal action and gives them an opportunity to respond. Rules regarding service of process specify acceptable methods of delivery, such as personal delivery by a process server, certified mail, or, in some jurisdictions, publication in a newspaper when the party cannot be located. Ensuring proper service is crucial as it upholds the legal rights of the other party to be informed and respond appropriately.

Discovery process: Discovery is the phase where parties exchange relevant information, including financial documents and communications. Procedural rules outline how discovery should be conducted, the types of discovery tools available (like interrogatories, depositions, and requests for production), and the timeline for completing discovery. Following these rules ensures both parties can access necessary information to support their cases.

Motion practice: Throughout the case, parties may need to file motions to request certain rulings or actions from the court, such as motions for temporary orders of support or custody, or motions to compel discovery when the other party is uncooperative. The rules for filing motions include specific requirements for the information that must be included, how the motion must be served on the other party, and how the motion is scheduled for hearing. Understanding motion practice is important for effectively managing the legal process and for addressing issues as they arise during the case.

Hearing and trial procedures: Family court hearings and trials have their own set of procedural rules, which govern how hearings are scheduled, the order of presenting evidence, and the conduct of parties and attorneys in the courtroom. Knowing these rules can help parties prepare adequately, whether they are representing themselves or are represented by an attorney. This includes understanding how to introduce evidence, how to question witnesses, and the proper decorum expected in the courtroom.

Post-trial motions and appeals: After a decision has been made, there may be additional procedural rules regarding post-trial motions and appeals. These may include motions for reconsideration or modification of an order, as well as procedures for appealing a decision to a higher court. These rules typically have strict deadlines and specific requirements for what must be included in the filings.

Importance of procedural compliance: Compliance with procedural rules is not merely a formality; it is a critical component of the legal process. Proper procedure ensures fairness by providing both parties equal opportunity to present their case and respond to the other party's claims. It also facilitates the efficient operation of the court system, helping to ensure that all parties receive timely resolutions to their disputes.

For individuals involved in family law disputes, understanding and following the procedural rules of the court is crucial. This knowledge not only prevents procedural missteps but also empowers parties to navigate the family court system more confidently and effectively.

As such, it is advisable for individuals to seek guidance from legal professionals familiar with the local court procedures and to actively engage in the process by staying informed and prepared.

Common Judicial Decisions

While every case is unique, there are often precedents that provide a baseline expectation for common issues. For example, courts frequently aim to maintain stability for children, which might mean favoring custodial arrangements that best preserve a child's current lifestyle and minimize disruption. Familiarity with precedent can provide a realistic framework for what to expect and help manage expectations.

Custody and visitation: Courts focus on the best interests of the child when deciding custody and visitation. They consider factors such as the child's age, health, emotional ties to each parent, and each parent's ability to meet the child's needs. Stability, continuity of care, and a nurturing environment are crucial. Judges often prefer arrangements that allow significant involvement from both parents, unless there are concerns about one parent's ability to provide a safe environment. Joint custody is becoming more common, but if sole custody is awarded, the non-custodial parent typically receives reasonable visitation rights to support the parent-child relationship.

Support obligations: Child support is usually determined using formulas that consider the parents' incomes, the number of children, and necessary expenses for their care. This aims to ensure financial responsibilities are shared based on each parent's ability to pay, helping maintain the child's standard of living. Spousal support, or alimony, is more discretionary and influenced by factors like the length of the marriage, the standard of living during the marriage, and each spouse's financial situation and future earning potential. Courts often grant transitional support to help the lower-earning spouse become financially independent. In long-term marriages, permanent alimony may be awarded, especially if age or health issues limit a spouse's ability to become self-sufficient.

Property division: In jurisdictions following equitable distribution laws, courts divide marital property based on what is deemed fair, considering factors like the duration of the marriage, the contributions of each spouse to the marital estate, and the economic circumstances of each spouse at the time of the division. Common judicial decisions often reflect an attempt to balance economic fairness with practical outcomes, ensuring that both parties can move forward with financial stability. In community property states, the division is more straightforward, with marital assets generally split 50/50, reflecting the view that both partners contributed equally to the marriage, regardless of individual income or asset accumulation.

Conclusion: The Legal Landscape

Judicial decisions in family law are guided by statutes, case law, and overarching principles aimed at fairness and the welfare of children. By understanding these common judicial decisions, parties in family law cases can better prepare their cases, set realistic goals, and make informed decisions. It's important to remember that while trends can indicate likely outcomes, each case is unique, and outcomes can vary based on the specifics of the situation and the discretion of the presiding judge.

Section II – Legal Documentation: Documenting Interactions and Gathering Evidence

In family court, evidence is key. The evidence you present is not just general supporting material to your commentary; it is often the cornerstone upon which cases are built and decided. You can argue all day long and share your views and opinions with the court, but unless there is evidence to back up your claims and concerns, most likely nothing will happen.

Effective documentation of interactions and meticulous gathering of evidence are not merely administrative tasks; they are strategic practices that can substantially influence the outcome of your case. This section outlines best practices for documenting interactions and gathering evidence, particularly in cases where it is crucial to objectively demonstrate the other parent's damaging and toxic behaviors.

Courts often dismiss subjective statements and accusations as biased or emotive. Arguing "your truth" to the court in the absence of facts and objective evidence is almost always a recipe for failure. To strengthen your case, focus on objective and precise documentation that illustrates the other parent's behavior. Focus on showing the court through direct evidence what you want the court to see, rather than just telling the court what you think and believe. Instead of merely claiming that your ex is uncooperative, provide specific examples, like texts that ignore agreed pickup times or emails that disregard your concerns about your child's well-being.

Keep a detailed log of all interactions with the other parent. Record dates, times, and contexts of conversations, and save all written communications, such as texts, emails, and social media posts. If allowed in your state, consider recording verbal exchanges when the other parent is making disparaging remarks in the presence of the children or threatening you. Maintaining a lot of interactions and major events creates a clear, chronological account of the other parent's actions that can be a useful roadmap for presenting your evidence in court.

Photos and videos can also be powerful evidence, especially to show conditions that appear harmful to the child's welfare or to document the parent's behavior. Additionally, keep records of interactions with third parties – like teachers, doctors, or family friends – who can support your observations with their direct witness testimony.

In gathering and presenting this evidence, it is crucial to adhere to legal standards to ensure its admissibility in court. This includes obtaining evidence legally, ensuring it's relevant and presented in a clear and organized manner. By providing concrete examples of harmful behaviors, you help create a compelling, factual basis for your claims, enhancing your credibility and strengthening your legal standing.

When sending or responding to messages from the other parent, avoid emotional responses or confrontations in your communications. Keep messages concise, factual, and neutral to prevent escalation and avoid giving the other party ammunition against you. Use communication platforms that save histories automatically, like emails or texts, and back up this data regularly. Always assume that anything you say or write can and will be used against you in court. What you want the court to see is that you consistently respond in simple, clear, normal, and professional ways, no matter what the other parent throws at you.

If legal in your jurisdiction, consider recording verbal communications, especially during exchanges involving custody handovers or other significant interactions. Always check local laws regarding consent for recordings. These practices ensure you have a robust evidence trail that demonstrates the other party's behavior without relying on subjective accounts.

Documenting Interactions

Documenting interactions with the other party, especially regarding your children, is essential. This provides a factual basis for any claims you may make in court. In custody disputes, showing patterns of behavior – such as attendance at child-related appointments or participation in educational activities – can influence the court's decisions about parental responsibilities.

When dealing with high-conflict individuals, it's important to document not only aggressive or abusive interactions but also more subtle forms of manipulation. Keep records of any attempts to undermine your parenting or violate agreements. Methodically logging dates, times, and details of conversations and incidents helps illustrate consistent behavior patterns over time. This thorough documentation is invaluable in court, where clear, detailed evidence can counter the manipulative narratives often presented by HCPs.

The importance of documentation in family law disputes, especially those involving a high-conflict, narcissistic party, cannot be overstated. Proper documentation creates a reliable, objective record that can help the court see patterns in behavior that may not be evident from isolated incidents. These patterns can significantly influence the court's understanding and decisions regarding custody, visitation, and other contentious issues.

Gathering Evidence

While every family law case is unique, gathering evidence is a central component for all cases that can significantly impact the outcome. Understanding the importance of various forms of evidence can help you navigate the legal process more effectively and set realistic expectations for your case.

Physical evidence: Physical evidence plays a crucial role in family court proceedings, particularly in cases involving custody, divorce, and property disputes. This type of evidence includes any tangible items that can substantiate claims made by either party. Common examples include financial documents such as bank statements, pay stubs, vehicle registrations, insurance policies, tax returns, property deeds, or personal belongings, which are essential for establishing financial status and obligations, because they help clarify the ownership and value of marital assets.

In cases where personal conduct is in question, physical evidence can also include photographs, clothing, or other personal items that might corroborate instances of behavior or presence at specific locations. For example, photographs from social media can be used to establish a person's whereabouts or actions at a given time. Properly collected and presented, physical evidence provides concrete proof that can support or refute claims, making it an indispensable component of the legal process in family law cases.

Digital evidence: Digital evidence has become increasingly critical in family law cases, reflecting the integral role that technology plays in our daily lives. This type of evidence includes emails, text messages, social media posts, and even data from various apps like GPS, and can provide insight into personal conduct, intentions, and interactions. For instance, text messages exchanged between parents can illustrate their communication regarding child custody arrangements or show evidence of harassment or abusive behavior. This type of evidence can also help establish timelines, state of mind, or prove/disprove allegations made by the other party.

Furthermore, financial transactions tracked through online banking or investment accounts can reveal undisclosed assets or spending patterns crucial in divorce settlements.

Social media platforms often serve as a rich source of information where posts, comments, and even "check-ins" can contradict statements made in court, such as claims about financial hardship or whereabouts on particular days.

When collecting digital evidence, it's essential to ensure it is obtained legally and ethically to maintain its admissibility in court. Proper documentation, including capturing metadata like the time and date stamps of communications, can bolster the credibility of digital evidence, making it a powerful tool in supporting legal arguments and claims.

Witness testimonies: Witness testimonies are a pivotal element of evidence in family law cases, providing firsthand accounts that can corroborate your claims about parenting abilities or the nature of the relationship with the other party, and refute the claims made by the opposing party. These testimonies can come from a variety of sources, including family members, friends, teachers, or healthcare professionals who have direct observations or interactions relevant to the case.

For example, a teacher or childcare provider might provide insights into a child's behavior and well-being, offering evidence about the child's home environment and the effects of parental behavior. Similarly, friends and family members can testify about a parent's character and daily interactions with the child, which can be crucial in custody disputes.

Professional witnesses such as psychologists or social workers can offer expert opinions on the psychological impact of certain parental behaviors on children or assess the capabilities of each parent to meet the child's needs. Ensuring that witness testimonies are credible, relevant, and unbiased is crucial, as they can significantly influence the judge's decisions regarding custody, support, and property division.

Legal Considerations in Documenting Interactions and Gathering Evidence

a. Legal Standards for Admissibility

In family court, as in all legal proceedings, not all evidence that a party wishes to present will be accepted by the court. Just because a party thinks something is important and wants the judge to know about it does not make it admissible. I have personally observed numerous times where the opposing party comes into court with stacks of papers and exhibits, none of which are admissible. I have also seen opposing parties come into court trying to rely on nothing other than inadmissible hearsay. Once objected to, they were essentially left with no case whatsoever to present to the court.

The admissibility of evidence is governed by specific legal standards that ensure fairness, reliability, and relevance to the case. Understanding these standards is crucial for effectively preparing and presenting a case in family law.

Relevance: The most fundamental criterion for admissibility is relevance. Evidence must be directly related to the matters at issue in the case. For instance, in a custody dispute, evidence that speaks to a parent's ability to provide a safe and stable environment for the child is relevant, whereas information about the parent's unrelated personal interests might not be. The relevance of evidence is considered in the context of whether it makes a fact more or less probable than it would be without the evidence.

Reliability: Evidence must not only be relevant but also reliable. This means it must come from a trustworthy source and be created or maintained in a way that ensures its accuracy. For example, financial statements must be authentic and unaltered to be admissible. Similarly, digital evidence such as emails or text messages must be shown to have been preserved in their original form and obtained in a manner that prevents tampering.

Procedural rules: Each jurisdiction has rules regarding how evidence should be collected, preserved, and presented. These rules often cover the technicalities of submitting documents, the process for disclosing evidence to the opposing party, and the protocols for witness testimony, including expert witnesses. Failing to follow these procedural rules can result in evidence being excluded, regardless of its relevance or reliability.

Constitutional considerations: In certain cases, constitutional issues such as the right to privacy can affect the admissibility of evidence. For instance, evidence obtained through illegal means, such as unauthorized recordings or violations of privacy, may be deemed inadmissible. Similarly, considerations under the Fourth Amendment (protection against unreasonable searches and seizures) can bar the use of certain evidence in court.

b. Relevance

Evidence must be relevant to the case and must be linked to the issues at hand. Irrelevant information can clutter your case, frustrate the judge, and distract from the key issues.

In legal proceedings, the concept of relevance is foundational to determining which pieces of evidence are permissible for consideration by the court. For evidence to be deemed relevant, it must directly relate to the facts at issue in the case and have the ability to make a fact more or less probable than it would be without the evidence. This criterion is vital to ensuring that the court's decisions are based on information that genuinely impacts the outcome of the case.

For example, in a custody dispute, direct evidence of a parent's interaction with the child, such as documented attendance at school events or medical appointments, directly aligns with claims regarding a parent's involvement and responsibility. Similarly, financial records that illustrate a clear picture of a spouse's earnings and assets are relevant in disputes over alimony and child support, as they directly affect determinations of each party's financial capabilities and needs.

Aligning direct evidence with your claims means meticulously gathering and presenting data, communications, or witness testimonies that directly support or refute the key issues under consideration. This approach not only strengthens your case but also streamlines the proceedings by focusing on the most impactful facts.

Ensuring that all presented evidence is relevant avoids the introduction of superfluous or distracting information, maintaining the focus on the essential elements that need adjudication. This strategic alignment helps the court understand the core of the dispute, facilitating a more efficient and effective decision-making process.

When collecting and organizing your evidence and witness testimony, always ask yourself whether what you want to present is relevant to the issues at hand. Does the evidence or testimony make a key fact more or less probable, or is it ultimately irrelevant to the court's decision? As you consider these questions, be brutally honest with yourself and challenge your assumptions about the relevance of each piece of evidence.

Another useful tool is to engage an attorney in a consulting role to play devil's advocate with your arguments and evidence. What objections might they raise? Can you overcome those objections? How would they challenge your evidence and testimony to keep it from being considered by the judge? Investing a few hours in consulting support can save you from having your case implode in open court.

Understanding the Element of Hearsay

In the context of family law, particularly in cases involving high-conflict dynamics such as those with a narcissistic party, the challenge of hearsay often comes to the forefront. Understanding what constitutes hearsay, why it is generally inadmissible, and how it can affect the proceedings is crucial for anyone navigating family court.

What is hearsay? Hearsay is any statement that was made outside of the courtroom and is brought in as evidence to prove the truth of the matter asserted in the statement. For example, if a parent in a custody dispute claims in court, "My child told me their other parent never feeds them dinner," that statement is considered hearsay if its purpose is to prove the other parent neglects their child's dietary needs. The primary reason hearsay is problematic is its lack of reliability. Since the statement was made outside of the court, it has not been subjected to cross-examination, and there is no way to verify the declarant's credibility, accuracy, or the circumstances under which the statement was made.

Why is hearsay generally inadmissible? Hearsay is typically inadmissible because it does not allow for the opposing party to challenge the veracity of the statement through cross-examination. The court cannot observe the demeanor of the person who originally made the statement, nor assess their sincerity or the conditions affecting the statement's reliability. This limitation undermines the fairness and integrity of the judicial process, which relies heavily on the ability to test evidence through direct examination.

Exceptions to the hearsay rule: While hearsay is generally inadmissible, there are numerous exceptions based on the presumption that certain circumstances or types of statements carry inherent reliability. For instance:

- **Statements made under oath:** Such as those in a previous legal proceeding.

- **Statements against interest:** Statements that would have been against the declarant's interest when made.

- **Excited utterances:** Statements made in response to a startling event or condition while the declarant was under the stress of excitement caused by the event.

- **Medical statements:** Statements made for purposes of medical diagnosis or treatment. These exceptions are based on the rationale that the conditions under which the statements were made lend credibility to their reliability.

Practical implications in family court: In family law, where much of the evidence may involve personal interactions and private conversations, navigating the complexities of hearsay is particularly important. Parties often attempt to use statements from children or other relatives as evidence. Understanding both the hearsay rule and its exceptions can empower a litigant to effectively challenge inadmissible evidence or argue for the admissibility of crucial information.

Moreover, when preparing for court, it is advisable to focus on gathering direct evidence – such as documented communications or testimony from witnesses who can speak from personal knowledge – rather than relying on hearsay. When hearsay seems unavoidable, consult with legal counsel to determine if an exception applies and how best to introduce that evidence in court.

Effectively managing hearsay in family court involves a clear understanding of what hearsay is, recognizing its limitations and exceptions, and preparing a case strategy that relies on admissible, reliable evidence. This preparation not only strengthens your case but also enhances your credibility and persuasiveness in the eyes of the court.

c. Credibility

Credibility is a crucial factor in legal proceedings, affecting both the acceptance of evidence and the overall perception of the parties involved. In family court, where personal testimony often plays a pivotal role, the credibility of the evidence and the individuals presenting it can significantly influence the case's outcome. It is essential to ensure that your sources are reliable and that the evidence is presented clearly and professionally.

Credibility refers to the trustworthiness or believability of a witness or a piece of evidence. For evidence, credibility is assessed based on its source, its consistency with other known facts, and its reliability in terms of how it was collected and presented.

For example, a financial statement that has been independently audited carries more credibility than a self-reported summary of expenses. Similarly, digital evidence such as texts or emails must be shown to have been preserved in their original form and obtained in a legally permissible manner to be seen as credible.

Witness credibility, on the other hand, is evaluated based on the consistency of the testimony, the demeanor of the witness, their ability to recall details, and their lack of bias. Witnesses who can provide consistent and detailed accounts that align with other evidence tend to be more credible. Furthermore, witnesses without a personal stake in the outcome of the case, or those who do not exhibit hostility or excessive emotionality, are often more persuasive.

Maintaining credibility in court involves careful preparation and honesty. Presenting evidence that is accurate, verifiable, and relevant, coupled with delivering consistent and measured testimony, helps establish a trustworthy narrative. This not only aids in winning the court's favor but also in achieving a just resolution based on sound and reliable testimonial and documentary evidence.

Best Practices for Evidence Management

1. Organizing Evidence

   Organizing evidence effectively is a crucial step in presenting a strong case in family court. Proper organization not only aids in creating a compelling narrative that supports your legal arguments but also ensures that the evidence can be easily accessed and understood by the court.

   Organize your evidence in a way that makes it easy to access and present. This can involve chronological organization or categorizing by type. Having a well-organized case file can save valuable time during court proceedings and increase your attorney's effectiveness. Focus on aligning it with your claims and prioritizing the quality of the evidence presented.

Aligning Evidence with Legal Claims

Organize your evidence chronologically or by theme, depending on what best supports the narrative. Chronological organization works well for showing patterns over time, such as the evolution of financial issues or demonstrating consistent parental behavior. Thematic organization, on the other hand, can be effective for complex issues like demonstrating the mental health impacts on children due to the other parent's behavior. Each category or file should directly correspond to a specific claim or aspect of the case, making the relevance clear.

Start by clearly understanding the legal claims and defenses in your case. Each piece of evidence should directly relate to and support these claims. For instance, if the claim involves demonstrating a parent's involvement in a child's life, direct evidence such as dated photographs at school events, copies of parental correspondence with teachers, or a log of daily care activities would be pertinent.

Prioritizing Quality of Evidence

Quality of evidence is paramount. Prioritize direct, current, and compelling evidence that provides explicit proof of the claims made. This includes documented communications, official records, and direct testimonies that are recent and relevant to the matters at hand. Direct evidence typically carries more weight as it does not rely on inference and directly establishes a fact.

Conversely, avoid relying heavily on old, speculative, or vague evidence. While historical context can be important, especially in demonstrating patterns, ensure that it complements strong, current evidence that directly addresses the legal issues. Speculative evidence, such as assumptions about behavior based on hearsay, should be minimized as it is generally weak and can undermine the credibility of your argument.

2. Presentation and Accessibility

Once organized, evidence should be presented in a format that is accessible and easy to understand. Use clear labels, concise descriptions, and an indexed system that allows for quick retrieval during court proceedings. Summaries or charts can be helpful in distilling complex information or extensive data into digestible formats that are immediately graspable by judges and attorneys.

By aligning evidence with legal claims and prioritizing its quality, you ensure that your presentation in court is both persuasive and credible. This strategic organization helps convey your narrative effectively, making a strong case for your position and increasing the likelihood of a favorable outcome.

Continuous Updating

Family law cases can extend over long periods, and new evidence can sometimes emerge on a daily basis. Continuously update your documentation and keep abreast of any new information that may be relevant to your case, especially in dynamic and ongoing cases that involve multiple significant issues. This practice ensures that the evidence remains relevant and reflects the latest developments in the situation, which can significantly influence the outcome of the case.

First, as new information or documents become available, they should be integrated into your existing body of evidence. This might include newly received communications, updated financial statements, recent photographs, or additional witness statements. Regularly adding to your evidence helps to build a comprehensive and current case file, which is crucial for responding effectively to changes in the legal landscape or the opposing party's strategy.

Second, continuous updating involves reviewing the existing evidence to assess its ongoing relevance and accuracy. As circumstances evolve – such as changes in a child's educational needs or a parent's financial status – previous evidence might become less pertinent or might need to be supplemented with newer information to maintain its impact.

Additionally, this practice helps in identifying gaps or weaknesses in your case that need addressing, allowing for timely corrections or enhancements. For example, if initial evidence of a parent's involvement in a child's life is deemed insufficient, more detailed and recent examples can be collected.

Staying proactive in updating and managing your evidence not only keeps your legal strategy aligned with the latest facts but also demonstrates diligence and thoroughness to the court. This can enhance your credibility and the persuasive power of your case, giving you a strategic advantage in negotiations or at trial.

Professional Evaluation

Professional evaluation of evidence before a hearing or trial is crucial to ensure that you present a robust and compelling case. This critical review, typically conducted by legal professionals, serves multiple purposes.

First, it verifies the relevance and admissibility of the evidence, ensuring that it meets legal standards and is likely to be accepted by the court. This step helps avoid the pitfall of relying on evidence that the court may dismiss due to procedural or substantive deficiencies.

Second, professional evaluation assesses the strength and persuasiveness of the evidence. Attorneys can identify potential weaknesses or gaps that might be exploited by the opposing side and suggest enhancements or additional evidence to reinforce the case. This process is vital for avoiding the scenario where a party shows up to court underprepared, potentially leading to unfavorable outcomes due to inadequately supported claims.

Moreover, a thorough evaluation ensures that the evidence aligns strategically with the legal arguments, enhancing the overall coherence and effectiveness of the case presentation. This alignment is crucial for making a convincing argument to the judge and jury, ultimately increasing the chances of a successful outcome.

Conclusion: Documenting Interactions and Gathering Evidence

Effective documentation and meticulous evidence gathering are critical to presenting a strong case in family court. They not only support your claims and demonstrate your commitment to the process but also prepare you to counter any allegations from the opposing party. By adhering to these practices, you ensure that your narrative is supported by solid, undeniable facts, thereby increasing your chances of achieving a favorable outcome in your family law dispute.

Section III – Legal Compliance: Legal and Moral Responsibilities

In the context of family court proceedings, particularly those fraught with conflict, understanding and adhering to both legal and moral responsibilities is paramount. This adherence not only ensures compliance with the law but also upholds a standard of conduct that can significantly influence the outcome and long-term implications of a case.

Legal Responsibilities

Compliance with Court Orders and Deadlines

One of the foremost legal responsibilities in any court proceeding is to comply with all court orders and meet prescribed deadlines. This includes orders for temporary custody arrangements, child support payments, or document submission deadlines. Failing to comply can lead to legal penalties, including fines or, in severe cases, charges of contempt of court. Moreover, adherence to court orders demonstrates respect for the judicial process and can positively influence the court's perception of your reliability and integrity.

This is especially important when dealing with HCPs, who may ignore court directives to assert control. Their disregard can undermine their credibility with the court.

For your part, it's crucial to follow all court orders and deadlines, regardless of the other party's actions. Doing so demonstrates reliability and respect for the law, setting you apart from any non-compliant behavior. By adhering strictly to these requirements, you uphold legal and ethical standards, strengthen your case, and position yourself favorably in the eyes of the court.

Truthfulness in Filings and Testimonies

All statements in court filings and testimonies must be truthful and accurate. Providing false information can lead to serious consequences, including perjury charges. Being truthful also extends to the disclosure of assets in divorce proceedings; hiding or undervaluing assets can result in unfavorable judicial decisions and legal action post-judgment.

Truthfulness is essential for maintaining integrity in legal proceedings. This is particularly important when dealing with a high-conflict ex who may use dishonesty to manipulate the situation, discredit you, or gain sympathy from the court.

For those on the receiving end of such tactics, it is vital to remain truthful in all legal documents and testimonies. Doing so upholds legal standards and establishes your credibility. Judges are skilled at detecting dishonesty, so consistently presenting the truth provides a reliable foundation for fair decisions and counters false narratives made by the opposing party. Adhering to truthfulness not only strengthens your case but also protects you from potential legal repercussions like perjury.

Respect for the Proceedings

Showing respect for the court and its processes is a crucial legal responsibility. This includes following courtroom etiquette, being punctual for hearings, and treating all parties – court staff and the opposing party – with respect. Such behavior maintains the dignity of the proceedings and positions you as a credible participant in the eyes of the court.

Respect is especially important when dealing with a high-conflict, narcissistic party, who may try to dominate proceedings or flout procedural norms to provoke emotional responses. In contrast, demonstrating respect is essential for those opposing such individuals. This means dressing appropriately, adhering to courtroom etiquette, and communicating professionally with everyone involved.

Maintaining professionalism not only showcases your maturity and reliability but also facilitates smoother interactions with judges and attorneys. When the court sees that you respect its time and resources, it is more likely to view your case favorably. This approach reinforces the legitimacy of your claims and establishes a positive rapport with the court, enhancing your overall legal strategy.

Courtroom Etiquette

Adhering to courtroom etiquette is essential in legal proceedings, especially in family court where emotions can run high. Proper behavior not only shows respect for the judicial system but also positively influences how judges and legal professionals perceive your seriousness and professionalism. Follow these guidelines when addressing the court and interacting with judges and other parties:

Addressing the court: Always use professional and respectful language. Avoid slang and focus on facts rather than emotions. Speak clearly and audibly so that everyone can hear you. When responding to questions, answer only what is asked to respect the court's time.

Properly addressing the judge: Address the judge as "Your Honor" to show respect. Avoid informal terms like "Mr." or "Ms." followed by the last name. Never interrupt the judge; wait for a pause to speak.

Importance of standing: Stand when addressing the court, especially during opening or closing statements. This shows your engagement and readiness to interact with the court. Remain seated and composed when your attorney or opposing counsel is speaking.

Interacting with court personnel and opposing counsel: Treat all individuals in the courtroom with respect, including court staff and opposing counsel. Acknowledge clerks and bailiffs politely. Use professional titles (e.g., Attorney [Last Name]) when addressing opposing counsel, and maintain a courteous tone, even in contentious situations.

Attire and physical demeanor: Dress formally, as you would for a significant business meeting. Men should wear suits and ties, while women should opt for suits or conservative dresses. Avoid casual clothing like jeans or t-shirts. Maintain a calm demeanor and avoid overt displays of emotion, such as frustration or anger. Non-verbal cues, like nodding politely and avoiding negative expressions, contribute to a respectful presence.

Mastering courtroom etiquette is vital for anyone involved in legal proceedings. It reflects respect and professionalism, helping to keep the focus on your case rather than any breaches of decorum.

Moral Responsibilities

Acting in the Best Interests of Children

In family law, especially in cases involving children, there is a strong moral obligation to act in their best interests. This means prioritizing their emotional, educational, and physical well-being over personal grievances. When making decisions about custody or visitation, it's essential to focus on the children's needs for stability and ongoing relationships with both parents, rather than viewing the situation through the lens of personal grievances or desires.

The best interests of the children should guide all decisions, with emphasis on their health and safety. Factors to consider include each parent's stability, involvement in the child's life, emotional bonds, and ability to meet the child's needs.

When parties genuinely prioritize the children's best interests, they make decisions that support healthy development. For parents, this may involve making personal sacrifices, such as accepting inconvenient visitation schedules or fostering the child's relationship with the other parent. Demonstrating commitment to the children's well-being not only helps achieve favorable outcomes in court but also establishes a positive foundation for co-parenting after litigation.

Fairness in Negotiations

Even when employing strong legal strategies, there is a moral imperative to engage in fair and honest negotiations. This means being open to compromise and avoiding tactics that seek to undermine the other party. Fair negotiations are especially important in divorce and custody arrangements, as their outcomes significantly impact everyone involved for years to come.

Honest negotiations should respect the rights and needs of all parties, particularly the children. However, dealing with a high-conflict ex can complicate this process.

HCPs often adopt a win-at-all-costs approach, prioritizing their desires over fair outcomes. They may withhold information, make unreasonable demands, or use the children as leverage, which undermines fairness and prolongs conflicts.

For the opposing party, it's essential to stay composed and committed to equitable solutions, regardless of the circumstances. This may involve using mediation, seeking judicial intervention when necessary, and advocating for arrangements that prioritize the children's best interests. Keeping this focus can help counteract the imbalance created by a high-conflict ex and lead to a more just resolution.

Avoidance of Unnecessary Conflict

Although conflicts are sometimes unavoidable, there is a moral obligation to avoid exacerbating disputes unnecessarily. This involves choosing strategies that aim to resolve issues through mediation or collaborative law rather than litigation, whenever possible. Reducing conflict not only minimizes the emotional strain on all parties but also helps preserve relationships post-litigation, which is particularly beneficial for co-parenting arrangements.

Conclusion: Adherence to Legal and Moral Responsibilities

In navigating family court proceedings, the interplay between legal and moral responsibilities is crucial for achieving favorable outcomes and fostering a respectful environment. Adhering to court orders, maintaining truthfulness in all filings, and demonstrating respect for courtroom procedures not only uphold the integrity of the judicial process but also enhance your credibility in the eyes of the court. Concurrently, prioritizing the best interests of children, engaging in fair negotiations, and striving to avoid unnecessary conflict reflect a commitment to ethical conduct that transcends legal obligations. By balancing these responsibilities, you position yourself not only for immediate success in your case but also for healthier relationships and co-parenting dynamics in the long run. Ultimately, a steadfast adherence to both legal and moral principles creates a foundation for a more positive future for all parties involved.

Section IV – Legal Planning: Strategic Considerations

In family law, strategic legal planning becomes critically important when dealing with a high-conflict, narcissistic party. For HCPs, it's not a matter of whether high-conflict games will be played, but a matter of when, how, and how severe. HCPs often bring chaos, disruptions, misdirection, and unpredictable and highly charged emotions into legal proceedings, making it essential to have a well-thought-out strategy that anticipates their antics and leverages legal tools effectively to protect yourself and your case.

To effectively manage such dynamics, it's crucial to anticipate the range of potential issues that will likely arise from their volatile (and predictable) behavior. This includes preparing for sudden changes in their legal strategy, false accusations, or attempts to manipulate the proceedings to their advantage.

Effective legal planning, therefore, must involve comprehensive preparation and the strategic use of legal tools to safeguard against these challenges. This approach ensures that your case progresses as smoothly as possible, with measures in place to counteract the disruptions and maintain focus on achieving the best possible outcomes for all involved, especially the children.

Understanding High-Conflict Behaviors

The first step in strategic legal planning is to understand the behaviors typically displayed by narcissists, which include manipulation, deception, and a penchant for creating chaos and high conflict. HCPs often view the legal system as something akin to a battleground, circus, and stage where they can assert and display their dominance rather than as a means to resolve disputes constructively. Recognizing these tendencies allows for better preparation and the development of tactics to mitigate their impact.

HCPs often display a lack of empathy and have a tendency to manipulate or exploit situations and people to their advantage. In the context of legal disputes, this might manifest as relentless litigation, twisting facts, or even making false allegations to avoid accountability and undermine the credibility of the opposing party. They are also prone to react aggressively to criticism or perceived slights, which can lead to unpredictable and highly charged responses during negotiations or court proceedings.

Moreover, HCPs may use charm or deceit as tools to sway opinions or garner support, making it challenging to maintain a clear and objective perspective in legal matters. Their behavior can create significant disruptions, prolonging the legal process and increasing the emotional and financial strain on all parties involved.

Developing an understanding of these behaviors allows for better preparation and the creation of effective counterstrategies.

This includes setting firm boundaries, maintaining meticulous documentation to counteract false narratives, and employing calm, factual communication to keep proceedings as rational and straightforward as possible.

Taking a Blunt and Honest Self-Inventory

In the midst of battling HCPs in family court, it's easy to become so focused on the other party's unpredictable behaviors that you neglect to examine your own actions and vulnerabilities. Taking a thorough and honest self-inventory is not only a crucial step in preparing for the legal battle ahead but also a key aspect of maintaining your integrity throughout the process.

Begin by asking yourself: What valid claims does the other side have against you? It's important to confront uncomfortable truths. Perhaps there are past actions or behaviors that could be leveraged against you. Maybe you've been less than perfect in your co-parenting, or perhaps there are financial decisions that might be scrutinized. Acknowledging these points is essential because they could be weaponized by your HCP counterpart.

Next, consider what you realistically need to be concerned about. Are there specific allegations that you believe might gain traction in court? Understanding which issues could realistically pose a threat will allow you to prepare effectively.

Finally, think about potential pitfalls that could arise. Are there emotional triggers that could lead to impulsive reactions? Could a moment of frustration lead to a misstep that the other party might exploit? Identifying these vulnerabilities helps to create a comprehensive strategy.

Once you've taken this inventory, the next step is to own those truths. Acknowledge any mistakes or shortcomings and take proactive steps to address them. This might mean making amends where possible, such as improving your communication with the other parent or ensuring that financial obligations are met promptly. The act of owning your issues not only reinforces your integrity but also reduces the ammunition available to your HCP adversary.

Mitigating potential damage involves implementing practical strategies to address your vulnerabilities. For instance, if you recognize that a history of conflict might come up in court, consider documenting positive co-parenting efforts or enrolling in parenting courses. This creates a counter-narrative that emphasizes your commitment to responsible parenting, thereby undermining any attempts to paint you negatively.

Additionally, it's vital to engage in emotional self-regulation. High-conflict situations can provoke strong emotions; therefore, developing techniques to manage stress and anger – such as mindfulness, therapy, or even support groups – can help you remain calm and collected when faced with provocations.

Integrity is more than just an ethical stance; it's a strategic advantage. By being honest about your vulnerabilities, you can craft a legal strategy that not only counters the HCP's tactics but also positions you as the more reasonable party in the eyes of the court. Judges are often wary of HCPs who resort to manipulative tactics. When you demonstrate integrity and accountability, it can enhance your credibility and reinforce your case.

Moreover, by maintaining a consistent commitment to your integrity throughout the process, you establish a foundation for effective communication and negotiation. This doesn't mean ignoring your own needs or rights, but rather approaching the situation with a level of honesty and respect that can diffuse tensions and lead to more productive discussions.

Taking a blunt and honest self-inventory may feel daunting, but it's a vital step in navigating the turbulent waters of family court against a high-conflict personality. By acknowledging your vulnerabilities, owning your truths, and strategically mitigating potential damage, you not only enhance your legal position but also cultivate a sense of personal integrity that will serve you well beyond the courtroom. As you move forward, keep your focus on your objectives and remain steadfast in your commitment to both your values and your strategy.

Setting Clear Objectives

Define clear legal and personal objectives at the outset of your case. In the context of a high-conflict divorce or custody battle, this might involve securing fair custody arrangements, protecting your financial interests, or ensuring personal safety in cases involving abuse. Additional objectives could include minimizing direct conflict, protecting yourself and your children from emotional abuse and trauma, and ensuring any communication is documented and limited to necessary interactions.

Objectives should be realistic, focusing on achievable outcomes that prioritize the well-being of children and your stability post-litigation; they should also be specific, measurable, and tailored to the unique circumstances of your case, ensuring they address both legal outcomes and personal well-being. Clearly defined goals provide a roadmap for your legal strategy and help maintain focus amid the complexities of litigation.

Your objectives should also include decisions about how much time you allocate to managing and developing your case. Family court litigation can easily become an all-consuming affair, taking over your life like an invasive species. It's important to set boundaries and establish rules early on to create clear distinctions between the time you dedicate to your case and the time you spend living your life. Setting these objectives and standards is crucial for protecting your time, relationships, and overall well-being – both mental and physical – during and after the litigation process.

Articulating these goals early on with your legal team helps ensure that every legal action taken is aligned with achieving these outcomes. It also aids in evaluating the progress of your case and adjusting strategies as needed to address new developments or challenges. It is also important to articulate your objectives to your coach, therapist, and family-member support team so they can help keep you aligned with your standards and goals.

Anticipating and Managing Conflict

Given the high-conflict nature of dealing with a narcissistic party, anticipate that they will use tactics designed to intimidate, harass, or wear you down emotionally as a means to assert control and gain an upper hand in legal disputes. It's what they do. They may engage in relentless criticism, public humiliation, and manipulative behaviors that are designed to destabilize your emotional state and distract from the legal issues at hand.

These tactics can manifest as excessive litigation, unfounded accusations, and continuous changes in legal demands – actions that not only prolong the legal process but also significantly increase your stress and legal costs.

By recognizing these potential behaviors in advance, you can strategize effectively to shield yourself and your loved ones. Such preparation involves setting strict boundaries, using communication channels that limit direct contact (relying instead on attorneys or mediators), and maintaining a strong support network.

Furthermore, keeping detailed records of all interactions provides a factual basis to counter any false narratives they might attempt to propagate in court.

Best Practices for Anticipating and Managing Conflict

Document everything: Documenting every interaction is essential in any high-conflict legal scenario. Meticulous records serve as objective evidence that can reveal patterns of behavior, which may be pivotal in court. This includes keeping copies of all written communications such as emails, texts, and social media exchanges, as well as detailed notes on verbal interactions, specifying dates, times, and the context of each conversation.

When possible, legal recordings of interactions can also be invaluable, provided they comply with local laws regarding consent. Such documentation provides a clear, unambiguous record that can counter the manipulative narratives often put forward by high-conflict individuals. It can also help the court see through attempts at deception, ensuring that the truth of the situation is accurately represented.

Use communication strategically: In legal disputes involving a high-conflict individual, strategically managing communication is crucial to maintain clarity and reduce emotional strain. HCPs often seek to dominate and manipulate conversations, especially in face-to-face settings, where they can use emotional manipulation to unsettle or provoke reactions. To mitigate this, it is advisable to limit direct verbal communication and favor written forms whenever possible.

Seek protective orders if necessary: If harassment or abuse is a factor, do not hesitate to seek protective orders. Courts can implement measures that limit the abuser's ability to inflict harm.

Protective orders, also known as restraining orders, are legal decrees issued by a court to prevent one person from contacting or coming near another. Documentation of threatening behavior, harassment, or abuse will support your request for a protective order, underscoring the seriousness of the situation to the court.

This legal tool is essential for immediate protection and can also impact the broader outcomes of your family law proceedings by formally recognizing the problematic behavior of the high-conflict individual.

Stay focused on the facts: Keep your interactions with the court factual and evidence-based. Avoid emotional pleas; focus instead on presenting clear, documented evidence and logical arguments.

This methodical, evidence-based strategy is not only more persuasive but also upholds the integrity of your case by aligning it with the rational, legal framework that courts rely on to make decisions.

Importance of an Evidence-Based Approach

The legal system is designed to adjudicate based on evidence, rules, and precedent, rather than emotional narratives. Judges are trained to be objective, and they assess cases based on the evidence presented.

In high-conflict scenarios, particularly those involving narcissistic individuals, there is often an attempt to shift the focus from factual evidence to emotional manipulation. An HCP might provoke emotional reactions intentionally to undermine your credibility or distract from the substantive issues at hand.

By staying focused on the facts, you counteract their strategies and reinforce the legitimacy of your claims.

Best Practices for Presenting Evidence in Court

Organize evidence logically: When presenting your case in court, organize your evidence clearly and logically. Structure your arguments to lead with strong, indisputable facts that directly support your claims. Use a calm, composed manner to discuss the evidence, demonstrating your rational approach and reliability as a witness.

Avoid emotional language: While it's natural to feel emotional about your case, particularly in family law matters, strive to keep your language in court neutral and professional. Focus on delivering your points with clarity and precision, avoiding overly emotional phrases that could detract from the strength of your factual reporting.

Point to specifics: When facing allegations or arguments from the HCP, focus on dismantling their claims with your evidence, rather than engaging in personal attacks or emotional rebuttals. Point to specific pieces of evidence that contradict their statements and reinforce your position with logical explanations.

Connect to legal precedents: Align your factual presentation with relevant legal standards and precedents. Show how the evidence you provide meets the legal criteria for your requests or defenses. This not only strengthens your case but also helps the judge see the alignment of your claims with the legal framework governing the case.

Maintaining a focus on facts and evidence in court proceedings, especially when opposing a high-conflict party, provides a solid foundation for your case. It minimizes the influence of emotional manipulation and focuses the court's attention on the legal merits of your position. By systematically presenting clear, documented evidence and logical arguments, you enhance your credibility and strengthen your chances of achieving a favorable outcome.

Long-Term Planning

Strategic legal planning, especially in disputes involving high-conflict, narcissistic individuals, requires a careful and thoughtful approach that extends beyond the immediate issues at hand. It is vital to consider the long-term implications of any legal decisions or agreements, particularly in how they affect co-parenting and parallel parenting arrangements and ongoing interactions with the other party.

Thinking long-term involves planning for sustainable co-parenting and parallel parenting structures that anticipate the challenging behavior patterns of a high-conflict ex. This includes setting up detailed parenting plans that specify boundaries and guidelines for handover protocols, setting rules for engagement in public spaces or during child exchanges, and other conflict resolution mechanisms. It may also involve structured communication methods, such as using specialized apps for messaging that keep records and can be monitored if necessary. These plans should be designed to minimize direct conflict and reduce the opportunities for the HCP to engage in manipulative behavior.

Utilizing experienced legal counsel is crucial in navigating these complexities. An attorney familiar with high-conflict cases can provide invaluable guidance in developing a legal strategy that not only addresses the immediate goals but also safeguards against future issues. They can help foresee potential challenges and prepare contingencies that protect your interests and welfare, as well as those of your children.

By understanding the nature of HCPs, anticipating challenges, and preparing meticulously, you can effectively manage the dynamics of your case. This comprehensive approach not only aims for a favorable resolution in the current legal battle but also establishes a foundation for managing future interactions, ensuring that the outcomes are sustainable and serve the best interests of all involved, especially the children.

Emotional Regulation During Legal Processes

Navigating the legal intricacies of family court can be an intensely emotional experience, particularly in high-conflict cases. While the focus is often on legal strategies and outcomes, it's crucial to recognize that your emotional well-being is an invaluable asset in these proceedings. Emotional regulation not only aids in making rational decisions during your case but also serves as a vital resource, defense, and weapon against the manipulative tactics often employed by HCPs.

Understanding Emotional Regulation

Emotional regulation refers to the ability to manage and respond to an emotional experience in an appropriate manner. It involves being aware of, understanding, controlling, and expressing emotions effectively. In the context of legal disputes, particularly those that are high-stress and emotionally charged, mastering this skill can prevent your emotions from clouding your judgment or undermining your case.

Effective emotional regulation helps individuals respond to stressful situations calmly and thoughtfully rather than reacting impulsively. It requires an awareness of one's emotional triggers and the ability to pause before responding, allowing time to process the situation and consider the consequences of various actions.

Techniques such as deep breathing, stepping away momentarily, or engaging in reflective thinking are useful. Developing these skills enhances one's ability to face challenging or provocative situations, like those often encountered in disputes with high-conflict individuals, without becoming overwhelmed or acting in ways that might undermine one's legal position.

The Importance of Emotional Stability in Family Court

When individuals maintain emotional stability, they are better equipped to think clearly and analytically, focusing on factual information and grounded legal advice rather than being swayed by temporary emotions or stressful situations.

This level of composure is essential in family court, where decisions need to be made with a long-term perspective in mind, considering the future well-being of children and the equitable distribution of assets.

Emotional stability helps prevent reactive decisions that might seem satisfying in the heat of the moment but could lead to regrettable outcomes or ongoing legal battles. By prioritizing a calm and measured approach to decision-making, parties are more likely to reach resolutions that are not only fair and just but also sustainable over time, ultimately leading to a more stable future post-litigation.

In the context of family court, where judges must often rely on testimonial evidence and personal assessments to make judgments, the credibility of each party becomes a central factor in the decision-making process.

Judges and other legal professionals are more likely to view you as reliable and credible if you present yourself as calm and composed. When individuals consistently demonstrate calmness, rationality, and the ability to articulate their concerns and responses without undue emotion, they are more likely to be viewed as reliable and truthful. Judges and mediators typically favor parties who can manage their emotions effectively, as this suggests a capacity for responsible parenting and rational decision-making.

On the other hand, emotional outbursts or overly emotional testimonies can be perceived as signs of instability, which might influence the court's decisions, especially in custody matters.

HCPs often try to provoke emotional responses as a way to manipulate situations in their favor. By maintaining emotional control, you prevent them from using your reactions against you, effectively neutralizing one of their key tactics.

To counter these tactics, it is essential to maintain a strategy of emotional detachment and strict adherence to facts and documented evidence. This approach minimizes the impact of their provocations and keeps the proceedings focused on verifiable information rather than emotional interplay. Additionally, consistently employing a calm and composed demeanor in response to a narcissist's attempts at manipulation can frustrate their efforts to dominate the situation, shifting the dynamic in your favor.

Anticipate potential lines of attack and have ready responses that are grounded in evidence and legal precedent. By staying emotionally regulated, you deprive the HCP of the emotional responses they seek, which can neutralize their tactics and maintain the focus on the substantive issues of the case.

Best Practices for Maintaining Emotional Regulation

Professional support: Engaging with mental health professionals such as therapists or counselors can be crucial. They can provide strategies for coping with stress, anxiety, and emotional upheaval that often accompany legal disputes. Cognitive Behavioral Therapy (CBT) and other therapeutic techniques can help you understand and manage your emotions effectively.

Mindfulness and meditation: Practices such as mindfulness and meditation can enhance your ability to remain calm and centered throughout the legal process. These practices help in focusing on the present moment and can reduce the impact of stress and anxiety.

Physical health: Physical activity and a healthy diet play significant roles in emotional regulation. Regular exercise, adequate sleep, and a balanced diet help improve mood, reduce anxiety, and enhance overall well-being, making it easier to handle stress.

Building a support system: Having a robust support system is essential. This can include friends, family, support groups, or anyone who provides emotional and practical support. Sharing your experiences and feelings with trusted individuals can alleviate the sense of isolation and help you navigate through difficult times.

Setting boundaries: Setting and maintaining clear boundaries with the narcissistic party is crucial. This may involve limiting direct communication to necessary interactions or using mediated communication platforms. Protecting your emotional space is vital for maintaining your mental health.

Legal and emotional preparedness: Prepare for each legal encounter, such as court appearances or mediation sessions, by reviewing what to expect and planning your responses. Being well-prepared can reduce anxiety and increase your confidence.

The Long-Term Benefits of Emotional Regulation

Successfully managing your emotions during legal disputes can lead to better outcomes and a more positive post-litigation life. It allows you to focus on healing and moving forward rather than remaining entangled in ongoing conflict. Emotional regulation not only impacts the immediate outcomes of your case but also lays the foundation for future interactions, especially in co-parenting scenarios.

While the legal aspects of family court are undeniably important, the ability to regulate your emotions is equally vital. It serves as your primary defense against manipulative tactics and is a critical resource that supports your overall strategy. By prioritizing your emotional health and stability, you enhance your ability to navigate the complexities of the legal process with strength and resilience, ultimately leading to more favorable outcomes for both you and your children.

Set clear objectives and organize an evidence-based approach to your case in anticipation of high-conflict tactics by your ex. Strategic planning and emotional regulation will further your goals and enhance your ability to execute with integrity in family court. By meticulously preparing your case, you not only strengthen your claims but also demonstrate your dedication to the legal process. This preparation equips you to address any counter arguments from the opposing party, ensuring that your narrative is backed by undeniable facts. Ultimately, adhering to these practices enhances your credibility and significantly increases your chances of achieving a favorable outcome in family law disputes.

Conclusion: Effective Legal Planning

In conclusion, effective legal planning in family law is essential for navigating the complexities and emotional turbulence that arise when dealing with high-conflict personalities. By understanding the traits of these individuals, conducting an honest self-inventory, and setting clear objectives, you create a strong foundation that anticipates and manages potential conflicts. An evidence-based approach further bolsters your case, while long-term planning allows you to prepare for future scenarios and implications of your legal decisions. Additionally, focusing on emotional regulation equips you to maintain your composure throughout the process, reducing the likelihood of reactive decisions. By addressing these distinct yet interconnected aspects, you empower yourself to mitigate chaos, protect your interests, and prioritize the well-being of all parties involved, especially the children. Ultimately, a well-structured legal strategy not only enhances your chances of success but also lays the groundwork for healthier relationships in the future.

Key Takeaways:

- **Recognize Legal Framework:** Understanding family court principles is essential for effective decision-making and managing expectations. Familiarity with family law basics helps navigate the process smoothly.

- **Focus on the Child's Best Interests:** Family court prioritizes the child's health, safety, and welfare. This principle is central to custody decisions and should guide your approach.

- **Different Courts, Different Goals:** Family courts aim for mediation and fair resolutions in family matters, while criminal courts handle crimes and penalties. Family court procedures are less formal and focus on negotiation.

- **Local Laws Matter:** Understand how your local laws impact divorce, property division, custody, and support, as these can vary by jurisdiction.

- **Comply with Court Orders:** Adhere to all court orders and deadlines, such as custody arrangements and support payments, to avoid penalties and show respect for the judicial process. Non-compliance can damage credibility and lead to legal consequences.

- **Respect Court Proceedings:** Show respect for the court by following etiquette, being punctual, and treating everyone involved courteously. This professionalism reflects positively on your case.

- **Recognize Manipulative Tactics:** HCPs often use manipulation, deception, and conflict to gain control. Knowing these behaviors helps you prepare effective counter strategies and maintain focus on your case.

- **Prepare Thoroughly:** Keep detailed records of all interactions, including dates and contexts. Use formal communication methods and back up all data regularly.

- **Get Expert Help:** Work with legal professionals experienced in family law and high-conflict cases. They can help ensure your evidence is strong and properly presented.

- **Minimize Unnecessary Conflict:** Strive to resolve disputes through mediation or collaboration rather than escalation. This reduces emotional strain and helps maintain relationships, especially for co-parenting.

- **Define Goals Clearly:** Set specific, achievable objectives for your case, such as fair custody arrangements or financial protection. Clear goals guide your legal strategy and ensure you stay focused.

- **Prioritize Evidence-Based Arguments:** Focus on clear, documented evidence and logical arguments in court. Avoid emotional appeals and let the facts drive your case.

3

RECOGNIZING AND COUNTERING MANIPULATIVE TACTICS

Family court presents a complex and emotionally taxing environment, especially when faced with an opponent who employs manipulative tactics, from subtle misinformation to outright deception and emotional provocation. Recognizing and effectively countering these strategies is essential for safeguarding your interests and ensuring a fair legal process.

This chapter delves deeply into the various forms of manipulation that can arise in family law disputes, offering insights into how to identify and understand the underlying intentions behind these behaviors. Whether through gaslighting, false accusations, or exploiting legal processes, these tactics are designed to disorient and destabilize, creating an unfair advantage in proceedings. Again, when dealing with an HCP, it's not a matter of whether they will employ these high-conflict and manipulative behaviors…it's a matter of when, how many, how often, and how severe.

Beyond mere recognition, you will be equipped with practical strategies to counteract these manipulations. From maintaining meticulous documentation to enhancing your communication techniques and securing skilled legal representation, the emphasis will be on building a proactive defense. These tools not only neutralize the effects of manipulation but also reinforce your case with integrity and resilience.

As we explore these critical aspects, the goal is to empower you with the knowledge and strategies necessary to effectively navigate manipulative legal landscapes, allowing you to maintain control over your case and work toward the best possible outcomes for yourself and your family.

Manipulative Tactics in Divorce and Custody Disputes

In the emotionally charged environment of custody disputes, manipulative tactics are frequently employed by parties seeking to sway outcomes in their favor. High-conflict individuals often use these tactics instinctively, as it is part of their nature. Understanding these manipulative strategies in detail is essential for any parent involved in such disputes, as recognizing them can aid in developing effective counterstrategies. To prepare yourself for all possibilities, let's take a closer look at some of the most common manipulative tactics encountered in custody disputes, along with a wide variety of solutions you can practice in order to limit or counteract the negative effects of manipulation by HCPs.

Gaslighting

Gaslighting is a psychological tactic commonly used in high-conflict custody disputes, aimed at making someone question their own memory, perception, and sanity. In custody disputes, one parent might contradict the other parent's account of events, insist that certain events did not happen or that the other parent's recollections are wrong, or dismiss the other parent's feelings and concerns as irrational or unfounded.

This tactic can be particularly destructive as it not only sows seeds of doubt and confusion in the victimized parent but also can undermine their credibility in legal settings. Victims of gaslighting may begin to question their own judgments and memories, which can impair their ability to advocate effectively for themselves and their children.

Countering gaslighting requires keeping detailed records of all interactions and communications, seeking corroborative evidence where possible, and relying on documented facts rather than subjective recollections in legal proceedings.

Examples of Gaslighting by HCPs in Family Court:

1. **Denial of events:** One party claims that certain events or conversations never happened, causing the other to question their memory and perception.

2. **Misrepresentation of evidence:** The HCP may twist or fabricate facts about incidents, presenting a distorted version of reality to the court.

3. **Accusations of mental instability:** They might label the other party as "unstable" or "irrational" to undermine their credibility and paint themselves as the more competent parent.

4. **Dismissing legitimate concerns:** When one parent raises valid concerns about the children's welfare, the other dismisses them as overreactions or paranoia.

5. **Blame shifting:** The high-conflict party blames the other for problems in the relationship or the divorce process, making them feel responsible for their own distress.

6. **Emotional manipulation in court:** They may use emotional outbursts or victimhood narratives in the courtroom to sway the judge's perception and garner sympathy.

7. **Selective memory:** The ex may conveniently forget their own negative behavior while vividly recalling the other party's mistakes, creating an unfair narrative.

8. **False allegations:** Making unfounded accusations of abuse or neglect to damage the other party's reputation and influence custody decisions.

9. **Undermining parenting skills:** They may criticize the other parent's parenting abilities in front of the children or in court, portraying them as unfit.

10. **Using children as pawns:** Manipulating children to relay messages or negative perceptions about the other parent, fostering confusion and emotional conflict in the kids.

Solutions to Counteract Gaslighting:

- Keep Detailed Records: Document every interaction you have with the other parent, including emails, texts, phone calls, and in-person exchanges. Time stamp and save important communications to create a reliable timeline. These records can serve as powerful evidence to counter false narratives and manipulation attempts during custody disputes.

- Collect Corroborative Evidence: Gather objective, third-party evidence such as school records, medical reports, and therapist evaluations to support your claims. These documents can verify your involvement in your child's life an d counteract any false accusations or distorted claims made by the high-conflict parent in court.

- Use Co-Parenting Apps: Utilize court-approved co-parenting apps like OurFamilyWizard or Talking Parents, which automatically log and time stamp all communications. This ensures that a clear, unaltered record of interactions exists, reducing the gas lighter's ability to manipulate or deny previous conversations and agreements in custody disputes.

- Seek Professional Support: Engage neutral professionals such as therapists, custody evaluators, or mediators who can provide an unbiased assessment of family dynamics. These experts can recognize and document manipulative behaviors, helping to counter gaslighting tactics while also offering insights that support the best interests of the child in court.

- Stay Calm and Focused: Gaslighting is designed to provoke you emotionally. Stay calm, respond only to factual issues, and avoid engaging in emotional battles. Keeping your composure not only preserves your own mental well-being but also demonstrates to the court that you are a reliable and stable parent, strengthening your case.

- Get Legal Representation: Hire an experienced family law attorney familiar with high-conflict custody cases. Your lawyer can help you respond effectively to gaslighting tactics, present your evidence clearly in court, and ensure that the other party's attempts to distort reality are countered with factual, legally sound arguments.

- Document Positive Parenting: Keep a detailed log of your involvement in your child's life, including school meetings, medical appointments, and extracurricular activities. Photos, receipts, and schedules can serve as evidence of your active role as a parent, countering false claims that you are uninvolved or neglectful in the child's upbringing.

- Use Witnesses: Where possible, have witnesses present during important interactions with the other parent. Whether it's a family member, friend, or professional, witnesses can offer objective testimony to support your version of events. This can help disprove the high-conflict parent's false claims and manipulation efforts.

- Focus on the Child's Best Interests: Throughout all interactions and court proceedings, prioritize the well-being of your child. Emphasize how your actions, decisions, and requests serve the child's needs. This approach contrasts with the high-conflict parent's manipulative behavior, which is often self-serving, and reinforces your stability and genuine concern for your child.

- Avoid Emotional Reactions: Gaslighting thrives on creating emotional responses. Practice emotional regulation techniques such as deep breathing, mindfulness, or consulting with a therapist. Staying composed in the face of provocation demonstrates maturity and level-headedness, helping you avoid being drawn into unproductive or damaging conflicts during legal proceedings.

- Prepare for Court: Come to court fully prepared with organized documentation, evidence, and any professional assessments you've obtained. Present a clear, factual narrative that contradicts the gas lighter's distortions. Your ability to provide solid evidence

and stay calm under pressure will strengthen your
credibility and position in the custody case.

Projection

Projection is a psychological defense mechanism often employed
by HCPs during family court disputes, where one parent
attributes their own undesirable feelings, thoughts, or behaviors
onto the other parent. In custody battles, this tactic can manifest
as accusations of neglect, anger, or inappropriate behavior
directed at the other parent, despite the accuser exhibiting
similar traits themselves. For example, a parent may accuse
their ex-partner of being emotionally unstable or unfit while
simultaneously displaying those very same characteristics.

This tactic is particularly harmful as it not only deflects
attention from the accuser's own shortcomings but also creates
confusion and mistrust between parents. By framing themselves
as the victim and the other parent as the perpetrator, they can
manipulate perceptions in court, undermining the accused
parent's credibility and potentially impacting custody decisions.

Counteracting projection involves maintaining clear,
factual documentation of behaviors and interactions, seeking
external validation from professionals or neutral third parties,
and presenting a coherent narrative that highlights the true
dynamics of the relationship. By focusing on evidence rather
than engaging in emotional counterattacks, the targeted parent
can better defend their position and protect their relationship
with their child.

Examples of Projection by HCPs in Family Court:

1. **Accusing the other parent of emotional instability**: A parent who struggles with emotional regulation might claim that the other parent is the one who is unstable or erratic.

2. **Claiming the other parent is unfit**: A parent may accuse their ex-partner of being unfit to care for the children, despite their own history of neglect or inadequate parenting.

3. **Alleging substance abuse**: One parent may project their own issues with substance use onto the other, asserting that the other parent has a problem even when they do not.

4. **Falsely accusing the other parent of manipulation**: A parent might accuse their ex of manipulating the children or using them as pawns, while they themselves engage in similar behaviors.

5. **Denying responsibility for conflict**: A parent who frequently instigates arguments may accuse the other parent of being confrontational or difficult, shifting blame onto them.

6. **Projecting jealousy**: A parent who feels insecure about their own relationships may accuse their ex of being jealous or overly possessive regarding new partners.

7. **Accusing the other parent of alienation**: One parent may claim that the other is alienating the children from

them, while they are the ones subtly undermining the other parent's relationship with the kids.

8. **Claiming the other parent is financially irresponsible**: A parent who is struggling with finances may accuse their ex of being irresponsible with money, even if the other parent is managing their finances well.

9. **Alleging controlling behavior**: A parent who exhibits controlling tendencies might accuse the other parent of being overly controlling or domineering in parenting decisions.

10. **Projecting aggression**: A parent who has exhibited aggressive behavior may accuse the other parent of being angry or hostile, redirecting attention from their own actions.

Solutions to Counteract Projection:

- **Mirror Back the Facts:** When the high-conflict parent projects their own undesirable behaviors onto you, calmly restate the facts of the situation. Avoid engaging in the emotional accusations. By sticking to objective details, you prevent yourself from getting caught in their false narrative and make it easier for others, such as legal professionals, to see through the projection.

- **Keep a Parallel Timeline:** Document key events with time-stamped records. When projection occurs, your detailed timeline will serve as a clear and objective way to show that the claims made by the high-conflict parent do not match reality. This can help expose their manipulation tactics and support your case in court.

- **Seek Third-Party Verification:** Involve neutral third parties – such as teachers, doctors, or therapists – who can offer an unbiased perspective on family dynamics. Their input can verify your parenting behavior and counter false claims that result from projection, providing the court with a more accurate understanding of the situation.

- **Use "I" Statements:** When responding to projected accusations, focus on "I" statements to clarify your perspective without escalating the conflict. For example, say, "I feel that my parenting decisions are focused on our child's best interests" rather than directly accusing the other parent of projecting. This allows you to maintain control and avoids falling into the trap of defensiveness.

- **Flip the Script with Humility:** When facing accusations rooted in projection, consider using humility to disarm the conflict. For example, if the other parent accuses you of being controlling, acknowledge the complexity of parenting and state that you are open to improving for the child's sake. This may shift the focus back to their behavior without you directly confronting the projection, reducing the power of the tactic.

- **Document Your Positive Actions:** Maintain a record of your positive parenting behaviors, including attendance at your child's activities, supportive communication, and everyday interactions. By consistently documenting your constructive actions, you create a counter-narrative that can easily refute accusations and expose the high-conflict parent's projection for what it is – misdirection.

- **Engage a Guardian ad Litem:** Request a guardian ad litem or custody evaluator to be appointed in your case. These professionals observe family interactions and report their findings to the court. Their unbiased observations can highlight the true behaviors of both parents, helping to dismantle the projections being made by the high-conflict parent.

- **Practice Empathy as Armor:** Understand that projection is often a reflection of the high-conflict parent's own insecurities or guilt. Practicing empathy can help you emotionally detach from the accusations. While it doesn't mean accepting the false narrative, it allows you to respond calmly and with resilience, reducing the power of their projections to disrupt your emotional balance.

- **Present a Consistent Narrative:** Consistency in your actions, communication, and behavior speaks louder than any accusations made through projection. Stick to your principles, and avoid shifting your parenting approach in reaction to the other parent's attacks. Over time, your reliability will contrast with their erratic behavior, which can influence court perceptions in your favor.

- **Consider Family Therapy:** Propose family therapy as a neutral space to address the projection in a controlled environment. While the high-conflict parent may resist, suggesting therapy demonstrates your commitment to resolving issues constructively. If therapy is pursued, it can help reveal the unhealthy dynamics created by projection and provide the court with an expert assessment.

- **Keep Emotional Distance:** Recognize projection as an emotional manipulation tactic and refrain from personalizing the attacks. The high-conflict parent's accusations are more about their internal issues than your actual behavior. By maintaining emotional distance, you avoid internalizing their projections and can continue focusing on your child's best interests.

- **Use Written Communication:** Whenever possible, communicate in writing through emails, texts, or co-parenting apps. Written communication not only creates a record but also allows you to carefully craft responses that avoid emotional engagement with the high-conflict parent's projections. Clear, concise written exchanges can help disarm their attempts to create confusion or cast blame.

- **Frame the Projection for the Court:** When it comes time to address the projection in court, carefully frame the behavior for the judge without directly accusing the other parent. For instance, you could say, "It seems there is confusion around certain events, and

I have documentation that clarifies my actions." This allows you to expose the projection without appearing combative.

- **Model Stability for Your Child:** Projections often attempt to undermine your credibility in your child's eyes. To counter this, consistently model calm, supportive, and stable behavior around your child. Over time, your child will likely see through the distortions created by the other parent and recognize your reliability and positive influence.

- **Highlight Inconsistencies:** Projection often involves inconsistent or illogical accusations. Politely highlight these inconsistencies in written communication or in court by presenting factual evidence that contrasts with the accusations. Pointing out contradictions in the high-conflict parent's narrative can help discredit their claims and expose the projection as a manipulation tactic.

- **Stay Focused on the Child:** Refocus any discussions on what truly matters – your child's well-being. If the other parent is projecting, steer the conversation back to practical matters related to your child's needs, such as schooling, health, and extracurriculars. By keeping the focus on the child, you defuse the personal attacks and redirect the conversation toward constructive solutions.

Triangulation

Triangulation is a manipulative strategy frequently employed by HCPs in family court disputes, where one parent creates an alliance with a third party – often the child or another family member – to undermine the other parent. This tactic involves drawing in the third party to relay messages, express grievances, or manipulate perceptions, effectively isolating the targeted parent and creating an emotional wedge between them and the child. For instance, a parent might encourage a child to share negative opinions about the other parent, or they might involve relatives to bolster their narrative, painting themselves as the victim and the other parent as the antagonist.

This tactic is particularly harmful as it disrupts healthy parent-child dynamics and fosters confusion and loyalty conflicts within the child. It can lead to increased tension and conflict between parents, complicating custody arrangements and affecting the child's emotional well-being.

Countering triangulation requires proactive communication strategies and establishing boundaries. Co-parents should strive to maintain direct communication with each other regarding parenting issues, utilizing structured methods such as co-parenting apps to minimize the potential for manipulation. Documenting instances of triangulation and seeking support from professionals can also help clarify the situation and reinforce the focus on the child's best interests. By addressing triangulation head-on, parents can protect their relationship with their children and foster a healthier co-parenting environment.

Examples of Triangulation by HCPs in Family Court:

1. **Involving the child in adult disputes**: One parent asks the child to relay messages or complaints about the other parent, creating unnecessary conflict and emotional burden for the child.

2. **Encouraging negative talk about the other parent**: A parent may encourage the child to voice negative opinions about the other parent, effectively undermining the child's relationship with them.

3. **Manipulating extended family**: A parent might enlist the support of grandparents or relatives to take sides, creating an alliance against the other parent and reinforcing their narrative of victimhood.

4. **Using the child as a messenger**: Instead of communicating directly, one parent sends the child with messages or requests, which can lead to misunderstandings and miscommunication.

5. **Turning the child against the other parent**: A parent may subtly or overtly suggest to the child that they should prefer one parent over the other, fostering loyalty conflicts.

6. **Creating scenarios for the child to witness conflict**: A parent might stage confrontations in front of the child or provoke situations where the child feels caught in the middle.

7. **Involving teachers or counselors**: One parent may go to teachers or counselors to express grievances

about the other parent, attempting to gain support and influence the child's perception.

8. **Fostering dependency on the third party**: A parent might encourage the child to rely on them or other family members for emotional support instead of fostering a healthy relationship with both parents.

9. **Accusing the other parent of alienation**: One parent claims the other is alienating the child, while they are actually the ones creating divisions and emotional distance.

10. **Manipulating court professionals**: A parent may attempt to sway the opinions of custody evaluators or social workers by framing their narrative through the experiences of the child or other relatives.

Solutions to Counteract Triangulation:

- **Strengthen Direct Communication Channels:** Eliminate the need for intermediaries by establishing clear, direct communication with the other parent through co-parenting apps or email. This reduces the opportunity for the other parent to use the child or others as messengers or manipulate interactions. Apps like OurFamilyWizard can track communication and minimize triangulation attempts.

- **Reinforce Positive Parent-Child Boundaries:** Model and reinforce healthy boundaries with your child. Let them know that adult issues, especially custody matters, are not their burden to carry. Reassure them that they are not responsible for relaying messages or resolving conflicts between parents. Maintaining clear boundaries helps protect the child from being drawn into triangulation.

- **Invite Neutral Third-Party Support:** Involve a neutral third party, such as a family therapist or mediator, to provide a balanced perspective on family dynamics. Having a professional present can neutralize the triangulation attempts, as they can observe interactions and provide guidance to keep the focus on the child's well-being, preventing one parent from dominating the narrative.

- **Model Healthy Communication for the Child:** Children learn by example, so model open, respectful communication in their presence. When your child sees you handling disagreements calmly and directly with the other parent, they are less likely to fall for manipulative tactics and can better differentiate between healthy and unhealthy interactions.

- **Keep Evidence of Attempts at Triangulation:** Document instances where the other parent tries to use third parties, such as the child, to create an alliance against you. Save texts, emails, or notes about conversations where this occurs. These records can be useful in court to show the triangulation pattern and its negative impact on the child.

- **Encourage Open Dialogue with the Child:** Maintain an open-door policy for communication with your child. If they come to you with messages or sentiments from the other parent, listen without judgment and calmly clarify any misunderstandings. Let them know it's okay to share their thoughts, but gently remind them that they shouldn't have to mediate between adults.

- **Counter Triangulation with Transparency:** Be transparent with everyone involved – your child, family members, and professionals – about your intentions and decisions. Open communication reduces the other parent's ability to manipulate or misrepresent your actions. When everyone knows the facts, the triangulator's false narratives lose power.

- **Use a "Referee" for High-Stakes Discussions:** For discussions that tend to get heated or emotionally charged, bring in a mediator or trusted third party to oversee the conversation. This can prevent one parent from ganging up on the other or pulling in additional family members to create an alliance against you.

- **Frame It for the Court:** If triangulation becomes a major issue, bring it to the court's attention by framing it as harmful to the child. Focus on how the behavior creates loyalty conflicts and emotional stress for the child and propose solutions that prioritize their well-being. Courts are often sensitive to tactics that drag children into parental disputes.

- **Anchor the Child in Stability:** Children thrive on consistency and security. Counteract triangulation by creating a stable, supportive environment where they feel emotionally safe. Establish reliable routines and reinforce that they are loved and valued by both parents, regardless of any conflicts between adults.

- **Turn to Family Therapy for a Neutral Perspective:** If the other parent consistently triangulates, consider requesting family therapy. A therapist can observe the dynamics and provide expert insight on how the behavior is affecting the child. In some cases, therapy can help reduce triangulation by holding both parents accountable for maintaining healthy interactions with the child.

- **Strengthen Your Alliance with the Truth:** Triangulators thrive on manipulation and creating confusion. To counter this, ensure your alliance is with truth and integrity. Speak calmly, stick to facts, and avoid retaliating in kind. By focusing on honesty and clarity, you make it harder for the triangulator to create divisions that stick.

- **Use "Child-Centered" Reframing:** When the other parent triangulates, consistently reframe the issue around the child's best interests. For example, if the other parent tries to involve a relative, calmly say, "I'd like to focus on what's best for [child's name]. Let's keep the conversation about what they need right now." This prevents distractions and keeps the child at the center.

- **Build Strong Ties with Extended Family:** If the high-conflict parent tries to involve extended family in the triangulation, strengthen your own positive relationships with those family members. Clear, respectful communication with in-laws or mutual relatives can prevent them from being swayed by the manipulator's narrative and give you allies who understand the full picture.

- **Encourage a Child-First Focus in Group Settings:** When group meetings or family gatherings occur, keep the conversation focused on the child's needs and well-being. Deflect attempts to shift discussions into blame or division by emphasizing collaborative efforts for the child's sake. Encourage neutral topics like school, activities, or shared family events that keep triangulation at bay.

- **Teach Your Child Critical Thinking:** Empower your child by encouraging critical thinking. Help them gently question why they're being put in the middle of adult conflicts and teach them to recognize manipulation. By equipping your child with emotional intelligence and problem-solving skills, you enable them to resist being used as a pawn in triangulation.

- **Maintain Open Lines with Other Third Parties:** Keep teachers, doctors, and other key adults in your child's life informed of the situation. Having open communication with these neutral third parties can counter any attempts by the high-conflict parent to influence or manipulate their perceptions. They can provide objective insights if needed in court.

- **Stay Above the Fray with Clear Boundaries:** Resist being drawn into the triangulation dynamic yourself. If the other parent enlists a third party, calmly communicate that any necessary discussions should involve all relevant parties directly. Avoid getting pulled into side conversations or hidden alliances that play into the triangulator's hands.

- **Use Written Agreements:** To minimize triangulation attempts, get key agreements in writing – whether they involve parenting schedules, responsibilities, or communication plans. Written agreements reduce ambiguity and limit the triangulator's ability to twist verbal commitments or create conflicts between you and other third parties.

- **Turn Loyalty Conflicts into Lessons:** If your child expresses confusion due to triangulation, use the opportunity to teach a life lesson about loyalty, honesty, and independence. Reassure them that it's okay to love both parents and that they don't have to take sides. Providing this emotional security helps reduce the power of triangulation and teaches healthy relational dynamics.

Exploiting Emotional Vulnerabilities

Exploiting emotional vulnerabilities is a manipulative tactic frequently used by HCPs during family court disputes. This strategy involves targeting the emotional weaknesses of the other parent – such as fear, guilt, or insecurity – to gain an advantage in negotiations or court proceedings. A high-conflict parent may leverage past traumas, highlight perceived failures, or instill doubt about the other parent's capability to care for the child, thereby undermining their confidence and decision-making abilities.

This tactic can be particularly damaging, as it not only exacerbates the emotional turmoil of the targeted parent but also diverts attention from the best interests of the child. By creating a sense of crisis or portraying themselves as the more competent parent, the HCP can manipulate perceptions and sway opinions, complicating custody arrangements and increasing conflict.

To counter this exploitation, it is essential for parents to recognize and validate their feelings while maintaining a strong sense of self-worth. Establishing firm boundaries, seeking emotional support from trusted friends or professionals, and focusing on the child's well-being can help mitigate the impact of such tactics. Keeping detailed documentation of interactions and emotional responses can also provide clarity and support during legal proceedings, ensuring that decisions remain grounded in objective evidence rather than emotional manipulation. By addressing these vulnerabilities head-on, parents can protect themselves and their children from the destructive effects of this manipulative behavior.

Examples of Exploiting Emotional Vulnerabilities by HCPs in Family Court:

1. **Highlighting past failures**: A parent may bring up past mistakes or failures of the other parent to instill feelings of inadequacy or guilt, undermining their confidence.

2. **Playing the victim**: One parent might portray themselves as the victim of the relationship or parenting situation, eliciting sympathy from the court or professionals while painting the other parent as the aggressor.

3. **Instilling fear**: A parent could threaten to take the child away or suggest that the other parent will lose custody if they don't comply with demands, exploiting fears about losing parental rights.

4. **Using guilt**: One parent might manipulate the other by making them feel guilty about spending time away from the child for work or personal reasons, complicating co-parenting decisions.

5. **Questioning parenting skills**: A high-conflict parent may undermine the other's parenting capabilities by pointing out minor mistakes or differences in parenting styles, creating self-doubt.

6. **Creating false narratives**: A parent might fabricate stories about the other's behavior or parenting to provoke anxiety or insecurity, affecting the targeted parent's ability to present their case effectively.

7. **Leveraging emotional attachments**: One parent could exploit the child's emotional bond with them, suggesting the child would be devastated by spending time with the other parent, thereby creating loyalty conflicts.

8. **Manipulating support systems**: A parent might turn friends, family, or even professionals against the other parent by exaggerating concerns about their parenting or mental health, isolating them emotionally.

9. **Using high-conflict communication**: By engaging in aggressive or accusatory communication, one parent can provoke emotional reactions in the other, distracting from constructive dialogue.

10. **Threatening legal action**: A high-conflict parent may threaten to initiate legal proceedings over minor issues, exploiting the other parent's anxiety about the legal system to gain compliance.

Solutions to Counteract Exploiting Emotional Vulnerabilities:

- **Turn Vulnerabilities into Strengths:** Acknowledge your emotional vulnerabilities and transform them into strengths. For example, if guilt about past mistakes is being weaponized against you, focus on how you've grown as a parent. Showing self-awareness and personal growth disarms the manipulator and turns what they see as a weakness into a strength.

- **Practice Radical Acceptance:** By practicing radical acceptance of the situation, you neutralize the emotional power the HCP holds over you. Accepting the present reality – without judgment or resistance – helps you detach from their manipulations. This mindset shift makes it harder for the HCP to exploit your emotions, as you stop reacting emotionally to provocations.

- **Arm Yourself with Emotional Intelligence:** Sharpen your emotional intelligence (EQ) by learning to recognize and label your feelings. This gives you power over your emotions, allowing you to stay composed in the face of manipulation. When you understand what triggers your emotions, you can develop strategies to manage them, preventing the HCP from using them against you.

- **Master the Art of Neutral Responses:** When the HCP attempts to provoke guilt or fear, respond with neutral, calm statements. For example, say, "I hear your concerns, but my focus is on what's best for our child." Neutral responses deflate emotional attacks, leaving the HCP with no leverage to manipulate you further.

- **Prepare Emotional Exit Strategies:** Before entering a negotiation or court proceeding, prepare an "emotional exit strategy." If you feel your emotions being triggered, take a pause, step outside, or ask for a break. This gives you the space to regain emotional control before reengaging, preventing the HCP from using your emotions against you in real-time.

- **Create an Emotional "Firewall":** Visualize an emotional firewall between you and the manipulator. This mental exercise helps protect you from absorbing their emotionally charged attacks. Picture yourself calmly observing their behavior from behind this shield, without internalizing their efforts to exploit your vulnerabilities.

- **Embrace Your Fear and Move Through It:** Rather than avoiding your fears, acknowledge them and face them head-on. By confronting and understanding your fears, you disarm the HCP's ability to use them against you. For example, if they exploit your fear of losing custody, prepare yourself with knowledge, legal advice, and a strong support network to counteract the fear.

- **Prepare for Psychological "Ambushes":** Anticipate the HCP's emotional manipulation tactics and be ready for them. Prepare a mental list of common provocations (guilt trips, fearmongering, etc.) and practice your responses. By expecting these "psychological ambushes," you'll be less likely to be caught off guard and can respond with calm clarity.

- **Surround Yourself with Emotional Anchors:** Build a support system of trusted friends, family, or a therapist who can act as emotional anchors. When the HCP tries to exploit your insecurities, these people help ground you in reality, reminding you of your worth, abilities, and strengths. Their encouragement reinforces your emotional resilience.

- **Shift to a Problem-Solving Mindset:** Instead of getting caught up in emotional games, focus on solutions. When the HCP uses guilt or fear to manipulate you, pivot the conversation toward practical resolutions. For example, if they say, "You never spend enough time with the kids," respond with, "Let's discuss how we can ensure balanced parenting time."

- **Redefine Your "Weaknesses":** Don't let the HCP define your emotional vulnerabilities as weaknesses. Reframe them as a natural part of being a caring parent. For instance, guilt about not being "perfect" only shows your commitment to being the best parent you can be. This perspective shift weakens their manipulative attempts.

- **Use Tactical Vulnerability:** In controlled situations, you can use vulnerability as a strength. Openly acknowledging your challenges – such as feeling overwhelmed but committed to improving – can disarm the manipulator. By owning your vulnerability, you take away the power the HCP hopes to gain by exposing it.

- **Consult a Therapist for Emotional Coaching:** Work with a therapist to identify and address emotional triggers the HCP may exploit. Therapists can help you develop techniques to manage these triggers, strengthening your emotional resilience and reducing the manipulator's ability to gain control over you in court or negotiations.

- **Focus on Your Child's Well-Being:** Keep your attention firmly on your child's best interests. When the HCP tries to manipulate you by tapping into fear or guilt, redirect your focus to what's most important: your child's well-being. This helps shift the conversation away from personal attacks and keeps you grounded in your parenting goals.

- **Stop Defending and Start Asserting:** Instead of defending yourself against emotional manipulation, assert your position clearly. If the HCP tries to make you feel guilty, for example, calmly state your boundaries: "I understand you may feel that way, but I'm making decisions in our child's best interest." Assertiveness leaves little room for manipulation.

- **Track Patterns of Emotional Manipulation:** Keep a written record of specific instances where the HCP has targeted your emotions, noting what was said and how it made you feel. Identifying patterns helps you recognize these manipulations faster and prepares you to respond more effectively the next time it happens.

- **Channel Emotional Vulnerability into Action:** Transform emotional vulnerability into motivation for positive action. For example, if guilt over a past mistake is being exploited, use it as fuel to demonstrate your commitment to improving your parenting. Taking proactive steps reinforces your progress and limits the manipulator's ability to exploit past regrets.

- **Deflect Emotional Attacks with Strategic Reframing:** When the HCP tries to exploit your fears or insecurities, reframe the conversation. If they say, "You're a bad parent," calmly respond, "I'm always looking for ways to improve, and I'm focused on doing what's best for our child." This reframes their attack as an opportunity for growth, reducing its emotional sting.

- **Detach from the Guilt Trap:** High-conflict parents often use guilt to control you. When you feel guilt being used as a weapon, mentally detach by asking yourself, "Is this guilt helping my child, or is it being used to manipulate me?" Recognizing when guilt is being misused helps you stop reacting and start acting in a balanced way.

- **Develop a Mindfulness Practice:** Regular mindfulness practice helps you stay centered and present, reducing the impact of emotional manipulation. By staying aware of your feelings and reactions in the moment, you can prevent the HCP from hijacking your emotions. Mindfulness also boosts your ability to pause and respond calmly, rather than react out of fear or guilt.

Victim Positioning

Victim positioning is a manipulative tactic often employed by HCPs in family court disputes, where one parent seeks to portray themselves as the victim in order to gain sympathy and leverage against the other parent. This strategy may involve exaggerating or fabricating claims of mistreatment, presenting themselves as helpless or oppressed, and shifting blame for conflicts onto the other parent. By positioning themselves as the victim, they aim to elicit sympathy from legal professionals, the court, and even the children, thereby diverting attention from their own behaviors and actions.

This tactic can be particularly harmful, as it distorts perceptions of reality and can lead to unjust outcomes in custody arrangements. The targeted parent may find themselves defending against false narratives, undermining their credibility and emotional well-being. Additionally, this dynamic can confuse the children involved, as they may feel torn between loyalties or pressured to align with the "victim" parent.

To counteract victim positioning, it is vital for the other parent to remain grounded in factual evidence and maintain clear, consistent communication. Keeping meticulous records of interactions, documenting events and behaviors, and seeking third-party corroboration can help establish a more accurate narrative. Moreover, working with experienced legal counsel can provide essential guidance in navigating these complex dynamics and ensuring that the focus remains on the best interests of the child, rather than getting sidetracked by manipulative tactics. By recognizing and addressing victim positioning, parents can better advocate for themselves and protect their children from the emotional fallout of such behaviors.

Examples of Victim Positioning by HCPs in Family Court:

1. **Exaggerating claims of abuse**: One parent may exaggerate or fabricate incidents of physical or emotional abuse to present themselves as a victim, thereby seeking sympathy and protective orders.

2. **Presenting false narratives**: A parent might tell a skewed version of events, painting themselves as the innocent party while blaming the other parent for all conflicts, diverting attention from their own actions.

3. **Emotional manipulation**: By crying or displaying emotional distress in court, a parent can manipulate the perceptions of judges and evaluators, enhancing their victim persona.

4. **Claiming helplessness**: One parent may repeatedly express feelings of being overwhelmed or helpless in the co-parenting situation, suggesting that they cannot cope without special consideration or support from the court.

5. **Disparaging the other parent**: This tactic involves painting the other parent as the source of all problems, fostering a narrative that positions oneself as the victim of their alleged wrongdoing.

6. **Using children as pawns**: A parent may position themselves as the victim by claiming that the other parent is damaging the children's well-being, thereby

garnering sympathy while not prioritizing the child's best interests.

7. **Seeking sympathy from family and friends**: By telling a biased version of events to mutual friends and family, one parent may garner support that reinforces their victim status, further isolating the other parent.

8. **Involving professionals**: A parent might manipulate therapists, teachers, or social workers into believing they are the victim, leading to biased reports that sway custody decisions.

9. **Publicly defaming the other parent**: By spreading negative stories or misinformation about the other parent in public or social media, one parent can craft a victim narrative that garners public sympathy.

10. **Refusing Cooperation**: A parent may refuse to cooperate with co-parenting agreements, then position themselves as the victim when the other parent reacts to the lack of compliance, portraying themselves as the wronged party.

Solutions to Counteract Victim Positioning:

- **Stay Focused on Facts, Not Feelings:** Victim positioning relies on emotional appeals to sway others. Counteract this by presenting clear, objective facts rather than getting caught up in emotional arguments. Keep documentation of all interactions and provide evidence that highlights the reality of the situation, allowing the court to see through the victim narrative.

- **Use the "Golden Rule" of Courtroom Behavior:** In court, always take the high road by remaining calm, respectful, and focused on your child's best interests. While the HCP plays the victim, your composed and solution-oriented demeanor will contrast with their emotional manipulation. This "golden rule" approach helps the court see who is truly focused on resolving issues.

- **Turn the Spotlight on Your Child:** Shift the focus away from the HCP's self-pity by consistently redirecting attention to the child's needs and well-being. Every time the other parent tries to paint themselves as the victim, bring the conversation back to what's best for the child. Courts prioritize the child's welfare, making this tactic effective in neutralizing victim positioning.

- **Document Your Positive Contributions:** Keep a detailed record of your contributions to your child's life – whether it's attending school events, helping with homework, or providing emotional support. By documenting your active role, you can demonstrate that you are a stable and involved parent, countering the manipulative victim narrative that seeks to portray you as neglectful or harmful.

- **Respond to Accusations with Calm Confidence:** When the HCP accuses you of wrongdoing while positioning themselves as the victim, calmly respond with confidence. For example, say, "I understand your perspective, but here is what I have done for our child." Providing clear, concise responses shows that you are not reactive to their emotional manipulation, weakening the power of their narrative.

- **Use Consistent, Measured Communication:** Maintain a steady tone in all communications, whether written or verbal. The more consistent and professional you are, the harder it becomes for the HCP to claim victimhood effectively. This approach not only contrasts with their emotional outbursts but also helps ensure that your communication stands up in court as measured and reasonable.

- **Propose Third-Party Involvement:** When victim positioning escalates, request the involvement of third-party professionals, such as mediators, family therapists, or custody evaluators. Their neutral perspective can help clarify the true dynamics of the situation and highlight when one parent is using victimhood as a manipulative tactic.

- **Prepare for Emotional Ambushes:** Victim positioners often try to provoke emotional responses from you to bolster their narrative. Be prepared for these "emotional ambushes" and don't take the bait. Practice deep breathing or mindfulness techniques before meetings or court hearings so that you stay grounded and avoid reacting to provocations.

- **Frame Yourself as Solution-Oriented:** While the HCP plays the victim, position yourself as solution-oriented. In all discussions, propose practical resolutions and collaborative approaches to co-parenting. Courts are more likely to favor the parent who is focused on resolving issues, rather than the one constantly portraying themselves as helpless or oppressed.

- **Avoid Engaging in Drama:** HCPs thrive on creating drama, so steer clear of any emotional back-and-forth. If they claim victimhood, don't engage or defend yourself excessively. Instead, say something like, "I understand this is a tough situation, and I'm focused on finding solutions for our child." This diffuses the tension and keeps you out of their emotional trap.

- **Highlight Inconsistencies in Their Story:** Victim positioning often involves inconsistencies or exaggerations. Gently highlight these inconsistencies when necessary, but do so without sounding accusatory. For instance, if they claim you never contribute financially, present records of payments or contributions that contradict their narrative. By pointing out contradictions calmly, you undermine their credibility.

- **Use Documentation to Discredit False Claims:** When the HCP claims victimhood in specific instances, counter their assertions with documentation. If they say you didn't follow through on an agreement, produce emails or text messages that show otherwise. Hard evidence discredits their victim narrative and exposes the manipulation for what it is.

- **Reframe Victim Claims as Child-Centered Concerns:** If the other parent constantly claims to be the victim, reframe their concerns in terms of the child's needs. For example, if they say, "I'm always the one who suffers in this arrangement," respond with, "Let's focus on what's best for our child moving forward." This strategy shifts the conversation away from their personal grievances and toward practical solutions.

- **Control the Narrative with Professionalism:** Portray yourself as the rational, composed parent by maintaining professionalism in all interactions. Avoid reacting emotionally or defensively to their victim claims. Instead, calmly and consistently advocate for what's best for your child. This reinforces your credibility and paints the manipulative tactics of the other parent in stark contrast.

- **Solicit Character Witnesses:** If the HCP is aggressively positioning themselves as the victim, ask friends, family members, or neutral third parties to testify on your behalf. Character witnesses can provide testimony that counters the false narrative being presented and reinforces your reliability and integrity as a parent.

- **Propose Solutions to Undermine Victimhood:** If the HCP constantly plays the victim by complaining about various aspects of the custody arrangement, propose practical solutions to these issues. For example, if they claim you're not cooperating with the parenting schedule, offer a structured plan to ensure consistency. By taking a proactive stance, you weaken their ability to maintain the victim role.

- **Counter Emotional Appeals with Logic:** When the other parent tries to pull the court or mediator into their victim story, counter emotional appeals with logic. Focus on concrete examples of your parenting involvement, contributions, and your child's needs. Courts are more likely to respond to logical, factual arguments than to one-sided emotional narratives.

- **Establish Boundaries Around the Narrative:** Set clear boundaries in discussions with the HCP. If they begin to spiral into victimhood, gently redirect the conversation by saying, "I understand you're upset, but let's focus on how we can move forward in a way that's best for our child." This boundary-setting keeps the discussion productive and disarms emotional manipulation.

- **Let the Court See the Pattern:** If victim positioning is a frequent tactic of the HCP, create a timeline or pattern of behavior that you can present in court. By showing a consistent strategy of victimhood over time, you expose the tactic as manipulative rather than genuine, and the court may be less inclined to sympathize with their claims.

- **Keep Your Own Emotions in Check:** Victim positioning is designed to provoke your frustration or defensiveness, so it's important to stay emotionally regulated. Practice mindfulness, meditation, or deep breathing techniques before meetings or court hearings. Staying calm and centered allows you to effectively counter the emotional manipulation and keeps the focus on the facts.

Smear Campaigns

Smear campaigns are a damaging tactic frequently employed by HCPs in family court disputes, where one parent actively seeks to undermine the reputation and credibility of the other parent. This can involve spreading false or exaggerated information about the other parent's character, parenting abilities, or behavior, often with the intent to sway opinions in their favor, including those of legal professionals and the court. By portraying the other parent as unfit or harmful, they aim to create a narrative that positions themselves as the more suitable caregiver.

This tactic is particularly insidious, as it not only damages the targeted parent's reputation but can also impact their relationship with their children, who may become influenced by the negative portrayals. Such campaigns can lead to significant emotional distress for the accused parent, making it difficult to focus on the best interests of the child during the legal proceedings.

Countering a smear campaign requires a proactive approach. It is essential to gather and document evidence that refutes the false claims, such as maintaining detailed records of interactions and behaviors, securing statements from neutral third parties, and engaging legal counsel experienced in dealing with high-conflict situations. Additionally, maintaining a calm and composed demeanor in court can help demonstrate the accused parent's credibility and stability, countering the negative narratives being propagated. By recognizing and addressing smear campaigns effectively, parents can protect their rights and ensure that the focus remains on the well-being of their children.

Examples of Smear Campaigns by HCPs in Family Court:

1. **False allegations of abuse**: One parent may falsely accuse the other of physical or emotional abuse, aiming to paint them as a dangerous figure in the eyes of the court and professionals.

2. **Misrepresenting parenting skills**: A parent might exaggerate incidents where the other parent was inattentive or irresponsible, claiming they are unfit to care for the children.

3. **Spreading misinformation to family and friends**: One parent may tell mutual acquaintances false or exaggerated stories about the other parent's behavior, creating a biased narrative that influences their social circles.

4. **Manipulating professional evaluations**: A parent might provide misleading information to therapists

or social workers, shaping their assessments to reflect poorly on the other parent.

5. **Documenting false incidents**: Some may go so far as to fabricate events or create false documentation to support their claims against the other parent in court.

6. **Using social media**: Parents can exploit social media platforms to publicly criticize or demean the other parent, furthering the smear campaign to a wider audience.

7. **Coaching children**: One parent may instruct the children to share negative stories or opinions about the other parent, thereby influencing their perceptions and undermining the targeted parent's relationship with the kids.

8. **Creating a victim narrative**: By positioning themselves as the victim of the other parent's supposed misdeeds, one parent can garner sympathy and sway opinions against the other.

9. **Highlighting minor incidents**: A parent may focus on isolated minor incidents and blow them out of proportion, framing them as evidence of neglect or unfitness.

10. **Disparaging comments in court**: In legal proceedings, one parent might make derogatory remarks about the other's character or parenting abilities, attempting to undermine their credibility before the judge.

Solutions to Counteract Smear Campaigns:

- **Build a Solid Evidence Bank:** Keep meticulous records of all your interactions with the other parent, including emails, texts, and other communications. Collect any documents that can serve as evidence of your positive parenting – school reports, medical records, and even photos of family activities. This "evidence bank" can discredit any false claims made during the smear campaign.

- **Enlist a Professional Shield:** Work closely with a therapist, counselor, or parenting coordinator who can document your interactions with your child and your co-parenting efforts. These professionals can provide neutral, expert testimony that directly counters the negative narrative being spread by the other parent.

- **Stay Above the Fray:** Avoid engaging with the smear campaign directly. Instead of responding to every accusation or defending yourself emotionally, focus on staying calm, composed, and factual. Smear campaigns thrive on provoking reactions, but by refusing to engage, you maintain your credibility and show that you're focused on what matters: your child.

- **Use Co-Parenting Apps for Transparency:** Conduct all communication through co-parenting apps like OurFamilyWizard or Talking Parents. These platforms provide time-stamped, unalterable records of communication, making it harder for the high-conflict parent to twist your words or spread misinformation.

If needed, this documentation can be used in court to refute false claims.

- **Gather Character References:** Ask friends, family members, teachers, or other community members who have observed your parenting firsthand to write letters of support or offer to testify on your behalf. Their positive testimonies can help restore your credibility and provide a direct counter-narrative to the false claims being spread.

- **Counter with Consistent Positive Actions:** Actions speak louder than words. Focus on consistently demonstrating responsible, attentive parenting. Attend school events, maintain strong relationships with teachers and medical professionals, and remain an active participant in your child's life. Over time, your positive actions will discredit the lies being spread and reinforce your integrity.

- **Let the Facts Do the Talking:** In court or in negotiations, respond to false accusations by calmly presenting the facts. For example, if the other parent claims you've neglected your child, show evidence of doctor visits, school reports, or co-parenting schedules that demonstrate your active involvement. By relying on facts, you dismantle the false narrative without engaging emotionally.

- **Document the Smear Campaign:** Keep a record of all instances where the other parent spreads false or damaging information. Save social media posts, texts, emails, or any other communication where the smear campaign is evident. By documenting these attempts, you create a paper trail that can be presented in court to show that the other parent is engaging in manipulative behavior.

- **Propose a Custody Evaluation:** Request a formal custody evaluation by a neutral professional. A custody evaluator will observe family dynamics, interview both parents, and assess the truth of each parent's claims. This can help expose false accusations made during the smear campaign and provide an unbiased perspective on your parenting abilities.

- **Stay in Control of Your Narrative:** Take control of your own narrative by calmly sharing your side of the story in court or in any legal discussions. Focus on your strengths as a parent and the efforts you've made to create a healthy, loving environment for your child. By defining yourself, you prevent the other parent from dictating the narrative.

- **Deflect Personal Attacks with Child-Centered Language: When** the smear campaign centers on attacking your character, redirect the conversation to your child's well-being. Say something like, "My focus is on what's best for our child." This not only takes the spotlight off the personal attacks but also reinforces your commitment to being a responsible, child-focused parent.

- **Seek Legal Action if Necessary:** If the smear campaign involves defamatory statements that are damaging your reputation, consider seeking legal recourse for defamation. Consult your attorney to determine whether the false statements are grounds for a defamation case. The threat of legal consequences may deter further damaging actions from the other parent.

- **Counter Smear Tactics with Transparency:** Be transparent with the court and legal professionals. If the other parent is spreading false accusations, proactively provide your side of the story backed by evidence. Acknowledging any past issues, if relevant, and showing how you've addressed them can defuse attempts to paint you in a negative light.

- **Use Psychological Distance to Stay Unaffected:** Visualize a barrier between you and the smear campaign. Recognize that the other parent's lies are not a reflection of your reality but their attempt to manipulate perceptions. By creating psychological distance, you stay emotionally grounded and prevent the smear campaign from affecting your sense of self-worth.

- **Counteract Misinformation with Community Support:** Maintain strong ties with your community – teachers, neighbors, coaches, and other parents. When these people see your consistent behavior and positive involvement with your child, they're less likely to believe the false narratives being spread.

Their support can also serve as a counterbalance to the smear campaign.

- **Address Lies Calmly in Court:** If a specific lie is brought up in court, address it calmly without sounding defensive. Simply present the facts and, if necessary, show documentation that disproves the claim. For example, if they say you missed important events, produce records or photos proving your attendance. Staying calm and factual enhances your credibility.

- **Be Mindful of Social Media:** Avoid posting anything on social media that could be twisted or taken out of context by the other parent. HCPs often use social media as part of their smear campaign. Keep your accounts private, avoid posting details about your case, and focus on maintaining a positive, neutral online presence.

- **Engage in a Reputation Repair Campaign:** If the smear campaign has damaged your reputation in your community, take steps to rebuild it. Engage in positive activities that reinforce your values and show your true character. Volunteering, participating in school events, and being active in your child's life can help repair any damage caused by the false narrative.

- **Document Your Child's Well-Being:** Track your child's well-being and progress under your care – whether it's school grades, extracurricular involvement, or doctor's visits. Positive reports about your child's health and happiness serve as indirect evidence of your positive

> parenting, making it difficult for the smear campaign to stick in court.
>
> - **Focus on Long-Term Reputation Building:** Understand that smear campaigns are temporary. Focus on building a long-term reputation as a responsible, loving parent. Over time, the court and others will see through the manipulation and recognize the truth based on your consistent behavior, integrity, and focus on your child's well-being.

Love Bombing and Devaluation

Love bombing and devaluation are manipulative tactics often employed by HCPs during family court disputes. Love bombing involves overwhelming the other parent with excessive affection, attention, and validation, creating an illusion of a perfect relationship or co-parenting dynamic. This initial phase can lead the victimized parent to lower their defenses and believe that reconciliation or cooperation is achievable.

However, this façade is frequently followed by devaluation, where the same parent shifts to criticism, contempt, and emotional withdrawal. This drastic change can leave the targeted parent feeling confused, unworthy, and emotionally destabilized, ultimately eroding their self-esteem and undermining their confidence in legal settings.

These tactics can have profound implications, as they not only disrupt the emotional well-being of the victimized parent but can also adversely affect the children involved, who may witness the fluctuating dynamics. The unpredictable nature of love bombing and devaluation can make it difficult for the affected parent to advocate for themselves and maintain focus on the children's best interests.

To counter love bombing and devaluation, it is essential for the targeted parent to establish firm boundaries and recognize these patterns as manipulative behaviors. Keeping detailed records of interactions and communications can help illuminate the cycle of affection and criticism, providing a factual basis for discussions in court. Seeking support from mental health professionals and legal counsel can also aid in navigating these emotional upheavals, ensuring that the targeted parent can remain strong and focused throughout the legal process.

Examples of Love Bombing and Devaluation by HCPs in Family Court:

- **Excessive flattery**: One parent may shower the other with compliments and expressions of admiration, portraying them as the ideal co-parent to foster a sense of false security.

- **Over-the-top affection**: A parent might express intense affection through gifts, messages, or gestures, creating an illusion of reconciliation and undermining the other parent's defenses.

- **Feigning cooperation**: Initially, one parent may agree to favorable custody arrangements or co-parenting plans, only to later backtrack and create conflict.

- **Public displays of support**: One parent may publicly praise the other in front of friends or family to reinforce a positive image, only to later criticize them privately.

- **Creating a false narrative**: A parent might recount past events in an overly positive light to manipulate perceptions, leading the other parent to feel special and appreciated.

- **Sudden emotional withdrawal**: Following a phase of affection, the same parent may suddenly become cold, distant, or critical, leaving the other parent confused and questioning their self-worth.

- **Criticizing parenting choices**: After initially supporting the other parent's decisions, one parent might later undermine them by voicing disapproval and casting doubt on their capabilities.

- **Gaslighting during court proceedings**: One parent may alternate between loving behaviors and derogatory comments about the other during court, creating an unstable emotional environment.

- **Manipulating children's perceptions**: A parent may engage in love bombing with the children, then devalue the other parent in front of them, creating loyalty conflicts and emotional distress.

- **Using court as a stage**: During legal proceedings, one parent might present themselves as overly caring and involved, only to later exhibit devaluation by neglecting communication or parenting responsibilities.

Solutions to Counteract Love Bombing and Devaluation:

- **Recognize the Cycle:** Understand that love bombing is often part of a larger cycle that includes devaluation. Recognizing this pattern helps you stay grounded in reality when the excessive affection begins. Remind yourself that the sudden flood of validation is a manipulative tactic, not a genuine change in behavior or intention.

- **Set Emotional Boundaries:** When the love bombing starts, set clear emotional boundaries. Politely decline over-the-top gestures or compliments, and avoid engaging with attempts to create a false sense of closeness. Say something like, "I appreciate your willingness to work together, but let's focus on what's best for our child."

- **Document the Shifts:** Keep a detailed log of the transition from love bombing to devaluation. Record any instances where the high-conflict parent suddenly shifts from overwhelming affection to criticism or emotional withdrawal. This documentation can be presented in court to show the manipulative nature of their behavior.

- **Don't Get Hooked by the "Idealized Phase":** Love bombing is designed to make you feel special or like the co-parenting relationship has improved. Stay cautious and resist getting hooked by this idealized phase. Instead, stay focused on the practical aspects of parenting, and avoid getting swept up in the illusion of harmony.

- **Turn Attention Back to the Child:** When the love bombing begins, redirect attention back to your child's needs. If the other parent showers you with excessive praise or affection, calmly shift the conversation: "I'm glad we're working well together, but let's discuss how we can support our child's school needs." This keeps the focus on what matters.

- **Be Wary of Grand Gestures:** Love bombing often includes grand, exaggerated gestures that feel too good to be true. Be wary of these actions, and resist feeling indebted or manipulated into reciprocating. Grand gestures are often followed by devaluation, so maintaining a cautious distance helps protect you from the emotional highs and lows.

- **Establish Clear Co-Parenting Boundaries:** Set firm co-parenting boundaries that emphasize direct, child-centered communication. For example, communicate exclusively through co-parenting apps where the focus remains on logistics and your child's needs. This structure prevents love bombing attempts from derailing you emotionally or leading to false reconciliation narratives.

- **Avoid Reciprocal Over-Engagement:** When the other parent overwhelms you with attention, resist the urge to reciprocate. Keep your responses neutral and measured. By maintaining emotional distance and not engaging in the love bombing dynamic, you prevent yourself from being drawn into the manipulation cycle.

- **Anticipate the Devaluation Phase:** Recognize that love bombing is often followed by devaluation, where the other parent abruptly shifts to criticism or emotional distance. Mentally prepare for this shift, so when it happens, you're not blindsided or emotionally destabilized. Knowing what's coming helps you maintain emotional equilibrium.

- **Don't Allow Love Bombing to Influence Court Decisions:** Love bombing can create the illusion that the co-parenting relationship has drastically improved, leading you to make decisions that benefit the other parent. Be cautious about making major decisions – such as custody agreements – during periods of excessive affection. Ensure all decisions are based on consistent behavior, not temporary love bombing.

- **Maintain Emotional Objectivity:** When the other parent lavishes you with attention, practice emotional objectivity. Instead of getting caught up in their words, remind yourself of their past behavior patterns. Emotional detachment helps you stay focused on reality and prevents you from being swayed by temporary affection.

- **Communicate in Writing:** Stick to written communication when possible. Co-parenting apps or email create a clear, trackable record of communication that makes it harder for the other parent to switch between love bombing and devaluation without leaving evidence. Written exchanges also reduce the emotional intensity of verbal love bombing.

- **Seek Professional Validation, Not Their Approval:** If you're feeling vulnerable to the validation that comes with love bombing, seek support from a therapist, counselor, or trusted friend. These individuals can help you process your emotions and provide the validation you need in a healthy, unbiased way, so you're less tempted to fall for the manipulative approval.

- **Test the Consistency:** Love bombing may feel like the beginning of positive change but test the consistency of the other parent's behavior over time. If their affection is quickly followed by devaluation, you'll see the pattern emerge, making it easier to recognize that the love bombing is a tactic rather than genuine improvement.

- **Use Mindful Reflection:** When you notice love bombing happening, take a mindful pause before reacting. Reflect on the intent behind the behavior and how it fits into the larger pattern of manipulation. Mindfulness allows you to process the situation without being overwhelmed by emotion, keeping you grounded and in control.

- **Rely on Professional Recommendations:** If the other parent's love bombing causes you to question your decisions or boundaries, rely on professional recommendations, such as a therapist, custody evaluator, or mediator. Their neutral guidance can help you avoid being swayed by manipulation and keep your focus on long-term co-parenting solutions.

- **Stay Focused on Long-Term Behavior:** Evaluate the other parent based on long-term patterns rather than isolated love-bombing episodes. Focus on whether their actions have consistently prioritized the child's well-being over time. Long-term behavior is a more accurate reflection of their intentions than short-term bursts of affection or validation.

- **Decline Unnecessary Intimacy:** Love bombing often includes attempts to reintroduce unnecessary intimacy or emotional closeness. Decline invitations for personal conversations or activities that go beyond the co-parenting dynamic. By maintaining appropriate emotional distance, you protect yourself from being drawn into the manipulative highs and lows.

- **Recognize Manipulative Timing:** Love bombing often occurs during key moments – such as just before a court hearing or during negotiations – where the other parent seeks to gain favor or influence outcomes. Recognize when the timing of their excessive attention feels strategic, and make decisions based on logic rather than temporary affection.

- **Stay Grounded in Your Co-Parenting Plan:** When love bombing occurs, rely on your pre-established co-parenting plan. Stick to the agreed-upon terms and maintain the boundaries you've set. A clear, structured plan prevents the other parent from manipulating the relationship dynamic and ensures that both parents are focused on the child's needs.

Utilizing Legal Systems as a Weapon

Utilizing legal systems as a weapon is a manipulative strategy commonly employed by HCPs during family court disputes. This tactic involves one parent exploiting legal processes and procedures to harass, intimidate, or exert control over the other parent. It may manifest as relentless filing of motions, unfounded allegations, or the use of custody evaluations to create a hostile environment, all aimed at destabilizing the other parent's position and draining their emotional and financial resources.

The repercussions of this strategy can be devastating. It not only prolongs the legal proceedings but also exacerbates tensions, leaving the targeted parent feeling overwhelmed and unsupported. This relentless barrage can distract from the substantive issues at hand, such as the well-being of the children, while simultaneously undermining the targeted parent's credibility in the eyes of legal professionals and the court.

Countering the weaponization of the legal system requires a proactive approach. It is crucial for the affected parent to work closely with a skilled family law attorney who can navigate these complexities, streamline responses, and ensure that all actions are strategically aligned with the goal of safeguarding their interests. Maintaining meticulous documentation of all interactions and legal filings can also help create a clear record that counters any attempts at manipulation. By remaining focused and organized, the targeted parent can protect themselves and prioritize their children's best interests throughout the tumultuous legal landscape.

Examples of Utilizing Legal Systems as a Weapon by HCPs in Family Court:

1. **Relentless motion filings**: One parent may continuously file motions for modifications or requests for hearings, creating an overwhelming legal burden on the other parent.

2. **Unfounded abuse allegations**: A parent might falsely accuse the other of abuse or neglect to trigger investigations and legal scrutiny, aiming to damage their credibility.

3. **Harassment through subpoenas**: One parent could issue excessive subpoenas for personal records, including financial documents or communications, to intimidate and disrupt the other parent's life.

4. **Custody evaluations as weapons**: Requesting custody evaluations based on flimsy justifications can lead to biased assessments, creating a hostile environment and affecting custody outcomes.

5. **Contempt motions**: Filing contempt motions for minor infractions or misunderstandings to assert control and pressure the other parent, even when no real violation occurred.

6. **Misuse of restraining orders**: One parent might file for a restraining order based on exaggerated or fabricated claims, effectively isolating the other parent and gaining an upper hand.

7. **Manipulating discovery requests**: Submitting overly broad or irrelevant discovery requests to burden the other parent with excessive paperwork and time-consuming responses.

8. **Threatening legal action**: Using threats of legal action as a means to coerce the other parent into compliance with unreasonable demands or agreements.

9. **Changing legal representation frequently**: Regularly switching attorneys to create confusion and prolong proceedings, making it difficult for the other parent to keep up with the changing dynamics.

10. **Exploiting child support modifications**: Unjustifiably seeking to modify child support payments to create financial strain on the other parent, thus exerting control and pressure.

Solutions to Counteract Utilizing Legal Systems as a Weapon:

- **Document Every Legal Interaction:** Keep detailed records of every motion, hearing, and legal filing initiated by the high-conflict parent. Track dates, times, and the nature of the filings. This paper trail can help establish a pattern of frivolous or excessive legal actions, which can be used to demonstrate to the court that the other parent is abusing the legal system.

- **Request Sanctions for Frivolous Filings:** If the high-conflict parent continually files unnecessary motions or frivolous claims, ask your attorney to request sanctions. Courts can penalize individuals who misuse legal processes to harass or prolong the case, deterring further abuse of the system and possibly recovering some of your legal costs.

- **Propose a "No New Motions" Agreement:** Suggest to the court that a mutual agreement be put in place preventing either parent from filing new motions without first attempting mediation or alternative dispute resolution. This reduces the number of unnecessary filings and makes it harder for the high-conflict parent to weaponize the legal process.

- **Keep Your Emotions in Check During Court Hearings:** HCPs often use legal tactics to provoke emotional responses, hoping you'll make mistakes under pressure. Stay calm, composed, and focused on the facts during hearings. This not only strengthens your position but also makes it clear to the court that you are the stable, reasonable party.

- **Leverage a Family Law Specialist:** Work with a family law attorney experienced in high-conflict cases. These professionals know the tactics HCPs use and can create strategies to counteract legal harassment. They can also help expedite the case, making it harder for the high-conflict parent to drag out proceedings unnecessarily.

- **Request Court-Ordered Communication Restrictions:** If the other parent is harassing you with excessive legal communications or using the court system to intimidate you, request that the court limit the forms of communication between you to specific platforms, like co-parenting apps. This limits their ability to overwhelm you with legal threats and filings.

- **Stay One Step Ahead with Proactive Legal Action:** If you anticipate a legal maneuver by the high-conflict parent, be proactive. File necessary motions early, address potential concerns head-on, and make your legal arguments airtight. By staying ahead of the curve, you reduce their ability to surprise or manipulate the legal process in their favor.

- **Use Alternative Dispute Resolution (ADR):** Propose mediation, arbitration, or other forms of ADR to resolve disputes outside the courtroom. ADR is less adversarial and may reduce the high-conflict parent's ability to misuse the legal system. Plus, courts often appreciate efforts to settle matters outside of litigation.

- **Expose the Pattern of Legal Harassment:** Compile evidence of repeated, frivolous legal actions and present it to the court. A pattern of harassing legal filings can lead to the court taking action, such as limiting the high-conflict parent's ability to file additional motions without judicial approval, reducing their ability to abuse the system.

- **Request a Court-Ordered Parenting Coordinator:** Ask the court to appoint a parenting coordinator, a neutral third party who helps manage co-parenting disputes. This reduces the number of issues that need to be resolved in court and can act as a buffer, minimizing the high-conflict parent's ability to file constant legal motions.

- **Implement Tight Legal Deadlines:** Request that the court enforce tight deadlines for legal responses or filings. By reducing the amount of time the high-conflict parent has to prepare motions or delay proceedings, you prevent them from dragging out the process unnecessarily. Courts appreciate efficiency, and this shows that you are eager to move things forward.

- **Prepare for Financial Abuse Through the Legal System:** High-conflict parents may try to drain your financial resources by dragging out legal disputes. Be prepared by budgeting for legal costs, exploring legal aid options, or discussing payment plans with your attorney. Consider also discussing contingency fee arrangements or pro bono services if available.

- **Keep the Focus on Your Child:** When faced with excessive legal tactics, consistently refocus the court's attention on what matters – your child's well-being. HCPs often use the legal system as a distraction. By emphasizing the child's best interests, you demonstrate that the case is about parenting, not legal gamesmanship.

- **Request a Judicial Pre-Filing Review:** Ask the court to require the high-conflict parent to obtain judicial permission before filing any new motions or legal actions. This tactic puts a legal gatekeeper in place, making it harder for the other parent to clog the court system with baseless filings meant to harass or intimidate.

- **Stay Organized with a Legal Binder:** Create a binder (physical or digital) that organizes all court documents, filings, communications, and orders in chronological order. Staying organized helps you respond quickly to legal maneuvers, saves time for your attorney, and shows the court that you are professional and prepared.

- **Push for Legal Limits on Discovery Requests:** The high-conflict parent may try to overwhelm you with excessive discovery requests. Work with your attorney to request limitations on discovery, ensuring that any document requests or interrogatories are reasonable and relevant to the case. Courts may limit discovery abuse to prevent legal harassment.

- **Maintain Emotional Distance from Legal Threats:** Recognize that legal threats from the high-conflict parent are designed to intimidate and control. Practice emotional detachment from these threats, focusing instead on factual responses. Legal harassment often loses its power when you refuse to be emotionally rattled by constant filings or motions.

- **Streamline Court Involvement with Narrow Focus:** Keep your legal arguments focused on the most critical issues, such as custody and child welfare. Avoid getting caught up inside issues the high-conflict parent may introduce to distract or confuse. This keeps the court focused on the core matters and reduces the opportunity for unnecessary legal battles.

- **Request Court Monitoring for Compliance:** If the high-conflict parent routinely violates court orders or agreements, request that the court monitor compliance. For instance, you can ask for regular check-ins or penalties for non-compliance. This shifts the burden onto the high-conflict parent to follow the rules and reduces their ability to use the system as a weapon.

- **Keep Your Focus on Long-Term Stability:** Remember that the high-conflict parent's misuse of the legal system is often a short-term strategy to wear you down. Stay focused on long-term goals: your child's well-being and a stable parenting arrangement. Patience, consistency, and a calm approach will eventually show the court that you are the more reasonable parent.

Parental Alienation

Parental alienation is a serious accusation in custody disputes, involving one parent influencing the child to reject the other parent without legitimate justification. However, a manipulative twist often employed by high-conflict individuals is to falsely accuse the other parent of alienation as a deflection tactic. This strategy can serve multiple purposes: It shifts the focus away from the narcissist's own harmful behaviors, places the other parent on the defensive, and creates confusion about the source of the child's distress or behavioral changes.

HCPs may make these accusations during legal proceedings to undermine the other parent's credibility and to paint themselves as the victim, which can garner sympathy from the court. This tactic can be especially effective if the HCP has been subtly engaging in true alienation themselves, as it projects their behavior onto the other parent, making it harder for professionals to discern the truth.

To counter false accusations of parental alienation, it is crucial for the accused parent to gather evidence of positive interactions with the child and to document any manipulative behaviors by the narcissist. Professional assessments from child psychologists or custody evaluators can also provide objective insights into the family dynamics, helping to clarify the situation for the court. This approach ensures that the focus remains on the child's best interests and helps prevent the narcissist from successfully using this deflection tactic.

Examples of Parental Alienation by HCPs in Family Court:

1. **Negative language about the other parent:** One parent consistently uses derogatory or hostile language

about the other parent in front of the child, fostering resentment.

2. **Limiting communication:** Actively obstructing or limiting the child's ability to communicate with the other parent, including refusing phone calls or messages.

3. **Forbidding contact:** Directly instructing the child not to have any contact with the other parent, framing it as a protective measure.

4. **Creating loyalty conflicts:** Manipulating the child into feeling guilty for wanting to spend time with the other parent, making them choose sides.

5. **False allegations of abuse:** Making unsubstantiated claims of abuse or neglect against the other parent to justify reduced contact and increase the child's fear or distrust.

6. **Reinforcing negative behaviors:** Encouraging or allowing the child to express hostility or anger toward the other parent, reinforcing negative feelings.

7. **Distorting reality:** Presenting a biased narrative to the child about the other parent's intentions or actions, framing them as harmful or uncaring.

8. **Playing the victim:** Portraying oneself as a victim of the other parent's supposed abuse or neglect to gain sympathy and support from the child.

9. **Coaching the child:** Coaching the child to say specific things during custody evaluations or court hearings that align with the alienating parent's narrative.

10. **Ignoring court orders:** Flouting custody agreements or visitation schedules to create a pattern of absence for the other parent, leading the child to believe they are unwanted.

Solutions to Counteract Parental Alienation:

- **Build a Positive Interaction Record:** Document every interaction you have with your child. Keep a journal with notes on activities, shared experiences, and communication, and save digital records like texts, emails, or photos of your time together. This evidence can demonstrate that you are maintaining a healthy, supportive relationship with your child, which counters false accusations of alienation.

- **Seek Neutral Third-Party Observers:** Engage neutral professionals, such as therapists, mediators, or parenting coordinators, who can observe family dynamics and interactions with your child. Their unbiased assessments can serve as critical evidence in court, showing that no alienation is occurring and that your relationship with your child is based on mutual respect and care.

- **Request a Custody Evaluation:** If falsely accused of parental alienation, request a custody evaluation by a licensed psychologist or family evaluator. This comprehensive evaluation assesses the mental health and behavior of both parents and the child, making it difficult for a high-conflict parent to sustain false accusations when the reality is professionally assessed.

- **Propose Family Therapy:** Suggest family therapy to work through any potential conflicts or misunderstandings. A therapist can help identify the actual source of tension and clarify whether alienation is happening. If the high-conflict parent resists this suggestion, it could signal to the court that their accusations of alienation are a manipulative tactic rather than a genuine concern.

- **Focus on Open Communication with Your Child:** Encourage open, honest conversations with your child. By fostering an environment where your child feels free to express their feelings, you create emotional safety and dispel the notion that you are influencing their opinions about the other parent. Open communication is a key counter to false alienation claims.

- **Use Co-Parenting Apps for Transparency:** Conduct all co-parenting communication through court-approved apps like OurFamilyWizard or Talking Parents. These apps create a clear, unalterable record of communication between parents, making it easier to show the court that your interactions are focused on your child's well-being and not on undermining the other parent.

- **Present Positive Co-Parenting Efforts:** Keep records of any efforts you've made to support your child's relationship with the other parent, such as facilitating visitation, encouraging communication, or attending joint school events. By demonstrating your support for the child's bond with both parents, you counter the false narrative that you are engaging in alienation.

- **Highlight the Absence of Manipulation:** If your child has expressed concerns or negative feelings about the other parent, present evidence that these feelings are based on the child's experiences, not your influence. Work with a therapist to highlight the child's perspective in an unbiased way, making it clear that any distancing behavior is not a result of your manipulation.

- **Use Character Witnesses:** Ask friends, family members, teachers, or other adults who have observed your interactions with your child to act as character witnesses. Their testimonies can provide a balanced view of your parenting, countering false accusations by highlighting your genuine care for your child and your encouragement of a healthy co-parenting relationship.

- **Dissect the Accusation in Court:** When faced with a false accusation of parental alienation, carefully dissect the accusation in court. Present evidence that contradicts the claim, such as your efforts to facilitate co-parenting, documentation of visitation exchanges, or text messages encouraging your child to spend time with the other parent. Logical, fact-based refutations help dismantle false allegations.

- **Expose the Projection:** High-conflict parents often project their own behaviors onto others. If the accusing parent is the one engaging in alienating behavior, document examples where they have interfered with your relationship with your child (such as refusing visitation or making negative comments about you to the child). Bring these examples to the court's attention.

- **Encourage Healthy Relationships with Extended Family:** Foster positive relationships between your child and extended family members on both sides, including those connected to the other parent. This counters the accusation that you are isolating the child from the other parent's world and provides additional evidence of your encouragement of a broad, supportive family environment.

- **Remain Calm and Professional in Court:** When faced with a false accusation of alienation, it's critical to maintain calm and professionalism. Respond to the accusation with logic and evidence, avoiding emotional outbursts. By demonstrating that you are focused on your child's well-being, you show the court that the accusation is unfounded and manipulative.

- **Request a Parenting Coordinator:** Suggest that a neutral parenting coordinator be appointed to oversee communication and co-parenting decisions. This neutral party can document and report on co-parenting dynamics, making it more difficult for the high-conflict parent to falsely accuse you of alienation without being contradicted by the coordinator's observations.

- **Stay Consistent with Boundaries:** Maintain healthy, respectful boundaries in your co-parenting relationship. If the high-conflict parent accuses you of alienation, remaining consistent with boundaries – such as clear communication and maintaining your child's routine – shows the court that you are focused on stability rather than manipulation.

- **Document Your Child's Well-Being:** Keep track of your child's emotional and psychological well-being, including school performance, participation in extracurricular activities, and general behavior. If your child is thriving under your care, this can be used as evidence to counter false claims of alienation. A happy, well-adjusted child is less likely to be the victim of alienation.

- **Expose Inconsistencies in the False Narrative:** Carefully examine the accusing parent's claims for inconsistencies. For example, if they accuse you of preventing visitation but also complain about frequent visitation issues, highlight this contradiction. Exposing inconsistencies weakens their credibility and makes it clear that their accusations are baseless.

- **Demonstrate Your Willingness to Co-Parent:** Show the court that you are committed to co-parenting and maintaining a healthy relationship between your child and the other parent. Propose solutions, such as mediation or joint counseling, to resolve any conflicts. Your willingness to collaborate and find solutions reinforces the fact that you are not alienating the other parent.

- **Don't Engage in Tit-for-Tat Accusations:** Avoid the temptation to respond to false accusations of parental alienation by accusing the other parent of the same. Instead, stay focused on presenting evidence and facts that demonstrate your positive involvement in your child's life. Engaging in back-and-forth accusations can create confusion and undermine your credibility in court, whereas a calm, factual approach shows the court that you are focused on the child's well-being.

- **Focus on Long-Term Stability:** Remind yourself that the court process is a marathon, not a sprint. High-conflict parents may attempt to wear you down with false accusations, but by remaining consistent, calm, and focused on your child's best interests, you demonstrate your commitment to being a stable, reliable parent. Over time, the truth will surface, and the manipulative tactics of the other parent will become more apparent to the court.

Using Children as Messengers

Another common tactic is using children as messengers between parents. This places an undue emotional burden on the child and puts them in the center of conflict. It can also be a way to miscommunicate or twist information, as messages delivered through children can be easily misconstrued or altered to create misunderstandings between the parents.

When a parent uses a child to convey messages about custody arrangements, support payments, or other sensitive issues, it not only burdens the child with adult responsibilities but also exposes them to the potential conflict between their parents. This practice can confuse and distress children, who may feel torn between their loyalties to each parent.

To counter this harmful tactic, it is vital for parents to establish direct lines of communication for all logistical and legal discussions, keeping such exchanges strictly between adults. Tools like court-approved communication apps specifically designed for co-parenting can ensure that all interactions are recorded and that the child is shielded from any parental conflict. Such measures help maintain the child's psychological well-being and uphold the integrity of parental communications.

Examples of Using Children as Messengers by HCPs in Family Court:

1. **Conveying messages about visitation:** One parent asks the child to relay changes to visitation schedules or arrangements instead of communicating directly with the other parent.

2. **Discussing financial issues:** Sending the child to discuss child support payments or financial disputes, placing the burden of adult concerns on the child.

3. **Informing about legal matters:** Using the child to communicate information about court dates, legal strategies, or other sensitive legal matters.

4. **Sending emotional messages:** Instructing the child to express feelings of anger or hurt about the other parent, effectively using them as a vehicle for emotional messages.

5. **Requesting behavior changes:** Asking the child to tell the other parent to change their behavior, such as requests to stop certain activities or habits.

6. **Reporting back:** Asking the child to report on what happens during visits with the other parent, placing them in a position of monitoring and scrutiny.

7. **Communicating preferences:** Instructing the child to convey their preferences regarding living arrangements or visitation to the other parent.

8. **Addressing conflicts:** Encouraging the child to communicate grievances or conflicts, such as disputes over rules or expectations, instead of addressing them directly.

9. **Misinformation:** Deliberately sending mixed or misleading messages through the child to create confusion or misinterpretation of intentions.

10. **Testing Loyalty:** Using the child to convey messages that test their loyalty, such as asking them to choose who they prefer to live with or spend time with more often.

Solutions to Counteract Using Children as Messengers:

- **Establish Direct Communication Channels:** To reduce the need for your child to relay messages, set up direct communication with the other parent through email, text, or co-parenting apps like OurFamilyWizard. These platforms ensure that all communication is clear, documented, and free from misinterpretation, eliminating the need for the child to act as a go-between.

- **Teach Your Child It's Not Their Responsibility:** Gently explain to your child that it's not their job to deliver messages between you and the other parent. Let them know that communication between parents should happen directly and that they should feel free to focus on being a kid. Reassure them that they don't have to take on the burden of adult problems.

- **Set Clear Boundaries with the Other Parent:** If the other parent is using the child as a messenger, set a firm but respectful boundary. Communicate directly, saying something like, "Let's make sure we handle communication between ourselves so that [child] doesn't have to be put in the middle." Reinforce that co-parenting conversations should remain between the adults.

- **Use Neutral Communication Tools:** Encourage the use of neutral, court-approved co-parenting apps to handle all logistical communication. These apps reduce the chance for messages to be altered or misunderstood, providing a clear, documented history of agreements and discussions, which reduces the other parent's ability to manipulate communication through the child.

- **Redirect Child-Delivered Messages Back to the Source**: When your child delivers a message from the other parent, gently redirect the responsibility. Say something like, "Thank you for letting me know, but I'll check in with your [mom/dad] about this directly." This approach keeps the child out of the middle and ensures that the message is handled properly.

- **Encourage Open Communication with the Child:** Let your child know that they don't need to withhold anything from you. Create an open environment where your child feels comfortable discussing any messages they've been given. By encouraging transparency, you reduce the other parent's ability to twist or manipulate information passed through the child.

- **Create a Co-Parenting Agreement:** Propose a formal co-parenting agreement that outlines direct communication protocols. Include a clause that states all parenting-related matters must be communicated directly between parents, not through the child. A legal agreement reinforces boundaries and can be presented to the court if the other parent continues the behavior.

- **Role-Model Healthy Communication:** Model positive, direct communication in front of your child. By seeing you handle discussions with the other parent calmly and directly, they will understand that communication between parents should be adult-to-adult, not channeled through them. This reinforces healthy boundaries and reduces the likelihood of manipulation.

- **Frame It as a Stress Relief for the Child:** If the other parent is resistant to direct communication, frame your request as being in the child's best interest. Say something like, "I think it would be less stressful for [child's name] if we communicated directly instead of using them to pass messages." Focusing on the child's well-being may make the other parent more willing to cooperate.

- **Respond Calmly to Miscommunication:** If a message delivered through the child is misconstrued or altered, respond calmly and directly to the other parent. Avoid blaming the child, and instead address the miscommunication clearly: "It seems there was some confusion about [issue]. Let's clarify directly so there's no misunderstanding."

- **Involve a Third Party for Contentious Communication:** If direct communication consistently leads to conflict, consider involving a neutral third party like a mediator or parenting coordinator to facilitate communication. This reduces the burden on the child and ensures that sensitive matters are handled in a structured, professional manner.

- **Encourage Emotional Boundaries in Your Child:** Help your child understand that they are not responsible for managing their parents' emotions or conflicts. Encourage emotional independence by teaching them that it's okay to step away from adult issues and that they don't need to feel responsible for relaying messages or solving problems between parents.

- **Praise Your Child for Being a Child:** Celebrate and reinforce your child's role as a kid. Encourage them to focus on their own activities, friendships, and interests. By emphasizing their role as a child, you make it clear that adult responsibilities like relaying messages should not be on their shoulders.

- **Propose a Structured Communication Schedule:** Create a regular communication schedule with the other parent for discussing co-parenting matters. This reduces the need for ongoing messaging through the child. For example, agree to have a weekly email exchange to go over schedules, activities, and other logistics, ensuring that everything is addressed without involving the child.

- **Redirect Emotional Conversations:** If the child expresses distress about being asked to deliver a message, validate their feelings and reassure them. Say something like, "I understand that might feel stressful. You don't have to worry about it – I'll talk to your [mom/dad] myself." This helps the child feel supported and removes them from the conflict.

- **Create a Parenting Log:** Maintain a parenting log that tracks important details about your child's schedule, activities, and any communication issues. This log can serve as evidence in court if the other parent continues to use the child as a messenger, showing that you've taken steps to handle communication in a more appropriate way.

- **Use Humor to Diffuse the Situation:** If your child comes to you with a message from the other parent, use humor to lighten the situation and subtly make your point. For example, you could say, "Wow, you must be the world's busiest messenger! I'll handle this one directly so you can take a break." This lightens the emotional burden while reinforcing the boundary.

- **Keep Your Child Out of Decision-Making:** Avoid discussing any co-parenting decisions or conflicts in front of your child. Even casual comments can make them feel like they're caught in the middle. Ensure that all decisions are made directly between parents, keeping the child out of adult conversations.

- **Encourage Healthy Self-Expression:** Support your child in expressing their feelings about being asked to deliver messages. Let them know it's okay to say "no" to either parent if they feel uncomfortable acting as a messenger. This empowers them to set boundaries and reduces the emotional pressure placed on them by the other parent.

- **Focus on Long-Term Emotional Health:** Remember that the emotional well-being of your child is a long-term priority. By consistently refusing to use them as a messenger, you reinforce healthy emotional boundaries and show them that their role is to grow, learn, and enjoy childhood – free from the stress of adult conflicts.

False Accusations

In some cases, one parent might falsely accuse the other of neglect, abuse, or other serious allegations to gain an upper hand in custody proceedings. These accusations can trigger a wave of legal scrutiny and investigations, which can be emotionally and financially draining for the accused parent, and potentially damage their reputation and standing in court – even if the accusations are eventually proven unfounded.

To effectively counter false accusations, it is crucial to maintain comprehensive documentation of all interactions and activities related to parenting and the child's welfare. This can include retaining receipts, emails, messages, and logs of phone calls, as well as securing statements from neutral third parties like teachers, doctors, or family counselors who can vouch for the accused parent's behavior and involvement.

Engaging legal representation experienced in handling such high-stakes family law matters is also vital, as they can guide the accused parent through the process of gathering and presenting evidence that refutes the claims and protects their rights and relationship with their child.

Examples of False Accusations by HCPs in Family Court:

1. **Allegations of physical abuse:** One parent falsely claims that the other has physically harmed the child or themselves, seeking to gain sympathy and legal advantages.

2. **Claims of emotional abuse:** Accusing the other parent of emotionally manipulating or psychologically abusing the child, often without evidence.

3. **Allegations of neglect:** Claiming that the other parent is neglecting the child's basic needs, such as food, shelter, or education, when this is not the case.

4. **Substance abuse accusations:** Falsely accusing the other parent of drug or alcohol abuse to undermine their credibility and fitness as a parent.

5. **Fabricated incidents of harm:** Creating a story about a specific incident where the child was allegedly harmed or endangered, leading to investigations that can be costly and stressful.

6. **Misrepresentation of parenting practices:** Accusing the other parent of unfit parenting behaviors, such as exposing the child to inappropriate situations or individuals.

7. **False claims of criminal behavior:** Alleging that the other parent has a criminal history or is engaged in illegal activities that would make them an unfit parent.

8. **Manipulating child statements:** Encouraging the child to make false statements about the other parent's behavior, effectively using the child as a tool for manipulation.

9. **Allegations of sexual abuse:** Serious accusations claiming that the other parent has engaged in inappropriate sexual behavior with the child, which can lead to severe legal consequences.

10. **Claiming parental alienation:** Falsely accusing the other parent of alienating the child against them, diverting attention from their own manipulative behavior.

Solutions to Counteract False Accusations:

- **Document, Document, Document:** Maintain a detailed log of all interactions with your child and the other parent. Keep records of medical appointments, school activities, and any relevant communications (texts, emails, etc.). Having a comprehensive documentation trail shows your ongoing involvement in your child's life and helps debunk false accusations.

- **Request a Custody Evaluation:** Proactively request a court-appointed custody evaluation. This neutral, professional assessment of your parenting abilities and home environment can provide concrete evidence that refutes false claims. Evaluators are trained to detect when accusations are exaggerated or fabricated.

- **Engage Professional Witnesses:** Involve professionals who regularly interact with your child, such as teachers, doctors, or therapists. Their testimonies and records can provide unbiased evidence about your child's well-being, school attendance, medical history, and general care, countering claims of neglect or abuse.

- **Consider Filing a Motion for a Guardian ad Litem:** Request the appointment of a guardian ad litem (GAL) to represent your child's best interests. GALs conduct thorough investigations into each parent's home environment and interactions with the child. Their reports can be crucial in refuting false accusations and demonstrating that your parenting is in the child's best interest.

- **Stay Calm and Collected During Investigations:** When under scrutiny, remain calm and composed. Treat investigations or social services visits as opportunities to present the truth. Overreacting or showing anger can inadvertently play into the hands of the accuser, making it appear as though you have something to hide. Calm cooperation shows confidence in your innocence.

- **Retain an Experienced Family Law Attorney:** Hire an attorney with experience in handling false allegations in family court. A skilled lawyer can help you navigate the legal challenges, prepare evidence, and file appropriate motions to expose the false claims for what they are. They can also protect you from further legal manipulation.

- **Demand Specificity in Allegations:** If the accusations against you are vague or ambiguous, demand that the accuser provide specific details. General accusations of neglect or abuse are often harder to prove, so by asking for specific dates, times, and events, you can pinpoint inconsistencies or fabrications in the other parent's claims.

- **Seek Legal Recourse for False Allegations:** If the accusations are blatantly false and intended to manipulate the legal process, discuss with your attorney the possibility of filing a motion for sanctions or even pursuing a defamation suit. Courts don't take kindly to false accusations, and legal consequences may deter further attempts at manipulation.

- **Work with a Therapist or Counselor:** Seek support from a therapist or counselor, not only to help you navigate the emotional toll of false accusations but also to provide professional insights into your relationship with your child. A therapist's documentation and testimony can serve as valuable evidence of your healthy parenting and stable home environment.

- **Prepare Character Witnesses:** Ask close friends, family members, or neighbors who have seen you interact with your child to provide written statements or testify on your behalf. Character witnesses can offer valuable testimony about your parenting style and refute false claims of neglect or abuse.

- **Propose a Third-Party Supervisor for Visitation:** If the false accusations are serious and lead to restricted visitation or supervised visits, consider proposing a neutral third-party supervisor who can objectively monitor your interactions with your child. Having a witness present during visitation can help protect against further false claims.

- **Stay Focused on Your Child's Well-Being:** Despite the emotional strain, stay focused on maintaining a stable, supportive environment for your child. Courts are more likely to side with a parent who consistently prioritizes the child's best interests over engaging in conflict. Showing that you are focused on your child's emotional and physical well-being can counteract false accusations.

- **Bring Up Prior False Allegations:** If the accusing parent has made false accusations in the past, present this history to the court. A pattern of making baseless allegations can undermine their credibility and demonstrate that they are using the legal system to manipulate the custody process rather than to protect the child.

- **Use Psychological Evaluations to Clarify False Claims:** Request a psychological evaluation for both parents and the child if necessary. A professional assessment can help determine if the accusations are based on reality or are being fabricated as part of a broader pattern of manipulation or alienation by the accusing parent.

- **Be Transparent and Cooperative with Investigators:** If social services or child protective services are involved, be transparent, cooperative, and respectful throughout the process. Provide clear access to documents, medical records, and proof of your involvement in your child's care. Cooperative behavior reinforces your credibility and can help discredit the allegations.

- **File a Motion for Dismissal:** If the false allegations are completely unsupported by evidence, your attorney can file a motion to dismiss the accusations early in the proceedings. If the court sees that there is no merit to the claims, it can help limit the emotional and financial toll of prolonged investigations.

- **Consider Court-Ordered Counseling for Both Parents**: If the accusing parent is weaponizing false claims to create division and conflict, suggest court-ordered co-parenting counseling. A trained counselor can help address communication issues, expose manipulation tactics, and bring to light the underlying motivations for false accusations.

- **Expose the Impact on the Child:** Demonstrate to the court that false allegations are harming the child by creating unnecessary conflict and tension between parents. Present evidence, such as school performance reports or statements from a therapist, showing how the custody battle is affecting the child emotionally or academically due to the other parent's false claims.

- **Stay Active in Your Child's Daily Life:** Even while under scrutiny, remain actively involved in your child's daily life, from attending school events to medical appointments. Visible, consistent involvement demonstrates your commitment as a parent and contradicts claims of neglect. Document these activities to show the court that you are fully engaged in your child's well-being.

- **Educate the Court on the Tactic of False Allegations:** In some cases, you may need to educate the court on how false allegations are used as a manipulation tactic in high-conflict custody cases. Provide relevant research or expert testimony on the misuse of such allegations and how they can be a form of emotional and legal abuse designed to gain an upper hand.

Withholding Information

A manipulative parent might withhold vital information about the child's health, education, or well-being to undermine the other parent's ability to participate fully in parenting. This might include failing to communicate about medical appointments, school meetings, or extracurricular activities, thereby limiting the other parent's involvement in important aspects of the child's life.

This tactic not only undermines the parental bond between the child and the non-custodial parent but also violates the spirit of co-parenting, which is based on mutual respect and shared responsibilities. It can cause significant disruptions in the child's life, as the uninformed parent may not be able to provide appropriate care or make informed decisions when needed.

To counter this tactic, it is essential for the affected parent to insist on written agreements that specify the terms of information sharing, utilize legal avenues to enforce these agreements, and, if necessary, seek court intervention to ensure that information is shared in a timely and comprehensive manner. Establishing these clear guidelines helps to maintain both parents' involvement in their child's life and upholds the child's best interests.

Examples of Withholding Information by HCPs in Family Court:

1. **Failure to communicate medical appointments:** One parent does not inform the other about the child's doctor visits, preventing them from participating in important health decisions.

2. **Not sharing school updates:** Withholding information about school events, report cards, or parent-teacher meetings, which affects the uninformed parent's ability to engage in the child's education.

3. **Omitting details of extracurricular activities:** Not communicating about sports, clubs, or other activities the child is involved in, leading to the other parent missing out on important experiences.

4. **Ignoring notification of changes in child's health:** Failing to share information regarding new medical diagnoses, allergies, or health issues, which can impact the child's care.

5. **Not providing contact information for caregivers:** Withholding details about babysitters, daycare providers, or other caregivers, making it difficult for the uninformed parent to stay involved.

6. **Failing to communicate travel plans:** Not informing the other parent about planned travel with the child, which can disrupt visitation schedules and parental involvement.

7. **Omitting information about the child's friends:** Withholding details about the child's friendships or social activities, which can affect the other parent's ability to support the child's social development.

8. **Not sharing behavioral concerns:** Failing to communicate about any behavioral issues at school or home that may require a unified approach to address.

9. **Withholding legal documents:** Not providing copies of relevant legal documents, such as custody agreements or court orders, that affect the parenting arrangement.

10. **Ignoring child's communication preferences:** Not sharing the child's expressed wishes or feelings about visits or custody arrangements, which can prevent necessary adjustments to the parenting plan.

Solutions to Counteract Withholding Information:

- **Create a Communication Protocol in Your Parenting Plan:** Request that your parenting plan explicitly outlines the requirement to share vital information about medical appointments, school meetings, and extracurricular activities. Include clear deadlines (e.g., "Both parents must notify the other of appointments or activities within 48 hours") to ensure timely communication. This makes withholding information a violation of the court order.

- **Use a Co-Parenting App for Shared Updates:** Implement a co-parenting app, like OurFamilyWizard or Talking Parents, where both parents are required to update information about the child's schedule, health, and education. These apps provide a transparent record of communication and make it easier to track whether vital information is being intentionally withheld.

- **Request Shared Access to Medical and School Records:** Ensure that both parents have direct access to the child's medical records, educational reports, and extracurricular schedules by contacting doctors, schools, and activity coordinators to set up individual parent accounts. This way, you can independently verify and monitor important information without relying on the other parent to share it.

- **Keep a Log of Missing Information:** Create a detailed log documenting every instance when the other parent withholds important information. Include dates, times, and specifics about the missed medical appointments, school events, or activities. This documentation can be presented in court to show a pattern of behavior and support your case for more structured communication.

- **Establish Relationships with Teachers and Coaches:** Develop strong relationships with your child's teachers, coaches, doctors, and other key figures in their life. By maintaining direct contact with these individuals, you can receive updates about your child's progress and important events directly, bypassing the manipulative parent's attempts to control the flow of information.

- **Propose a Parenting Coordinator or Mediator:** If the issue of withholding information persists, propose the appointment of a parenting coordinator or mediator. This neutral third party can oversee communication between parents, ensure that important information is shared, and document any failures to communicate, helping to create a more cooperative parenting dynamic.

- **Encourage Direct Communication with Professionals:** Request that your child's medical providers and teachers send appointment reminders and progress reports directly to both parents. This ensures that you receive the same information as the other parent, preventing them from acting as a gatekeeper. Most schools and medical practices are accustomed to handling co-parenting situations.

- **Request Court Orders for Joint Decision-Making on Key Issues:** Ask the court to issue a joint decision-making order on major issues like health, education, and extracurricular activities. This legal mandate ensures that both parents must be involved in decisions, and failure to consult or share information can lead to legal consequences for the non-cooperative parent.

- **Stay Proactive in Requesting Information:** Don't wait for the other parent to share information – proactively reach out to schools, doctors, and extracurricular coordinators to ask for updates. Take the initiative to schedule parent-teacher conferences or medical consultations and include the other parent in the invitations. This proactive approach makes it harder for them to withhold information.

- **Use Shared Calendars:** Set up a shared online calendar (such as Google Calendar) for important events, appointments, and activities. Encourage the other parent to update the calendar with relevant information. If they refuse to do so, you'll have a clear record showing that they are withholding updates, which can be presented in court if necessary.

- **Request Independent Medical and Educational Consultations:** If you suspect that the other parent is withholding critical information, request independent consultations with your child's doctors, teachers, or counselors. These professionals can provide an objective assessment of your child's well-being, ensuring that you remain fully informed and involved, even if the other parent is trying to block access.

- **Bring the Issue to Court if Necessary:** If withholding information becomes a recurring issue that affects your ability to parent, raise the issue with your attorney and request a court hearing. Courts generally prioritize the involvement of both parents in key decisions about their child's life, and repeated failure to share information can be seen as parental alienation or bad faith.

- **Involve the Child in a Healthy Way:** As your child grows older, encourage them (in an age-appropriate way) to share their schedules and experiences with both parents. If they mention an upcoming event or appointment that you weren't told about, gently confirm the details with them and follow up directly with the other parent or relevant parties.

- **Propose Joint Attendance at Key Events:** Whenever possible, propose that both parents attend medical appointments, school meetings, and extracurricular activities together. This reduces the likelihood of one parent withholding information and ensures that both parents have access to the same details and feedback about their child's well-being and progress.

- **Keep Calm and Document All Communications:** When confronted with a situation where the other parent has withheld important information, remain calm and professional in your response. Send a written communication (via email or co-parenting app) requesting the missing information and keep a record of their response. Courts tend to favor the parent who remains solution-focused and non-reactive.

- **Engage in Regular Meetings with Your Child's Professionals:** Schedule regular check-ins with your child's doctors, teachers, or coaches. Having a recurring dialogue with these professionals ensures that you stay informed about your child's progress and activities, regardless of whether the other parent is sharing information.

- **Focus on the Child's Well-Being in Court:** If the issue of withholding information escalates to court, focus on how it impacts your child's well-being. Highlight how being kept out of the loop prevents you from making informed decisions that support your child's health and education, which can undermine their development and stability.

- **Address Miscommunication Calmly:** If the other parent claims that the failure to share information was a simple oversight, address the situation calmly and propose ways to prevent future lapses in communication. Suggest using written communication (like email) for updates or setting up a weekly check-in to ensure all important details are shared.

- **Propose Consequences for Non-Compliance:** If the other parent consistently withholds information, work with your attorney to propose consequences for non-compliance in your co-parenting plan. This could include penalties such as make-up parenting time, financial consequences, or a modification of custody if one parent is intentionally undermining the other.

- **Maintain a Focus on Cooperation:** Throughout the process, consistently frame your efforts as being in the best interest of your child. By showing the court and other professionals that your goal is to foster open communication and collaboration, you position yourself as the cooperative parent, strengthening your case if the issue escalates to court.

Financial Manipulation

Financial manipulation is a tactic that involves using economic resources as a means to exert control or inflict hardship on the other parent. such as delaying child support payments or manipulating expenses that affect the child's welfare. This can manifest as one parent withholding child support to strain the financial stability of the custodial parent, deliberately failing to disclose or lying about financial assets during divorce proceedings, or incurring debts that unfairly bind the other party. Financial manipulation can also extend to using legal financial obligations as threats during negotiation processes. These actions are often intended to limit the other parent's ability to adequately care for the child or to force them into a less advantageous position during negotiations.

Countering this form of manipulation requires meticulous financial documentation and, often, the involvement of forensic accountants who can uncover hidden assets or undisclosed income. Legal measures such as court orders for the disclosure of financial information and penalties for non-compliance can also be critical.

Securing experienced legal representation can help navigate the complex financial aspects of the case, ensuring that all financial dealings are transparent and fair, safeguarding the economic well-being of the child and both parents.

Examples of Financial Manipulation by HCPs in Family Court:

1. **Delaying child support payments:** One parent intentionally delays or refuses to make child support payments, creating financial strain on the custodial parent.

2. **Underreporting income:** A parent deliberately underreports their income or fails to disclose sources of income to reduce their child support obligations.

3. **Hiding financial assets:** One party conceals financial assets, such as savings accounts or investments, during divorce proceedings to avoid equitable distribution.

4. **Inflating expenses:** Manipulating financial documents to show inflated living expenses, thereby justifying reduced support payments or financial contributions.

5. **Creating unnecessary debt:** Incurring debt in the name of the other parent or jointly held accounts to create financial burdens that affect negotiations.

6. **Threatening to withhold financial support:** Using financial support as leverage during custody

negotiations, threatening to withhold funds unless certain demands are met.

7. **Failing to disclose bonuses or windfalls:** Not informing the other parent about bonuses, inheritances, or unexpected financial gains that could affect support calculations.

8. **Manipulating tax returns:** Misrepresenting tax returns to show lower income or claiming deductions that unfairly benefit one parent over the other.

9. **Using child-related expenses as leverage:** One parent exaggerates the costs of the child's expenses (like medical or educational costs) to pressure the other parent into higher support payments.

10. **Engaging in financial coercion:** Using financial threats or manipulation to coerce the other parent into unfavorable agreements or concessions regarding custody or visitation.

Solutions to Counteract Financial Manipulation:

- **Document All Financial Transactions:** Keep a detailed record of all financial interactions, including child support payments, shared expenses, and any financial agreements. Use tools like spreadsheets, bank statements, and payment apps to create a clear financial trail. This documentation can serve as evidence if the other parent manipulates payments or misrepresents financial information.

- **Use Legal Channels for Child Support Enforcement:** If the other parent is withholding or delaying child support payments, contact your local child support enforcement agency. These agencies can enforce court-ordered support through wage garnishment, tax refund interception, or other legal measures to ensure consistent payments.

- **Request a Forensic Accountant:** If you suspect that the other parent is hiding or underreporting financial assets during divorce proceedings, request that a forensic accountant be brought in. These financial experts can track down hidden assets, uncover undisclosed income, and provide a thorough financial analysis that prevents the other parent from manipulating the system.

- **Propose Direct Payment Platforms:** To avoid delays or manipulation of child support payments, suggest using a direct payment platform such as Wage Garnishment or an escrow account. These platforms ensure that payments are automatically transferred and leave less room for the other parent to withhold or manipulate funds.

- **Establish a Court-Ordered Payment Schedule:** If the other parent frequently delays child support or other financial contributions, request a court-ordered payment schedule with strict deadlines. Courts can impose penalties or interest on late payments, incentivizing the other parent to comply and preventing financial instability for you and your child.

- **Set Up Separate Accounts for Shared Expenses:** If shared expenses (such as school fees or medical bills) are being manipulated, open a separate account specifically for child-related expenses. Both parents can contribute to this account as needed, providing transparency in spending and reducing the likelihood of financial manipulation or refusal to pay.

- **Seek Legal Advice on Debt Liability:** If the other parent is attempting to incur joint debts to bind you financially, consult with a family law attorney. Depending on your situation, you may be able to request a court order that holds each parent responsible for their own debts or prevents the other parent from accumulating new debts during the divorce process.

- **Request Financial Transparency in the Divorce Settlement:** During divorce proceedings, ask for full financial disclosure from both parties. This includes tax returns, bank statements, investment accounts, and debts. If the other parent fails to disclose assets or lies about their finances, you can file a motion to compel disclosure or seek sanctions for financial dishonesty.

- **Use Co-Parenting Apps for Shared Financial Responsibilities:** Co-parenting apps like OurFamilyWizard often have built-in expense tracking features. These tools allow both parents to track and document child-related expenses, upload receipts, and request reimbursements. The app creates a clear record of financial transactions, making it harder for the other parent to manipulate or delay payments.

- **Highlight the Child's Best Interests in Court:** When addressing financial manipulation in court, focus on how the other parent's actions are impacting the child's well-being. Highlight how delayed payments or hidden financial resources directly affect the child's quality of life – whether it's related to housing, education, or medical care. Courts are more likely to intervene when a child's welfare is at stake.

- **File a Motion for Contempt:** If the other parent consistently fails to make child support payments or comply with court-ordered financial obligations, file a motion for contempt. This legal action can result in fines, penalties, or even jail time for the non-compliant parent, helping to enforce financial responsibility.

- **Request Retroactive Child Support:** If the other parent has been underpaying or avoiding child support, request retroactive payments to cover the shortfall. Courts can order the delinquent parent to pay back child support, including interest, ensuring that your child receives the full financial support they are entitled to.

- **Protect Your Credit Score:** If the other parent's financial manipulation is affecting your credit (e.g., joint debts going unpaid), take proactive steps to protect your credit score. Close joint accounts if possible and monitor your credit reports for any unauthorized financial activity. If necessary, dispute any inaccurate entries caused by the other parent's manipulation.

- **Propose Mediation for Financial Disputes:** If financial manipulation is creating ongoing conflict, suggest mediation to resolve disputes. A neutral mediator can help both parents come to a fair agreement regarding financial responsibilities, making it harder for the manipulative parent to control finances or withhold information without oversight.

- **Seek Temporary Spousal or Child Support Orders:** If financial manipulation is causing immediate hardship, request a temporary support order from the court. Temporary orders provide financial stability while divorce or custody proceedings are ongoing, ensuring that the manipulative parent cannot starve the other parent out financially during the legal process.

- **Report Financial Manipulation to the Court:** If the other parent is deliberately withholding financial information, hiding assets, or delaying payments, report this behavior to the court. Financial manipulation can be seen as bad faith in custody proceedings, and the court may impose penalties or adjust custody arrangements to reflect the manipulative behavior.

- **Plan for Emergency Expenses:** Create a financial buffer for yourself by setting aside emergency funds to cover child-related expenses in case the other parent delays or refuses payments. Having a safety net can help alleviate stress and ensure that your child's needs are met, even when financial manipulation is at play.

- **Establish Financial Boundaries:** Set clear financial boundaries with the other parent. Establish which expenses are shared and which are not, and communicate these boundaries in writing (via email or co-parenting apps). By formalizing these boundaries, you reduce the likelihood of financial disputes and make it easier to address issues in court if manipulation continues.

- **Seek Modifications Based on Financial Changes:** If the other parent is intentionally misrepresenting their financial situation to avoid paying child support, request a child support modification. Courts can investigate changes in income or hidden assets to ensure that child support is fairly adjusted based on the true financial situation of both parents.

- **Present a Budget to the Court:** If financial manipulation is creating significant hardships, present a detailed budget to the court showing your actual expenses related to your child's care. This budget can help demonstrate the financial impact of the other parent's manipulation and support your request for enforcement or modification of support orders.

Sudden Compliance or Agreement Reversals

Sometimes, a manipulative parent might suddenly agree to terms during negotiations only to backtrack later. This tactic is often used to prolong legal proceedings and increase the other parent's legal costs and emotional distress.

To effectively handle sudden compliance or agreement reversals, it's crucial to have all agreements formally documented and legally ratified. This involves making sure that any consent or agreement reached outside of court is quickly turned into a court order or written agreement, which can then be enforced legally.

Having a skilled attorney is vital, as they can ensure that all communications and agreements are meticulously recorded and can move swiftly to secure court approval, reducing the opportunity for reversals and minimizing their disruptive impact on the case and the children involved.

Examples of Sudden Compliance or Agreement Reversals by HCPs in Family Court:

1. **Last-minute agreement in mediation:** One parent suddenly agrees to a custody arrangement during mediation, only to later retract their consent, claiming they felt pressured.

2. **Unexpected reversal of child support terms:** A parent initially agrees to a specific child support amount but later demands a lower amount, citing changed circumstances.

3. **Changing visitation schedules:** After agreeing to a visitation schedule, one parent may abruptly refuse to adhere to the agreed times, claiming new conflicts.

4. **Withdrawal of consent to shared expenses:** A parent initially agrees to share certain child-related expenses, only to later refuse, arguing that they cannot afford it.

5. **Agreement on educational choices:** A parent agrees to enroll the child in a specific school, then reverses this decision, insisting on a different educational path without prior discussion.

6. **Temporary custody changes:** A parent agrees to a temporary custody arrangement during a hearing but later contests the arrangement, citing "new evidence" or feelings of being undermined.

7. **Altering terms of joint decisions:** After agreeing to make joint decisions regarding the child's healthcare, one parent suddenly insists on unilateral decision-making.

8. **Reversal on relocation agreements:** A parent initially consents to a planned move for the other parent but later opposes it, claiming it negatively impacts the child's welfare.

9. **Backtracking on communication protocols:** After agreeing to communicate through a co-parenting app, one parent may later insist on direct communication, complicating interactions.

10. **Refusing to sign a final agreement:** A parent may verbally agree to a divorce settlement, then refuse to sign the final documents, citing "regrets" or misgivings about the terms.

Solutions to Counteract Sudden Compliance or Agreement Reversals:

- **Get All Agreements in Writing:** Immediately follow up verbal agreements with written summaries via email or co-parenting apps. Write something like, "I'm glad we agreed on [terms]. Please confirm that this is accurate." This creates a paper trail and puts pressure on the other parent to commit to the agreement.

- **Request Court Approval for Agreements:** Once you've reached an agreement during negotiations, request that the court approve and formalize it as a court order. This reduces the other parent's ability to backtrack without facing legal consequences. Courts tend to frown on parties who try to reverse decisions after they've been formalized.

- **Use Mediation to Lock in Terms:** Suggest mediation with a neutral third-party mediator to facilitate negotiations. Mediators can help solidify agreements in a structured environment, making it harder for the other parent to backtrack. Mediated agreements can also be submitted to the court for approval, adding an extra layer of accountability.

- **Propose Binding Arbitration:** If the other parent has a history of backtracking on agreements, propose binding arbitration. In arbitration, a neutral arbitrator makes final decisions on disputed issues, and the decisions are legally binding. This prevents the manipulative parent from changing their mind once the terms are set.

- **Request "No Backtracking" Clauses in Agreements:** Incorporate "no backtracking" clauses into written agreements, stating that once both parties agree to terms, neither can retract or alter the agreement without significant cause. This can be included in court orders or mediation agreements and deters the other parent from reneging on terms.

- **Set Clear Deadlines for Agreement Finalization:** Ask for strict deadlines to be set for finalizing agreements during negotiations. Deadlines prevent the manipulative parent from drawing out the process indefinitely and force them to commit to the agreed terms within a specific time frame, reducing the chance of backtracking later.

- **Submit Agreed-Upon Terms to the Court Immediately:** After reaching an agreement, file the agreed-upon terms with the court as soon as possible. This makes the agreement part of the official record, and it's much more difficult for the other parent to reverse their position once it's been submitted and approved by the court.

- **Request Interim Orders During Negotiations:** If the other parent has a pattern of backtracking, ask the court for interim orders on key issues (such as custody or child support) while negotiations are ongoing. Interim orders ensure that at least temporary terms are in place and enforceable, preventing the other parent from using backtracking as a delay tactic.

- **Use Video or Voice Recordings of Negotiations:** If allowed in your jurisdiction, consider recording negotiation sessions with the other parent's consent. This provides evidence of the agreements made during discussions and makes it harder for the other parent to claim they never agreed to certain terms. Always consult your attorney before recording to ensure it's legal.

- **Include Financial Consequences for Backtracking:** Propose including financial penalties in your parenting plan or settlement agreement for instances where one party backs out of agreed terms without good cause. For example, the party that backtracks may be required to cover additional legal costs incurred due to their change of position.

- **Bring in a Parenting Coordinator:** If the issue involves custody or co-parenting terms, suggest bringing in a parenting coordinator. This neutral third party can oversee parenting agreements, ensure both parents follow through on their commitments, and document any instances of backtracking for the court.

- **Stay Firm and Non-Reactive:** When the manipulative parent backtracks, don't get drawn into emotional arguments. Stay firm, calmly reiterate the terms that were agreed upon, and focus on moving forward. Remaining calm under pressure weakens their tactic of prolonging the process through emotional manipulation.

- **Request Judicial Involvement in Negotiations:** If negotiations are consistently derailed by backtracking, ask for judicial involvement. A judge can directly oversee negotiations or impose deadlines and requirements for finalizing terms. This prevents the other parent from playing games with the process and forces a resolution.

- **Document All Backtracking Incidents:** Keep a detailed record of every instance where the other parent agrees to terms only to backtrack later. Include dates, specific terms that were agreed upon, and any communication showing their reversal. This documentation can be presented to the court to demonstrate bad faith negotiations and request more structured proceedings.

- **Set Up Negotiation Meetings with a Court Reporter:** In particularly contentious cases, consider having a court reporter present during negotiation sessions. This creates an official record of the discussions, making it difficult for the other parent to claim they didn't agree to certain terms. A court reporter's record is an authoritative source in case of disputes.

- **Request Sanctions for Prolonging Proceedings:** If the other parent's backtracking is clearly a delay tactic, work with your attorney to request sanctions for prolonging the legal process. Courts may impose fines or order the backtracking parent to cover additional legal fees as a deterrent to this manipulative behavior.

- **Frame the Backtracking as Emotional Harm to the Child:** If the constant backtracking is causing instability or stress for your child (e.g., inconsistent custody arrangements), bring this to the court's attention. Courts prioritize the child's best interests, and showing that the other parent's actions are harming your child's emotional well-being can motivate the court to intervene.

- **Request Regular Status Conferences with the Court:** If negotiations are dragging out due to the other parent's backtracking, request regular status conferences with the court to monitor progress. Regular check-ins can help keep the other parent accountable and give the court insight into the delay tactics being used.

- **Use Court-Appointed Negotiators:** Ask the court to appoint a neutral negotiator or settlement officer to handle the discussions. These professionals can document the terms agreed upon during negotiations and provide reports to the court if one parent later attempts to backtrack, adding credibility to your position.

- **Remain Solution-Oriented:** Throughout the process, consistently position yourself as the solution-oriented parent. Show the court that you are committed to reaching fair agreements and moving forward in a timely manner. The manipulative parent's backtracking will stand in stark contrast to your reasonable, cooperative approach, enhancing your credibility with the court.

Excessive Litigation

A favorite tactic of the high-conflict personality is to engage in excessive litigation, often as a means to harass or exhaust the opposing party emotionally and financially. In family law, this can manifest as a relentless filing of motions, appeals, and other legal actions that may not necessarily have substantial merit but serve to prolong the legal process. The underlying goal is often to wear down the other party, pushing them to capitulate to demands just to bring an end to the constant legal battles.

To counter excessive litigation, it is crucial to work with an experienced family law attorney who understands the dynamics of high-conflict cases. Such legal professionals can help streamline responses and ensure that actions are efficient and directly address the issues without getting drawn into unnecessary skirmishes. Additionally, courts can sometimes be petitioned to impose sanctions or set specific limits on frivolous filings if one party is clearly using the legal system abusively. Effective legal representation can advocate for these measures, aiming to mitigate the draining impacts of excessive litigation on both financial resources and emotional well-being.

Examples of Excessive Litigation by HCPs in Family Court:

1. **Frequent motions for modification:** One parent files repeated motions to modify custody or support arrangements, even when no significant changes in circumstances warrant such actions.

2. **Frivolous appeals:** After a ruling, a parent files multiple appeals on minor issues that have already been decided, dragging out the process unnecessarily.

3. **Continuous motion filing:** A parent inundates the court with motions related to trivial matters, such as minor scheduling conflicts or requests for documentation that have already been provided.

4. **Repeated requests for discovery:** One party continuously demands discovery of the same information, even after previous requests have been fulfilled, creating unnecessary legal work.

5. **Excessive requests for mediation:** A parent insists on mediating every minor disagreement, regardless of whether mediation is appropriate or effective for the issues at hand.

6. **Unwarranted contempt motions:** One party files contempt motions against the other for perceived violations of court orders that are minor or non-existent, aiming to intimidate and harass.

7. **Multiple petitions for protective orders:** A parent files several petitions for protective orders over minor

disagreements, attempting to leverage the legal system for control.

8. **Strategic delay tactics:** One party purposefully delays proceedings by repeatedly requesting continuances or postponements, often to frustrate the other party.

9. **Excessive communication with the court:** One parent inundates the court with letters, emails, or other communications, attempting to gain the court's attention and sway opinions.

10. **Endless modification of parenting plans:** A parent persistently seeks to modify the parenting plan for trivial reasons, creating ongoing conflict and stress rather than allowing stability for the child.

Solutions to Counteract Excessive Litigation:

- **Request a Court-Imposed "Litigation Gatekeeper":** Ask the court to appoint a gatekeeper or require judicial approval for any new motions filed by the high-conflict parent. This prevents frivolous filings and ensures that only motions with substantial merit make it to court, significantly reducing the excessive litigation tactic.

- **File for Sanctions on Frivolous Motions:** Work with your attorney to request sanctions against the other parent for filing frivolous motions. Courts can impose financial penalties or require the high-conflict parent to cover your legal fees for repeatedly filing baseless legal actions, discouraging future attempts to abuse the system.

- **Seek a "No Re-Filing" Clause in Agreements:** Include a "no re-filing" clause in any settlement or court order, stating that once a particular issue has been resolved, it cannot be re-litigated without substantial new evidence. This prevents the high-conflict parent from continually reopening resolved matters to create more legal battles.

- **Document the Pattern of Excessive Litigation:** Keep a detailed record of every motion, filing, and legal action initiated by the other parent, along with dates and outcomes. If you can show the court a clear pattern of excessive and frivolous litigation, the court may impose restrictions or sanctions on the other party.

- **Request a Court-Appointed Attorney for the Child:** Involve a court-appointed attorney for your child (if applicable). These attorneys act in the child's best interests and can help push back against excessive litigation by showing how the constant legal battles are harmful to the child's emotional well-being, prompting the court to limit further unnecessary actions.

- **Propose a Parenting Coordinator or Mediator for Disputes:** Suggest appointing a parenting coordinator or mediator to handle future disputes before they escalate to court filings. This reduces the number of legal motions filed and encourages resolution through alternative dispute resolution (ADR) methods. It also makes it harder for the high-conflict parent to manipulate the system.

- **Ask for a Forensic Accountant if Financial Misconduct Is Involved:** If the excessive litigation involves disputes over financial matters, request a forensic accountant to audit the financial claims being made. This prevents the high-conflict parent from filing frivolous financial motions and provides clear evidence to address financial disputes efficiently.

- **Use Co-Parenting Apps to Resolve Minor Issues:** Suggest using co-parenting apps like OurFamilyWizard to resolve minor disputes outside of court. These apps offer structured communication, track exchanges, and document agreements, making it easier to avoid escalating minor issues into costly legal battles.

- **Request Strict Deadlines and Court Supervision:** Ask the court to impose strict deadlines for legal filings and responses. Courts can set tight schedules for resolving issues, preventing the high-conflict parent from dragging out proceedings unnecessarily. Regular court supervision can also keep the case on track and limit excessive delays.

- **Propose Binding Arbitration for Major Disputes:** If the high-conflict parent continues to litigate the same issues, propose binding arbitration for major disputes. Arbitration decisions are legally binding and can't be appealed, which prevents the other parent from repeatedly filing motions or re-litigating resolved matters.

- **File a Motion to Limit Filings:** Work with your attorney to file a motion requesting that the court limit the number of filings the high-conflict parent is allowed in a given time period. This limits the barrage of legal actions and forces the other parent to prioritize genuine disputes over harassment tactics.

- **Present the Impact on Your Child to the Court:** Highlight the emotional and financial toll that the excessive litigation is having on your child's well-being. Courts are particularly sensitive to issues that negatively affect children, and demonstrating how the constant legal battles are disrupting your child's life can motivate the court to intervene and curb the excessive filings.

- **Request a Stay of Proceedings:** If the high-conflict parent is filing excessive motions with little merit, your attorney can request a stay of proceedings, halting any further legal actions until the court has time to assess the situation. This puts an immediate stop to frivolous motions and prevents the high-conflict parent from overwhelming the system.

- **Seek Early Resolution Conferences:** Ask for early resolution conferences to address issues before they escalate to formal litigation. These conferences provide an opportunity for both parties to present their positions, often leading to faster resolution and preventing unnecessary motions from being filed.

- **Use a Court Reporter for Accuracy:** For hearings or negotiations, request a court reporter to record all proceedings. Having a clear, official record of what was agreed upon makes it harder for the high-conflict parent to twist facts or manipulate outcomes in future filings, and it can discourage them from filing unnecessary motions.

- **Show Bad Faith Behavior to the Court:** Document and present evidence of bad faith litigation tactics, such as filing motions purely to harass or delay the process. Courts frown upon parties who abuse the legal system and may impose penalties, sanctions, or limits on future filings to stop the bad faith behavior.

- **Request Costs for Vexatious Litigation:** Work with your attorney to request that the court impose costs on the other parent for vexatious litigation. Courts can require the high-conflict parent to cover your legal fees for frivolous motions or unnecessary appeals, discouraging them from filing excessive legal actions.

- **Suggest Mediation Before Court Filings:** Propose that all disputes go through mediation before either party can file a motion. Mediation often resolves issues more quickly and amicably, preventing the high-conflict parent from turning every dispute into a drawn-out court case. Courts appreciate parties who try to settle outside of litigation.

- **Push for Final Orders Instead of Temporary Ones:** Where possible, push for final orders instead of temporary ones. High-conflict parents often exploit temporary orders by filing motions to modify them or delay proceedings. A final order makes it harder for them to continuously reopen settled matters and prolong the legal battle.

- **Stay Emotionally Detached from the Tactic:** Recognize that excessive litigation is designed to wear you down emotionally. By staying emotionally detached and focused on facts, you can approach each motion or filing with calm professionalism. This not only preserves your emotional well-being but also helps the court see that the other parent's actions are intended to harass, not to resolve real issues.

Countering Manipulative Tactics by HCPs

When dealing with the challenges posed by HCPs in divorce and custody disputes, it's crucial to equip yourself with effective strategies to counter their manipulative tactics. These individuals often employ various psychological maneuvers aimed at undermining your confidence and destabilizing your position. To successfully navigate this complex landscape, cultivating a proactive mindset and developing a toolkit of counter strategies is essential.

The effectiveness of these strategies lies in their ability to disrupt the manipulative patterns that HCPs rely on. By fostering emotional resilience and focusing on factual evidence, you can mitigate the impact of tactics like gaslighting and projection, which are designed to create doubt and confusion. This approach not only empowers you to advocate more effectively for yourself and your children but also establishes a buffer against further manipulation, ultimately promoting healthier co-parenting dynamics.

Additionally, these strategies enhance self-awareness and critical thinking, allowing you to respond thoughtfully rather than react impulsively to provocations. By setting clear boundaries and prioritizing open communication, you can create an environment that discourages manipulative behaviors and encourages cooperative co-parenting. The recommendations that follow apply broadly to the range of manipulative tactics discussed above, providing you with a comprehensive framework for navigating high-conflict situations effectively.

1. Document Everything

Keep comprehensive notes of conversations or messages to establish a clear account of events and a factual basis for your experiences.

Create a structured system for documenting all interactions with the other parent. Use a notebook or digital app to log dates, times, locations, and the nature of conversations or exchanges. Save all communications, including emails, texts, and social media messages. Print out conversations when necessary and categorize them by topic (e.g., custody, finances, child-related matters).

Documenting everything during a contentious divorce or custody case not only serves as a practical legal strategy but also significantly benefits your mental health and emotional stability. By maintaining comprehensive notes and a structured system for recording interactions, you create a sense of order in an otherwise chaotic situation. This structure helps alleviate anxiety by providing clarity and a tangible reference point amidst the emotional turmoil. When you can visually see the facts laid out, it counters feelings of helplessness and confusion, reinforcing your understanding of the situation and your role within it.

Additionally, thorough documentation acts as a powerful form of self-validation. When faced with the emotional manipulation often employed by high-conflict ex-partners, it's easy to question your perceptions and memories. By keeping detailed records, you affirm your experiences and feelings, which can bolster your self-esteem and confidence. This process can reduce self-doubt, as you have concrete evidence to back up your narrative, reminding you that your account is legitimate and grounded in reality.

Furthermore, knowing that you have a well-organized archive of evidence can provide a sense of empowerment. This preparation allows you to approach court proceedings with greater confidence and stability, minimizing emotional volatility. When you are equipped with the facts, you are less likely to be swayed by the

220 | Family Court Solutions

opposing party's manipulative tactics, allowing you to maintain a more composed and resilient demeanor. Ultimately, this proactive approach not only safeguards your legal interests but also fosters a healthier mindset, enabling you to navigate the challenges of divorce and custody disputes with greater emotional resilience.

Comprehensive records provide objective evidence that can be crucial in court, helping to establish a timeline and counter any false narratives, thereby reinforcing your credibility. Having a well-organized archive of evidence can discredit false claims made by the other parent, leading to more favorable rulings in custody or support decisions.

2. Maintain a Journal

Maintaining a journal is a powerful countering tactic against manipulation during contentious divorce and custody cases. By consistently documenting your interactions, feelings, and observations, you create a factual record that can serve as a vital resource in navigating high-conflict situations. This practice not only enhances your self-awareness but also provides clarity in a tumultuous environment.

A journal allows you to capture details about interactions with the other parent, including instances of manipulation or unreasonable behavior. By recording specific events, dates, and conversations, you establish an objective timeline that can be invaluable in legal proceedings. This structured documentation helps counter false narratives and protects your credibility, demonstrating to the court your commitment to transparency and your child's best interests.

Moreover, journaling offers an effective outlet for processing emotions, which can be particularly beneficial in managing stress and anxiety. Writing about your experiences can foster a greater sense of control over your circumstances, alleviating feelings of overwhelm. As you reflect on your journey, you can identify patterns in behavior and develop strategies to respond more effectively, empowering you to navigate conflicts with greater resilience.

Additionally, maintaining a journal can facilitate clearer communication with legal professionals. By providing them with documented evidence of relevant incidents, you enable them to better advocate for your interests. This proactive approach not only enhances your case but also helps ensure that important details are not overlooked, ultimately contributing to a more favorable outcome.

When you consistently maintain a journal, it sets a precedent for accountability and responsible behavior in co-parenting. This commitment to documenting your experiences showcases your dedication to creating a stable and nurturing environment for your child.

Furthermore, a well-maintained journal can influence how the court perceives your ability to manage conflict and prioritize your child's welfare, potentially leading to more favorable custody arrangements. Ultimately, by investing time in this practice, you bolster your emotional resilience and support a healthier co-parenting dynamic, ensuring the best interests of your child remain paramount.

3. Reaffirm Reality and Challenge Fabrications in Court

Stick to the facts and calmly refute false claims. Use your documentation as evidence to support your narrative. Whenever possible, gather additional evidence such as photographs, videos, or witness statements from friends, family, or professionals who can verify your account of events. It's crucial to assert your version of events clearly and confidently.

Going through this process can also significantly benefit your mental health and enhance your sense of stability. By consistently sticking to the facts and confidently asserting your version of events, you regain a sense of control over your narrative. This process helps counteract the feelings of confusion and self-doubt that can arise when facing manipulative tactics from a high-conflict ex-partner. When you confront false claims with evidence, it not only reinforces your credibility in the eyes of the court but also fosters a more resilient mindset, helping you feel more empowered and less victimized.

Additionally, actively refuting false narratives can help alleviate feelings of isolation and vulnerability. It serves as a reminder that your experiences and perceptions are valid, countering any attempts to make you question your reality. This validation can have a grounding effect, allowing you to maintain clarity in your emotions and decisions. As you consistently present factual evidence, you cultivate a mental framework that emphasizes truth over manipulation, which can be incredibly reassuring during emotionally turbulent times.

Overall, this practice not only protects your legal interests but also nurtures your mental well-being. It reinforces your identity and perspective in a situation that can feel disorienting and distressing. By focusing on your narrative and surrounding it with corroborative evidence, you create a buffer against emotional upheaval, allowing you to compartmentalize your feelings more effectively while navigating the complexities of divorce or custody disputes. This stability ultimately contributes to a healthier environment for both you and your children.

Corroborative evidence strengthens your position and provides tangible proof that may influence the court's perception, increasing the likelihood of a favorable outcome. This approach reinforces your credibility and helps the court recognize inconsistencies in the other parent's claims. By establishing a clear, factual narrative, you not only protect your interests but also create a more stable environment for your children.

4. Engage a Neutral Third Party

Consider involving a mediator, counselor, or therapist who specializes in high-conflict situations. This professional can facilitate discussions and provide guidance on navigating conflicts.

Engaging a neutral third party during contentious divorce or custody cases not only facilitates healthier communication but also significantly benefits your mental health and sense of stability. When navigating high-conflict situations, emotions can run high, leading to stress and anxiety. A mediator or therapist provides a structured environment where discussions can occur in a more controlled manner. This reduces the potential for explosive confrontations and allows you to express your concerns and feelings in a safe space, which can alleviate emotional burdens and foster a greater sense of security.

Additionally, having a neutral facilitator can help validate your feelings and experiences. When you're constantly faced with manipulation or invalidation from a high-conflict ex, it's easy to feel isolated or misunderstood. A professional third party not only listens but also helps to affirm your perspective, reinforcing that your concerns are legitimate. This external validation can boost your self-esteem and confidence, allowing you to feel more grounded in your own reality.

Moreover, the involvement of a neutral party can provide much-needed perspective. They can help you see beyond the immediate conflict, reminding you of the ultimate goal: the well-being of your children. This focus can create a sense of purpose and direction, helping you compartmentalize the emotional challenges you face. By encouraging constructive dialogue and collaboration, a mediator can help you navigate the complexities of co-parenting with less emotional upheaval, leading to a more stable and peaceful co-parenting arrangement. Ultimately, this support not only aids in resolving disputes but also contributes to your overall mental well-being, allowing you to approach the situation with greater resilience and clarity.

A neutral third party can help de-escalate tensions and foster healthier communication, making it easier to focus on co-parenting arrangements that serve the child's best interests.

5. Consult Legal Counsel

Working with an attorney experienced in high-conflict cases is essential for effective advocacy. Your attorney can navigate the complexities of manipulation tactics, helping you formulate a strategic approach that addresses these challenges head-on. Provide them with all documentation and updates regarding your situation so they can build a robust defense.

Consulting an experienced attorney during contentious divorce or custody cases not only provides essential legal guidance but also significantly enhances your confidence and sense of empowerment. When facing a high-conflict ex, it's common to feel overwhelmed and uncertain about your rights and options. An attorney well-versed in high-conflict situations can demystify the legal process, equipping you with knowledge about your case and the steps you need to take. This understanding empowers you to make informed decisions and assert your rights more effectively.

Moreover, having a skilled advocate by your side reinforces your position, allowing you to focus on the facts rather than getting lost in emotional turmoil. Your attorney's expertise in handling manipulation tactics means you'll have someone who not only believes in your narrative but also knows how to present it compellingly in court. This support alleviates the burden of having to navigate the legal system alone, fostering a greater sense of control over your circumstances.

Additionally, the process of collaborating with an attorney helps you build a strategy that aligns with your goals, giving you a proactive role in your case. As you engage in the legal process, you'll likely experience a renewed sense of agency, knowing that you are actively working towards a resolution that prioritizes your and your children's well-being. This shift from a passive to an active role can significantly enhance your emotional resilience, making it easier to face the challenges ahead with determination and clarity. Ultimately, effective legal representation not only protects your interests but also bolsters your confidence, empowering you to advocate for yourself and your children in a meaningful way.

Effective legal representation is crucial in countering manipulative tactics and ensuring your case is presented clearly and compellingly. An experienced attorney will strengthen your ability to refute false claims and protect your rights throughout the process, ultimately leading to more favorable custody arrangements and support decisions.

6. Educate Yourself

Educating yourself about the legal processes, psychological dynamics, and practical strategies involved in divorce and custody cases is a crucial countering tactic against manipulation. By arming yourself with knowledge, you can navigate the complexities of high-conflict situations more effectively, making informed decisions that prioritize your well-being and that of your child.

Understanding the legal framework surrounding custody and divorce helps demystify the process, reducing anxiety and uncertainty. Familiarizing yourself with relevant laws, your rights, and the potential implications of various actions empowers you to advocate confidently for yourself and your child. This knowledge can also deter manipulative behaviors from the other parent, as they may be less likely to exploit your lack of understanding.

Moreover, educating yourself about the psychological tactics often employed in high-conflict scenarios can enhance your resilience. By recognizing manipulative strategies, you can develop strategies to counteract them effectively. This awareness allows you to remain grounded and focused, rather than reacting impulsively to provocations, thereby modeling emotional regulation for your children.

In addition to legal and psychological knowledge, learning about co-parenting strategies and child development can significantly benefit your relationship with your child. This understanding enables you to create a supportive environment that fosters emotional security, helping to mitigate the impact of the conflict. When you prioritize your child's well-being, you not only strengthen your bond with them but also reinforce your position as a responsible and caring parent in the eyes of the court.

Ultimately, by committing to continuous education, you position yourself as an informed participant in the process. This proactive approach not only safeguards your interests but also demonstrates your dedication to fostering a healthy co-parenting dynamic. Educating yourself sets a positive precedent for respectful interactions, influencing how the court views your capability to provide a stable environment for your child. In doing so, you enhance your chances of achieving a favorable outcome while ensuring that the best interests of your child remain at the forefront.

7. Establish Boundaries

Clearly communicate what behaviors are acceptable and unacceptable regarding interactions with the other parent and communicate consequences for violations. Stick to these boundaries consistently. Use structured communication methods, such as co-parenting apps, to minimize direct contact.

Consistently enforce these boundaries to demonstrate that manipulative tactics will not be tolerated. This approach not only protects your emotional well-being but also models appropriate behavior for your children, fostering a healthier co-parenting dynamic. Firm boundaries can deter high-conflict behaviors, making interactions more manageable and focused on the child's best interests.

Establishing clear boundaries during contentious divorce or custody cases not only helps reduce opportunities for manipulation and conflict but also significantly benefits your mental health and sense of stability. By defining acceptable behaviors and consistently enforcing these limits, you create a structured environment that minimizes stress and uncertainty.

This structure can lead to a greater sense of control over your circumstances, helping to alleviate feelings of anxiety and overwhelm. Knowing that you have set and communicated these boundaries can foster a sense of empowerment, allowing you to focus on your well-being and that of your child. Ultimately, maintaining firm boundaries contributes to a healthier co-parenting dynamic and enhances your emotional resilience throughout the process.

Additionally, a consistent enforcement of boundaries can reduce conflicts that might otherwise result in legal disputes or emotional outbursts, thereby preserving valuable resources – both emotional and financial – that can be better spent on your child's well-being. Ultimately, maintaining firm boundaries not only protects your interests but also reinforces a positive narrative in your case, contributing to a healthier outcome for all involved.

When boundaries are communicated clearly, it sets a precedent for respectful interactions and demonstrates to the court your commitment to a healthy co-parenting dynamic. This proactive approach can influence how the court views your ability to provide a stable environment for your child, potentially leading to more favorable custody arrangements.

8. Prepare Thoroughly for Court

Thoroughly prepare for court to effectively counter manipulation during contentious divorce and custody cases. This preparation involves gathering all relevant documentation, including communication records, financial statements, and evidence of positive parenting practices. By being well-organized and informed, you position yourself as a credible and responsible parent, making it more difficult for manipulative tactics to take hold.

Consistent and diligent preparation not only strengthens your case but also helps mitigate the impact of high-conflict behaviors from the other parent. This proactive approach demonstrates your commitment to prioritizing the best interests of your child, fostering a healthier co-parenting dynamic. When you present clear, well-supported arguments in court, you reduce opportunities for the other parent to manipulate the narrative or undermine your credibility.

Establishing a thorough preparation process significantly enhances your sense of stability and confidence. By knowing that you are equipped with the necessary evidence and a well-structured argument, you can alleviate feelings of anxiety and uncertainty leading up to your court appearance. This sense of control allows you to focus on your child's well-being and the key issues at hand, rather than getting sidetracked by the emotional turmoil often associated with contentious disputes.

Furthermore, preparing thoroughly for court helps preserve valuable resources – both emotional and financial – that might otherwise be spent on unnecessary legal battles. By presenting a well-prepared case, you are more likely to reach favorable outcomes, thus minimizing the duration of proceedings and associated costs. This focus not only protects your interests but also reinforces a positive narrative in your case, contributing to a healthier outcome for everyone involved.

When you demonstrate a strong commitment to preparation, it sets a precedent for responsible and respectful interactions. This not only showcases your dedication to the court but also influences how legal professionals perceive your ability to provide a stable environment for your child. Ultimately, thorough preparation can lead to more favorable custody arrangements and help you navigate the complexities of the legal process with greater ease and confidence.

9. Practice Self-Care

Practicing self-care is essential for effectively countering manipulation during contentious divorce and custody cases. By prioritizing your mental and emotional well-being, you build resilience against the stress and turmoil that often accompany high-conflict situations. Self-care encompasses a range of activities, from physical exercise and healthy eating to mindfulness practices and seeking emotional support from friends or professionals.

Consistent self-care helps mitigate the emotional impact of manipulative tactics, allowing you to maintain clarity and composure. When you invest time in your own well-being, you are better equipped to navigate conflicts without being overwhelmed by anxiety or frustration. This stability not only protects your mental health but also serves as a positive model for your children, demonstrating the importance of emotional resilience in challenging circumstances.

Establishing a self-care routine fosters a sense of control and empowerment over your circumstances. Knowing that you are actively taking steps to care for yourself can alleviate feelings of helplessness often experienced during divorce proceedings. This proactive approach allows you to focus on your well-being and the needs of your child, ensuring that you remain present and engaged in their lives despite external conflicts.

Moreover, prioritizing self-care can preserve valuable emotional and financial resources. By managing stress and maintaining a balanced perspective, you reduce the likelihood of emotional outbursts that could escalate conflicts or lead to unnecessary legal disputes. This focus not only protects your interests but also reinforces a positive narrative in your case, contributing to a healthier outcome for all involved.

When you demonstrate a commitment to self-care, it sets a precedent for respectful interactions and showcases your dedication to providing a stable environment for your child. This proactive approach can positively influence how the court perceives your ability to co-parent effectively, potentially leading to more favorable custody arrangements. Ultimately, prioritizing self-care not only enhances your emotional resilience but also supports a healthier co-parenting dynamic, ensuring the best interests of your child remain at the forefront.

10. Maintain Focus on the Best Interests of the Children

Clearly prioritize the best interests of your children in all interactions and decisions regarding custody and co-parenting. Communicate to the other parent that any behavior that detracts from this focus is unacceptable, and outline the consequences for such actions. Use structured communication methods, such as co-parenting apps, to minimize direct contact and ensure that discussions remain centered on the children's needs.

Consistently emphasizing the best interests of your children can help deter manipulative tactics, signaling that such behaviors will not be tolerated. This approach not only safeguards your emotional well-being but also serves as a model for appropriate behavior for your children, fostering a healthier co-parenting dynamic. By keeping discussions focused on what benefits the children, you minimize opportunities for conflict and manipulation.

Maintaining this focus also significantly enhances your mental health and sense of stability. By defining clear priorities and consistently reinforcing them, you create a structured environment that reduces stress and uncertainty. This focus can help you regain a sense of control over your circumstances, alleviating feelings of anxiety and overwhelm.

Knowing that your decisions are rooted in what is best for your children fosters a sense of empowerment. It allows you to advocate effectively for their needs while reinforcing your commitment to their well-being. Ultimately, this focus contributes to a healthier co-parenting dynamic and enhances your emotional resilience throughout the process.

Moreover, prioritizing the best interests of your children can help prevent conflicts that may escalate into legal disputes or emotional turmoil. This preservation of resources – both emotional and financial – can be redirected towards your children's needs and well-being. By consistently reinforcing this focus, you not only protect your interests but also promote a positive narrative in your case, leading to better outcomes for all involved.

When the focus on the children is clearly communicated, it sets a precedent for respectful interactions and demonstrates to the court your commitment to providing a stable and nurturing environment. This proactive approach can significantly influence how the court views your capability as a parent, potentially resulting in more favorable custody arrangements.

Build Your Psychological Resilience

Building psychological resilience is crucial for maintaining focus and composure in the emotionally challenging landscape of divorce and custody cases. Resilience empowers you to recover from setbacks, manage stress effectively, and stay centered on your goals, especially when facing a manipulative or high-conflict opponent. It's essential to explore four key areas to strengthening your resilience: emotional intelligence, strategic communication, professional support, and support networks.

Strengthening resilience can involve practices like mindfulness meditation, which helps in managing stress and maintaining mental clarity. Regular physical exercise and a healthy diet also contribute to psychological resilience by enhancing your overall well-being and ability to cope with stress.

Seeking support from friends, family, or mental health professionals can also strengthen your resilience. These support networks provide emotional comfort and practical advice, helping you to navigate the challenges of the legal process more effectively and with greater confidence. To develop resilience, it's important to foster a positive mindset that focuses on solutions and growth rather than dwelling on difficulties and conflicts.

By focusing on these four areas, you can enhance your mental and emotional well-being, enabling you to effectively counter manipulative tactics and work toward the best possible outcomes for yourself and your family.

1. Emotional Intelligence

Improving your emotional intelligence is essential for effectively navigating custody disputes and managing high-conflict interactions. Emotional intelligence encompasses the ability to recognize, understand, and regulate your emotions, as well as to empathize with others. By enhancing this skill, you can better anticipate the emotional triggers and tactics used by the opposing party, allowing you to respond calmly and strategically rather than react impulsively.

One powerful way to boost your emotional intelligence is through mindfulness exercises. Mindfulness meditation encourages you to stay present in the moment, fostering awareness of your thoughts and feelings without judgment. This practice helps you recognize emotional patterns and triggers, making it easier to detach from manipulative behaviors. Incorporating mindfulness into your daily routine – whether through guided meditation, mindful breathing, or simply taking a few moments to observe your surroundings – can significantly enhance your emotional regulation.

In addition to mindfulness, physical health strategies play a critical role in supporting emotional well-being. Regular physical exercise, such as walking, yoga, or strength training, releases endorphins that improve mood and reduce stress.

Exercise not only strengthens your body but also helps clear your mind, making it easier to manage emotional responses during challenging situations. A balanced diet rich in nutrients, including omega-3 fatty acids, antioxidants, and vitamins, can also positively impact your mood and cognitive function, further enhancing your resilience.

Furthermore, establishing a consistent sleep routine is vital for emotional health. Quality sleep improves cognitive processing and emotional regulation, allowing you to face challenges with greater clarity and composure. Techniques like setting a regular sleep schedule, creating a calming bedtime routine, and limiting screen time before bed can contribute to better sleep quality.

Finally, integrating techniques such as deep breathing and reflective pauses can strengthen your ability to respond thoughtfully. When faced with provocation, taking a moment to breathe deeply and assess the situation can help you maintain control over your emotional responses. Reflecting on the long-term consequences of your actions allows you to approach interactions with a strategic mindset, reinforcing your position and protecting your emotional well-being.

By incorporating mindfulness practices, physical health strategies, and emotional regulation techniques into your daily life, you can significantly improve your emotional intelligence, enabling you to navigate custody disputes with greater confidence and composure.

2. Strategic Communication

Strategic communication is a cornerstone strategy for building resilience in family court scenarios, particularly when confronting manipulative tactics. By choosing your battles wisely and knowing when to engage or withdraw, you create a buffer against emotional turmoil and maintain focus on your objectives. Utilizing written correspondence as much as possible not only minimizes direct conflict but also provides a clear, documented record of exchanges, which can be invaluable in legal proceedings.

In high-conflict custody disputes, strategic communication involves planned interactions that emphasize firm boundaries and reduce personal contact, particularly when dealing with manipulative or narcissistic ex-partners. Establishing and maintaining these boundaries is crucial for protecting your emotional well-being and reducing the likelihood of being exploited for your vulnerabilities.

When implementing strategic communication, favor written forms such as emails or text messages. This approach allows you to respond thoughtfully rather than react impulsively, decreasing the emotional intensity that often accompanies face-to-face or telephone conversations. It also empowers you to maintain control over the narrative and the flow of information.

During necessary verbal interactions, keep your communications concise and focused solely on essential matters, such as the custody or care of the children. Avoiding personal topics helps prevent escalation and unnecessary conflict. By setting these clear boundaries, you not only reduce opportunities for manipulation but also reinforce your autonomy and control in the communication process.

Ultimately, these practices foster resilience by creating a structured environment in which you can operate effectively, manage stress, and focus on achieving the best outcomes for yourself and your children.

3. Professional Support

Engaging with therapists or counselors who specialize in high-conflict relationships is an essential strategy for building resilience in family court settings. These professionals provide valuable insights and tailored strategies to help you navigate the emotional turbulence often associated with custody disputes. They can guide you in effective communication techniques, setting healthy boundaries, and protecting your emotional and mental well-being throughout the legal process.

Seeking professional support not only equips you with coping mechanisms but also enhances your understanding of how to manage your reactions to manipulative behaviors. Mental health professionals, such as psychologists or therapists, can help you develop strategies to communicate effectively, even under stress, fostering a sense of control and clarity during interactions with a high-conflict ex-partner.

In addition to emotional support, consulting with legal professionals experienced in high-conflict cases is crucial. These experts arm you with the necessary legal strategies and knowledge to safeguard your rights and interests, enabling you to anticipate and prepare for potential maneuvers by the opposing party. This proactive approach helps mitigate the emotional strain of unexpected legal challenges.

Together, these forms of professional support create a strong foundation for resilience, allowing you to maintain your well-being and navigate the complexities of custody disputes with confidence. By leveraging expert guidance, you not only bolster your emotional strength but also ensure a strategic, well-informed approach to achieving the best outcomes for yourself and your children.

4. Support Networks

Building a strong support network of friends, family, and peer groups is essential for fostering resilience in contentious family court cases, as they provide both emotional sustenance and practical advice. Sharing your experiences with those who care about you can alleviate feelings of isolation and offer emotional relief, while also equipping you with valuable coping strategies.

Engaging with a diverse circle of friends and family creates a sense of solidarity that is particularly important when navigating the emotional turmoil of high-conflict custody disputes. These individuals can offer different perspectives and insights that help inform your decisions, while their presence can serve as a comforting buffer against the stress of legal proceedings.

Moreover, your support network can assist with practical matters, such as helping with childcare or accompanying you to court sessions, which can ease the burden during challenging times.

Ultimately, relying on friends and family strengthens your emotional resilience and provides the resources needed to manage and counter manipulative tactics effectively. By cultivating these relationships, you can stay focused on achieving the best possible outcomes for yourself and your children, guided by clarity and deliberate action rather than reactive emotions. This approach highlights the importance of resilience as a long-term strategy in navigating family court complexities, empowering you to withstand challenges and advocate for your family's best interests.

Conclusion: Navigating Manipulative Tactics with Resilience and Strategy

A high-conflict custody dispute necessitates more than just legal knowledge; it calls for emotional resilience, strategic communication, and strong support systems. This chapter has highlighted key strategies for identifying and countering the manipulative tactics often used by narcissistic or high-conflict individuals. By enhancing your emotional intelligence, establishing clear communication boundaries, and leveraging both professional and personal support networks, you can effectively safeguard your interests and those of your children in a balanced manner.

It's important to remember that while the journey through such disputes can be challenging, you are not without tools and resources. Building and maintaining psychological resilience will help you to remain focused and effective, even under pressure.

As you move forward, keep in mind the ultimate goal: achieving a resolution that serves the best interests of your children and ensures their well-being. Armed with knowledge, strategies, and support, you are better prepared to face the challenges of high-conflict custody disputes and emerge with your dignity and your family's future intact.

Key Takeaways:

- **Recognize Manipulative Tactics:** Be aware of common tactics like gaslighting, false accusations, and parental alienation. Identifying these behaviors early can help you respond more effectively.

- **Document Everything:** Keep meticulous records of all interactions and communications. This documentation can provide crucial evidence to counter manipulative behaviors and false claims.

- **Establish Formal Agreements:** Ensure all verbal agreements are put into writing and legally ratified. This helps prevent sudden reversals and provides a clear, enforceable record of terms.

- **Counter False Accusations:** Gather evidence and seek professional assessments to refute false allegations. Comprehensive documentation and neutral third-party testimonials are vital.

- **Avoid Using Children as Messengers:** Communicate directly with the other parent through written channels to prevent putting children in the middle of conflicts and avoid miscommunication.

- **Address Financial Manipulation:** Document financial transactions and involve forensic accountants if necessary to uncover hidden assets or financial manipulation.

- **Prepare for Excessive Litigation:** Work with an experienced attorney to manage and streamline responses to unnecessary or frivolous legal motions, and petition for sanctions if needed.

- **Build Psychological Resilience:** Engage in self-care practices such as mindfulness, exercise, and healthy eating to maintain mental clarity and stress management.

- **Enhance Emotional Intelligence:** Develop skills to manage your own emotions and understand the emotional triggers of the opposing party. Use techniques like deep breathing and reflective thinking to respond calmly.

- **Use Strategic Communication:** Limit direct verbal interactions and rely on written correspondence to maintain a clear record and reduce emotional conflicts.

- **Seek Professional Support:** Consult with mental health professionals and legal experts specializing in high-conflict cases to gain strategies and support for managing manipulative behaviors.

- **Leverage Support Networks:** Build a robust support network of friends, family, and advisors to provide emotional and practical assistance, helping you navigate the complexities of the legal process.

4

CROSS-EXAMINING AN HCP IN FAMILY COURT

As a litigator, cross-examination is my hands-down favorite tool to use in high-conflict cases. Cross-examining a narcissist in a courtroom setting presents unique challenges and requires meticulous preparation as well as an understanding of the common behavioral patterns they display. Narcissistic individuals often possess a heightened sense of self-importance, a delicate ego, and a propensity for manipulation, which they try to use to their advantage during testimony. Their tendency to distort facts, evade accountability, and manipulate narratives necessitates a strategic approach to cross-examination. Here, we explore effective techniques for setting up questions, catching them in lies, and impeaching their credibility to undermine their testimony effectively.

Preparation is Key

Before stepping into the courtroom, thorough preparation is crucial. Review all available evidence meticulously, including communications, previous testimonies, and any documented instances of past behavior that could be relevant. Understanding the HCP's typical patterns of behavior and previous statements allows you to anticipate possible answers and plan your questions accordingly. It's important to familiarize yourself with every detail that the HCP might refer to, ensuring that no statement goes unchecked.

Create a comprehensive timeline of events and gather all forms of communication, including emails, texts, and recorded conversations, if available and legally obtained. Understand the legal boundaries and past precedents that might influence the case. By anticipating the narcissist's potential responses, you can formulate questions that preemptively counter their typical manipulative responses.

Also, consult with psychologists or experts on narcissism to better understand the psychological aspects of their behavior. This knowledge can give you an edge in predicting how they might try to distort facts or manipulate perceptions, enabling you to craft your questions and responses to expose these tactics effectively. Preparation not only equips you with the knowledge and tools to maintain control during cross-examination but also instills confidence, a crucial element when facing a challenging opponent in court.

Additionally, understanding the HCP's psychological profile – particularly their need for admiration, tendency to distort facts, and sensitivity to criticism – can guide the framing of your questions to exploit these traits. Prepare a list of potential questions that align with known facts and contradictions in the narcissist's past statements. Practicing these questions and possible follow-ups can ensure you are not caught off guard and can maintain control during the cross-examination. This level of preparedness not only boosts your confidence but also positions you to navigate the unpredictable nature of a narcissist's testimony effectively.

Setting Up Questions

When cross-examining an HCP, the way questions are structured is critical. Start with general questions that establish the baseline of their testimony, which you can reference later if their story changes. Use open-ended questions initially to let them speak; often, HCP's will reveal more than they intend through their desire to be seen and heard.

Transition gradually to more specific, pointed questions that box them into a narrative. This technique is known as funneling; begin broad, then narrow down to specifics that are harder for the HCP to manipulate without contradicting earlier statements. It's essential to remain calm and composed, regardless of the provocations, maintaining a professional demeanor throughout.

EXAMPLE SCENARIO #1: QUESTIONING ON PARENTAL RESPONSIBILITIES

Broad Opening Question:

"Can you describe your typical weekday interactions with the children?"

Purpose: This open-ended question gives the witness a chance to discuss their involvement broadly, setting the stage for more detailed inquiries.

Follow-Up Questions:

"Which days of the week are you responsible for taking the children to school?"

"What time do you drop the children off at school?"

Purpose: These questions begin to introduce specifics, which are easier to verify against known facts or other testimonies.

Narrowed Down Specific Questions:

"You stated earlier that you take the children to school every morning. How do you reconcile this with the school's records showing frequent tardiness on days you purportedly drove them?"

Purpose: These highly specific questions require precise answers. Discrepancies between the witness's responses and documented facts or previous statements can be highlighted, challenging the credibility of their broader claims.

EXAMPLE SCENARIO #1: QUESTIONING ON FINANCIAL CONTRIBUTIONS

Broad Opening Question:

"Could you outline how you have financially supported the family?"

Purpose: This question allows the witness to claim a general level of support, setting a baseline for their financial involvement.

Follow-Up Questions:

"What are the usual monthly expenses for the household?"

"How do you typically manage these expenses?"

Purpose: Moving to specifics about the nature and management of expenses narrows the scope and prepares the ground for contradiction.

Narrowed Down Specific Questions:

"On your statement, you claimed to handle utility bills. However, the utility company's records show late payments for several months. How do you explain this discrepancy?"

Purpose: These detailed, documentable questions are designed to catch the HCP in a lie or inconsistency. By directly confronting their general statements with specific, verifiable facts, you expose gaps in their narrative and impeach their credibility.

Effective Funneling Technique

In both examples, the technique of starting broad and then funneling down to specifics is crucial. It allows the examiner to first let the narcissist build a narrative and then use their own statements against them by introducing facts that contradict their broad claims. This strategy not only exposes inconsistencies but also effectively challenges the HCP's reliability as a witness, significantly weakening their position in the eyes of the court.

Catching Them in Lies

To effectively catch an HCP in a lie, you must pay close attention to their answers and be ready to reference specific evidence that contradicts their statements. Documentation is your ally; have all relevant communications, previous contradictory statements, and other evidential documents ready for quick reference. When they make a claim, counter it with documented evidence and ask them to clarify the discrepancies.

This method not only highlights the inconsistencies in their testimony but also traps them in their narrative, making it difficult to backtrack without losing credibility. It's crucial to conduct this calmly and systematically, as showing any emotional reaction can be twisted by the HCP to their advantage.

Catching a high-conflict witness in lies during cross-examination requires astute observation and a strategic use of evidence. To effectively expose falsehoods, you should be intimately familiar with all the details of the case, including timelines, communications, and any previous statements made by the witness.

When the HCP provides an answer, compare it immediately against documented evidence. For instance, if they claim they were at a child's school event, have attendance records or photographs ready to prove otherwise. If they state a particular financial contribution, be prepared with bank statements or receipts that contradict their claim.

To catch them in a lie, present the evidence directly after they make a conflicting statement. Ask them to clarify or explain the discrepancy: "You mentioned you were at the school play Thursday night; however, we have a photo from the event that doesn't include you. Can you explain why that might be?" This direct approach leaves little room for evasion and effectively highlights their dishonesty, undermining their credibility in front of the court.

Impeaching Their Credibility

Impeaching the credibility of an HCP involves highlighting their unreliability, dishonesty, or bias to the court. Utilize prior inconsistent statements; these are particularly powerful as they directly undermine the witness's reliability. If they've lied under oath or provided different accounts at different times, highlight these instances clearly and concisely.

Question their motives for testifying. HCPs often have a clear agenda, and exposing this can help illustrate their bias. If the HCP stands to gain significantly from a particular outcome of the case, make sure the court is aware of this. Additionally, if there are any psychological evaluations or third-party observations that suggest manipulative tendencies or dishonesty, these can be introduced as evidence to further question their credibility.

Controlling the Courtroom Dynamics

Maintaining control of the courtroom dynamics is crucial when dealing with an HCP witness. Speak clearly and authoritatively, establishing control of the dialogue. Do not let the HCP steer the conversation away from the topic at hand. If they attempt to evade a question, gently steer them back to the topic without aggression. Remember, the court is likely to view your demeanor as well as your words.

When they attempt to manipulate or charm the court, counteract this by bringing the focus back to the facts of the case. Keep your questions direct and grounded in evidence, and always bring any deviations back to the point of law or fact you are addressing.

Controlling the courtroom dynamics is crucial when cross-examining an HCP, particularly because individuals with high-conflict or narcissistic traits may attempt to dominate the proceedings or evade direct questions. An effective tool in maintaining courtroom control is the timely use of objections, specifically objecting with "non-responsive" when the witness avoids answering the question posed. This legal tactic helps keep the testimony relevant and focused, preventing the HCP from derailing the proceedings with tangential or evasive responses.

Using "Objection, Non-Responsive" Effectively

When an HCP witness begins to stray from answering the question directly, or starts to introduce unrelated information to manipulate the narrative, a well-placed "objection, non-responsive" serves several purposes:

1. It signals to the judge that the witness is not providing the information requested. This draws the court's attention to the fact that the witness is avoiding a direct answer, which can affect the witness's credibility.

2. It interrupts the flow of the HCP's testimony. HCPs often use courtroom testimony as a stage for self-aggrandizement or manipulation. Interrupting this with an objection forces them to refocus on the specific question at hand, disrupting their strategy of evasion or narrative control.

3. It reinforces the authority of the questioner. Consistently objecting to non-responsive answers underscores your role in directing the examination and asserts control over how information is presented in court. It sends a clear message that attempts to divert the conversation will not be tolerated.

Strategic Application

To apply this objection effectively, be vigilant and listen carefully. You must be fully attentive to every part of the witness's answer to quickly identify when they deviate from a direct response.

Act quickly but calmly. Timing is crucial. Object immediately after a non-responsive portion of the testimony to prevent the witness from building momentum with irrelevant information.

Follow up with a precise reiteration of your original question. After the objection is sustained, rephrase or repeat your original question to guide the witness back to the topic you need them to address. This not only keeps your line of questioning clear but also limits the witness's ability to stray from the subject.

Example in Practice

If you ask, "What time did you arrive at the event?" and the witness begins discussing the importance of the event rather than stating a time, you would immediately say, "Objection, non-responsive." Upon the judge acknowledging the objection, you would then repeat, "Please state the specific time you arrived at the event."

By employing "objection, non-responsive" effectively, you can help maintain a disciplined and focused examination, preventing the HCP from using evasive tactics and ensuring that the testimony remains pertinent to the case at hand. This strategy not only aids in revealing the truth but also underscores your competence and control in handling the complexities of legal dynamics.

The Art of Using Leading Questions with an HCP on the Witness Stand

When cross-examining an HCP witness in court, one of the most effective techniques at your disposal is the use of leading questions. Leading questions are phrased in such a way that they suggest the desired answer or contain the information the examiner is looking to have confirmed. This method is particularly useful with narcissistic individuals, who may be prone to manipulation or evading direct answers.

Purpose and Power of Leading Questions

Leading questions serve several strategic purposes in the courtroom. Firstly, they can help control the narrative flow and keep the testimony focused and efficient, preventing the HCP from diverting the topic or embellishing the truth. Secondly, they allow the attorney to steer the witness towards specific details, making it harder for them to avoid accountability or construct a false narrative.

Leading questions also expedite the process of extracting relevant information by bypassing unnecessary narrative and focusing directly on specific points that need confirmation or clarification. This is particularly useful in revealing inconsistencies in the witness's story or in pinning down details that the witness might otherwise overlook or avoid. By constraining the witness's answers to a specific framework, these questions can expose contradictions and undermine attempts at deception, enhancing the clarity and effectiveness of the cross-examination process.

Best Practices for Crafting Effective Leading Questions

To craft effective leading questions for an HCP witness:

1. **Be precise:** Ensure that each question is narrowly focused and directs the witness to a specific point. This limits their ability to provide broad, generalized answers that dodge the question. For example, instead of asking, "What did you do that day?", you might ask, "You were at the office until 5 PM on that day, correct?"

   In another example, instead of asking a vague question like "How do you handle responsibilities?" which allows for a broad and subjective answer, a precise question would be, "Did you attend the scheduled meeting on July 7th at 10 AM?" This type of question demands a specific and easily verifiable response. It limits the witness's ability to stray into irrelevant details or create a narrative that serves their agenda.

   Being precise in crafting leading questions for an HCP witness is crucial for effective cross-examination. Precision in questioning not only focuses the testimony but also minimizes the witness's ability to provide evasive or overly broad answers that can obfuscate the truth. Precise questions are directly linked to specific facts, requiring the witness to address those facts without the opportunity for diversion or generalization.

   By carefully phrasing questions to elicit exact information, you effectively close off avenues for an HCP witness to manipulate the dialogue, ensuring that their responses remain relevant and factually grounded. This precision is vital in establishing a clear and factual record in the courtroom, directly impacting the credibility of the testimony and the overall outcome of the case.

2. **Incorporate known facts:** Embed undeniable facts into your questions to box in the witness. This approach leaves little room for deviation without contradicting established evidence. For instance, "Isn't it true that you sent an email stating you would not attend the meeting?" Or, instead of broadly querying, "What did you communicate to the team?" you could ask, "On March 15th, you emailed the team to postpone the project deadline, didn't you?"

   This approach not only reinforces the factual basis of your questioning but also traps the witness into acknowledging these facts. It significantly reduces the scope for manipulation, as the witness must align their responses with the concrete evidence already accepted by the court, thus maintaining the integrity and focus of the testimony.

   Incorporating known facts into your leading questions is a powerful technique for anchoring the cross-examination in undeniable reality, which is particularly effective against HCP witnesses prone to distorting the truth. By weaving incontrovertible details directly into your questions, you constrain the witness's ability to deviate from established truths.

3. **Anticipate their narrative:** Utilize your understanding of the HCP's common tactics and narrative strategies to foresee how they may attempt to manipulate their responses during questioning. This foresight empowers you to craft questions that directly counteract their typical approaches, effectively limiting their ability to evade the truth.

For example, HCP witnesses often employ deflection by focusing on peripheral issues rather than addressing the core question. To counter this, you might anticipate their tendency to speak broadly and ask, "You reviewed my credit report on December 1st, correct?" This directs them to a specific event, preventing them from wandering off-topic.

Another common tactic is to present themselves as well-meaning but ultimately misguided. To address this, frame your questions in a way that highlights their responsibility: "You chose not to disclose the potential impact of the business credit card on my personal credit, isn't that true?" This confronts them with their own decisions and diminishes their ability to shift blame.

Additionally, HCP witnesses may attempt to downplay their errors or miscommunications. By asking questions like, "You sent an email on December 5th stating that my credit score would not be affected, correct?" you bring their own words into the spotlight, making it difficult for them to minimize their prior assurances.

By anticipating these narrative strategies, you can effectively structure your questions to maintain focus on the specific facts and hold the witness accountable for their statements. This approach enhances the clarity of the testimony, ensuring that the dialogue remains centered on the critical issues at hand.

4. **Limit answer choices:** Phrase your questions in a way that requires a simple "yes" or "no" or another very specific answer. This technique minimizes the opportunities for the witness to stray into tangential or misleading territory.

Limiting answer choices in your questions is a strategic move that curtails a witness's ability to steer the conversation away from uncomfortable truths, particularly effective when dealing with manipulative or evasive individuals like narcissists. By designing questions that require a simple "yes" or "no," or a specific, predefined option, you can significantly reduce the scope for ambiguity and prevent the witness from expanding into a broader narrative that may not be relevant or truthful.

For example, rather than asking an open-ended question such as "Can you describe what happened?", you might ask, "Did you call Mr. Smith on the night of the incident? Yes or No?" This method forces the witness to commit to a concise answer, providing less room to manipulate facts or dodge the question. Such precision in questioning is vital for maintaining the focus of the testimony on the actual evidence and for effectively managing the testimony of a narcissistic witness who may seek to obfuscate or mislead through more elaborate responses.

Using Leading Questions to Impeach Credibility

Leading questions are also invaluable for impeaching the credibility of a high-conflict or narcissistic witness. By carefully constructing questions based on discrepancies in their previous statements or evidence, you can highlight inconsistencies and deceit.

For example: "You previously stated under oath that you were unaware of the financial issues, yet this document shows you were emailed about them over a month ago. How do you reconcile these two conflicting statements?"

Likewise, if a witness previously stated in a deposition that they were out of town during a critical event but later posts on social media suggest otherwise, a leading question like, "You stated under oath you were out of town on June 5th, yet your Facebook post shows you at a local restaurant that evening; how do you explain this discrepancy?" can be very effective.

Such questions not only force the witness to confront their prior statements but also put them in a position where any attempt to reconcile their conflicting accounts can further erode their trustworthiness. This method effectively utilizes the inherent power of leading questions to corner the witness into admitting falsehoods or demonstrating unreliability, thereby undermining their overall credibility in the eyes of the court.

Effectively using leading questions requires a blend of sharp legal acumen, psychological insight, and strategic phrasing. When dealing with an HCP witness, these questions become tools to subtly but firmly control the testimony, guiding it towards the truth despite the witness's inclinations towards self-serving distortion. By mastering this technique, you can significantly enhance your ability to expose falsehoods and assert the truth in high-stakes legal environments.

Conclusion: Cross-Examining a Witness with Confidence

Cross-examining an HCP requires a blend of psychological insight, legal acumen, and strategic questioning. By carefully structuring your approach, maintaining a repository of evidence, and methodically challenging their statements, you can effectively dismantle their testimony and expose the flaws in their narrative. This not only serves to impeach their credibility but also enhances the integrity of the legal process, ensuring that justice is served based on truth and facts.

Key Takeaways:

- **Thorough Preparation:** Review all evidence, communications, and past behaviors related to the narcissist. Understanding their patterns and statements helps anticipate their responses and strategize questions effectively.

- **Create a Detailed Timeline:** Organize events and gather relevant communications to use as evidence. This helps in presenting a coherent narrative and challenging inconsistencies in their testimony.

- **Consult Experts:** Work with psychologists or experts on narcissism to understand their behavior and psychological tendencies. This insight assists in crafting questions that expose manipulative tactics.

- **Structured Questioning:** Begin with broad, open-ended questions to establish a baseline, then use funneling techniques to narrow down to specific details, making it harder for the narcissist to manipulate their answers.

- **Catch Lies with Evidence:** Compare their statements to documented evidence immediately. Present conflicting evidence directly and ask for clarification to highlight discrepancies and catch them in lies.

- **Impeach Credibility:** Highlight prior inconsistent statements and question their motives. Use psychological evaluations or observations to expose manipulative tendencies and bias.

- **Control Courtroom Dynamics:** Maintain authority by keeping the focus on relevant facts. Use objections, like "non-responsive," to manage evasive or manipulative responses and maintain control of the examination.

- **Effective Use of Objections:** Object to non-responsive answers to disrupt the narcissist's attempts to divert or manipulate. This reinforces your control over the questioning and helps keep the testimony relevant.

- **Leading Questions:** Use leading questions to guide the witness's responses, control the narrative, and expose contradictions. This method helps in obtaining clear, focused answers and revealing inconsistencies.

- **Address Evasion Tactics:** If the narcissist tries to evade questions, gently steer them back to the topic. Remain calm and assertive to prevent them from manipulating the court's perception.

- **Maintain Professionalism:** Stay composed and professional throughout the cross-examination. Emotional reactions can be used against you, so focus on systematically addressing inconsistencies and falsehoods.

- **Prepare for Psychological Manipulation:** Understand that narcissists may use charm or manipulation in court. Counteract this by sticking to facts and evidence, and keep the proceedings focused on the case at hand.

5

PRESENTING YOUR CASE IN FAMILY COURT

In the courtroom, the power of a well-constructed, evidence-based narrative cannot be underestimated. A coherent narrative in legal arguments does more than convey the facts; it weaves those facts into a compelling story that resonates with the judge and jury, making it easier for them to understand the issues at hand and the justice being sought.

Here we will delve into the art and science of building an effective narrative for legal arguments, exploring how to structure your case as a coherent story, one that not only adheres to the legal framework but also captures the emotional and ethical dimensions of the dispute. By linking credible and compelling evidence seamlessly into this narrative, you can illuminate the facts in a way that is both persuasive and memorable. A strong narrative enhances the clarity of your argument, reinforces the credibility of your case, and significantly boosts your chances of a favorable outcome.

This chapter will provide you with the tools and insights necessary to master this crucial aspect of legal strategy.

Build a Storyline

Building an effective storyline for a legal narrative involves crafting a sequence that is logical, compelling, and easy for the court to follow. This sequence serves as the backbone of your narrative, providing a structure that helps the judge and jury understand the progression of events and their relevance to the legal issues at hand.

Start by establishing a clear, chronological framework that includes relevant dates, actions taken, and decisions made. For instance, in a custody case, significant events may include the child's birth, changes in living arrangements, any incidents of parental conflict, and school or medical milestones.

Next, identify the central theme of your case. This theme should resonate with the core legal and moral questions at stake and will guide the presentation of your evidence and arguments.

In a divorce settlement, the theme might be "fairness and equity," highlighting contributions of both parties and the importance of a balanced division of assets. Alternatively, you may wish to focus on "financial responsibility," using income, expenses, and the child's needs to argue for an appropriate support amount.

In a custody dispute, the theme might revolve around the best interests of the child, with each piece of evidence and testimony strategically chosen to reinforce this point, demonstrating stability, a nurturing environment, and the child's needs. An alternative theme might center on "maintaining parent-child relationships," focusing on the importance of the child's emotional connections with both parents and how visitation supports that.

Conclude your narrative by summarizing the key points and reiterating your central theme. Clearly state what you are asking the court to decide, linking it back to your storyline. Example: "Given the evidence presented and the overarching theme of the child's best interests, we respectfully request the court to grant primary custody to the petitioner, ensuring a stable and nurturing environment for the child's development."

By thoughtfully constructing your narrative around a clear timeline and a resonant theme, you can create a compelling legal story that effectively communicates your case's merits to the court.

Linking Evidence to Narrative

Linking evidence to your narrative effectively is crucial in reinforcing your legal arguments and ensuring that each piece of information presented resonates with the storyline you are building. To accomplish this, each item of evidence should not merely be presented in isolation but should be clearly connected to specific aspects of your narrative. Select evidence that not only supports your claims but also aligns with the emotional undertones of your narrative.

Start by mapping out your main narrative points, then strategically align evidence that supports these points. For example, if your narrative is about demonstrating a breach of contract, align emails, contract drafts, and witness testimonies directly with the timeline and actions that led to the breach. This approach transforms abstract legal concepts into a tangible storyline that the judge and jury can easily understand and remember. Alternatively, if your theme is focused on the best interests of the child, present testimonies from teachers or childcare providers who can speak to the child's well-being in your care, contrasted with evidence of instability in the other parent's environment.

Furthermore, when presenting each piece of evidence, explicitly state how it connects to your narrative. For instance, when introducing a financial statement, you might say, "This document shows the transaction that took place on X date, which is crucial because it directly contradicts the defendant's claim of ignorance about the account's existence." Such statements make it clear why each piece of evidence is relevant and how it supports the broader story, enhancing the persuasiveness of your case.

By meticulously linking evidence to your narrative, you reinforce the coherence and credibility of your legal arguments, making a stronger case for your position.

Emotional Resonance

Emotional resonance is a powerful component of persuasive storytelling in the courtroom, particularly when balanced with factual integrity. The key to harnessing this emotional power is not to manipulate feelings but to let the most emotionally charged facts speak for themselves, thus naturally eliciting a genuine emotional response from the judge or mediator.

When crafting your narrative, identify the facts that inherently carry emotional weight. Just as a personal injury case may be focused on the details of the physical pain and emotional distress experienced by the plaintiff, a family law case will typically highlight the impact of the dispute on the children. These facts should be presented clearly and vividly, allowing the reality of the situation to make a deep impact.

While maintaining a logical framework, don't hesitate to weave in emotional elements. Family court often involves deeply personal issues, and resonating with the court's emotional sensibilities can enhance your narrative. In a divorce case, share personal stories that illustrate the impact of the relationship dynamics on the children's well-being, helping the judge understand the human element behind the facts.

However, it's crucial to maintain a balance. The narrative should not stray into overt emotional manipulation. Instead, it should remain grounded in the truth, with the emotional aspects naturally emerging from the factual content, and maintain a positive tone. For example, if the issue at hand is harassment by an HCP, the theme should emphasize "safety and peace of mind," showing how the behavior of the other party creates a hostile environment that necessitates legal intervention.

By carefully selecting and showcasing the facts that match the tone of your theme, you enhance the emotional appeal of your narrative without compromising its factual integrity. This approach not only engages the court emotionally but also reinforces the credibility of your case, making it both compelling and believable.

Addressing Counter-Narratives

Addressing and countering the opposing narrative in a legal dispute, especially when dealing with a narcissistic opponent, requires keen observation and strategic preparation. Narcissists often reveal their counter-narratives long before they are articulated in court. They tend to be repetitive, relying on a limited set of themes or excuses that they believe are effective. This predictability is both a challenge and an opportunity.

Firstly, it's crucial to thoroughly document all instances where the opposing party has previously articulated their narrative, whether in written communications, during depositions, or in earlier court appearances. This record will show the recurring themes and arguments they depend on, which often include playing the victim, shifting blame, or other manipulative tactics to deflect responsibility.

Once these patterns are identified, you can prepare specific strategies to dismantle their narrative effectively. This involves gathering concrete evidence and witness testimonies that directly contradict their repeated claims. It's also beneficial to prepare questions that anticipate their typical responses, designed to expose inconsistencies and reduce their narrative's credibility.

Additionally, during your presentation, proactively address these expected counter-narratives by showing how they are based on distortions or selective recollections of facts. Use clear, objective evidence to undermine their claims and strengthen your narrative.

It's also critical that you anticipate the opposing side's narrative and counter arguments, particularly if an ex is emotionally manipulative. A strong storyline acknowledges potential weaknesses in your case and addresses them proactively.

For instance, if you expect the opposing party to falsely claim that you're an unfit parent due to a past mistake, frame that event within the context of personal growth and change, emphasizing how it has informed your current parenting. If your HCP ex has a tendency to use parental alienation as a tactic in family court, focus your narrative on "the importance of both parents in a child's life," emphasizing how one parent's actions may harm the child's relationship with the other.

By preparing to turn their predictable strategies against them, you can maintain control of the narrative flow and keep the focus on the factual truth, significantly diminishing the impact of their manipulative tactics in the eyes of the court.

Using Evidence to Demonstrate the HCP's Negative Impact on Children

In family court disputes, particularly those involving custody and parenting issues, the primary concern of the court is the well-being and best interests of the children involved. While it may be useful to illustrate how a narcissistic ex-partner's behavior affects you, it is far more critical and compelling to effectively demonstrate how these behaviors adversely affect the children. The following strategies for gathering and presenting evidence will help you highlight the negative impact of an HCP's behavior on children, which can be pivotal in influencing court decisions.

1. **Documenting Behavioral Patterns:**

    Start by maintaining a detailed record of incidents that showcase the narcissist's harmful behaviors. This includes keeping a diary or log of dates, times, descriptions of incidents, and their immediate effects on the children. For instance, if the narcissist frequently cancels visitations at the last minute, record each occurrence and note any emotional responses from the children, such as disappointment, confusion, or distress.

    To effectively demonstrate the narcissist's negative impact on the children, it is essential to meticulously document all instances of behavior that could affect them. This documentation should be detailed and organized chronologically, capturing both the behavior and its immediate effects on the children. Include specific dates, times, and a thorough description of each incident.

For instance, if the narcissist exhibits verbal outbursts during custody exchanges, note each occurrence, the specifics of what was said, and how the children reacted – whether they became visibly upset, cried, or expressed confusion or fear. Similarly, if the narcissist fails to adhere to agreed-upon schedules, document each instance, including any explanations given and the children's reactions to these disruptions.

Additionally, maintain records of any indirect behaviors such as derogatory remarks made about you in front of the children, or inappropriate discussions about court matters, noting how each event impacts the children emotionally and behaviorally. This comprehensive log will serve as a critical piece of evidence, demonstrating patterns that highlight the ongoing emotional toll on the children due to the narcissist's actions.

2. Educational and Health Records:

Gather evidence from the children's educational and health records that may indicate a decline in their well-being correlated with the narcissist's behavior. This could include school reports showing a drop in academic performance, increased absences, or notes from teachers about changes in the child's behavior or mood. Medical records that show increased visits to healthcare providers for stress-related issues, anxiety, or depression can also be compelling.

Educational and health records serve as crucial evidence in illustrating the impact of a narcissist's behavior on children involved in family court disputes. Begin by securing copies of the children's school reports, which might reveal a decline in academic performance, increased absences, or notes from teachers about changes in behavior such as withdrawal, aggression, or anxiety. These records often provide objective data that correlate school-related stress with custody issues or parental conflicts.

Similarly, obtain health records that detail any visits to healthcare providers that may be linked to stress, such as appointments for anxiety, depression, or somatic complaints like headaches and stomachaches. These documents can demonstrate a direct connection between the narcissist's behavior and the children's physical and mental health issues.

Presenting these records in court can powerfully substantiate claims about the detrimental effects of narcissistic behavior, providing concrete examples of how disruptions and stress manifest in significant areas of the children's lives.

3. Expert Testimonies:

Expert testimonies from psychologists, child therapists, or counselors who have interacted with the children are invaluable in family court cases. These professionals can provide authoritative insights into the psychological impact of a narcissist's behavior on children. By presenting detailed assessments and evaluations, experts can discuss the specific effects of stress, anxiety, or emotional trauma observed in the children, linking these directly to behaviors exhibited by the narcissistic parent.

For instance, a child psychologist might testify about signs of regression, anxiety, or behavioral disorders in the children, and offer a professional opinion that these issues are exacerbated by the unstable or harmful environment created by the narcissist. Experts can also speak to the resilience strategies that could be beneficial for the children, which further underscores the need for a stable and supportive home environment.

Such testimonies are critical as they provide the court with a scientifically backed perspective on the children's well-being, helping judges make informed decisions based on the best interests of the children.

4. Witness Statements:

Statements from people who have observed the children's behavior can be valuable. This might include relatives, school staff, neighbors, or family friends who can testify about what they have observed firsthand regarding the children's reactions to certain behaviors exhibited by the narcissist. For example, a grandparent might provide a statement about how the children express fear or anxiety about visitations.

Witness statements in family court should focus on firsthand observations of the children's behaviors and emotional states, rather than hearsay or second-hand information. These statements can be provided by individuals who have direct, regular interactions with the children, such as family members, teachers, coaches, or neighbors. These observers can testify to specific incidents where they have seen the children's reactions to certain behaviors exhibited by the narcissistic parent, or changes in the children's demeanor and behavior over time.

For example, a teacher might provide a statement describing how a child becomes withdrawn or agitated on days following visits with the narcissistic parent, or how their academic performance declines in correlation with ongoing parental conflicts. Similarly, a family friend might recount specific instances where they observed the children displaying signs of stress or recounting troubling interactions.

These firsthand accounts are powerful as they provide tangible, observed evidence of the impact of the narcissist's behavior on the children, avoiding the pitfalls of hearsay by sticking strictly to witnessed facts and personal observations, which hold more credibility in court.

5. **Direct Observations from Children:**

If appropriate and conducted under professional supervision, obtaining insights directly from the children can be powerful. This must be handled delicately and ethically to avoid further trauma. Courts sometimes appoint special advocates or psychologists to interview children and provide reports to the court, ensuring that the children's voices are heard without exposing them to direct court proceedings.

Gathering insights directly from children, when appropriate and done under professional supervision, can provide compelling evidence in family court cases. This method should be approached with caution to ensure it does not cause additional stress or trauma to the children. Professionals such as child psychologists or appointed special advocates can conduct interviews in a safe, supportive environment, allowing children to express their feelings and experiences related to their interactions with the narcissistic parent.

These professionals can then relay the children's statements to the court, providing a child-centered perspective that directly reflects their emotional and psychological state. This testimony is highly valuable because it offers the court a direct window into the personal impact of parental behavior from the children's own viewpoint, which is critical in assessing their best interests.

6. Correlation of Narcissist's Behavior with Children's Stress Events:

Establish clear connections between the narcissist's specific actions and stressful events in the children's lives. For instance, you might correlate a significant behavioral outburst from the narcissist with a child's subsequent school suspension or a visit to a healthcare provider for stress-related symptoms. This timeline can help illustrate cause and effect more clearly for the court.

Demonstrating a direct correlation between the narcissistic parent's behavior and specific stressful events in the children's lives is a critical aspect of presenting a compelling case in family court. This approach involves meticulously linking specific actions or patterns of behavior exhibited by the narcissist with concrete incidents of stress, anxiety, or behavioral changes observed in the children.

For example, documenting instances where the narcissist's aggressive or dismissive behavior coincides with significant events such as the child's birthdays, school performances, or other important milestones can be telling. Noting how these behaviors impact the child – perhaps leading to emotional withdrawal, academic issues, or health concerns like anxiety attacks – provides clear evidence of the negative influence.

It's beneficial to maintain a detailed timeline that aligns the narcissist's specific actions with subsequent reactions or conditions in the children. For instance, if a child exhibits signs of distress or behavioral regression following a particularly volatile altercation witnessed during custody exchanges, this should be clearly documented and presented. This evidence not only supports claims about the harmful impact of the narcissist's behavior but also helps the court understand the urgency and necessity of protective measures for the children's well-being.

7. **Focusing on Patterns Rather Than Isolated Incidents:**

While individual incidents can be telling, patterns of behavior have a much stronger impact in court. Demonstrating that the narcissist's harmful behaviors are consistent and ongoing offers stronger evidence of potential future risks to the children.

Demonstrating a consistent pattern of behavior by a narcissistic parent can be more influential than isolated incidents, no matter how severe. Patterns provide clear evidence of ongoing behavior that can predict future actions and their impacts on the children involved. This approach involves compiling multiple instances of behavior that collectively indicate a trend or habitual actions by the narcissist, thus offering a broader context of their impact on the children's welfare.

For example, instead of focusing solely on a single outburst or negative interaction, compile evidence showing how repeated emotional outbursts, neglect, or manipulation occur and the corresponding adverse effects on the children over time. This might include recurring disruptions in the children's routines, consistent signs of stress around custody exchanges, or a pattern of derogatory remarks made in the children's presence.

Presenting this information in a systematic, chronological format helps the court see not just snapshots but a continuous storyline that more accurately reflects the living conditions and emotional climate the children endure. This method strengthens the case by showing that these are not one-off events but rather part of a detrimental environment created by the narcissistic parent, emphasizing the need for court intervention to protect the children's long-term emotional and psychological health.

When presenting your case in court, your objective is to paint a clear and truthful picture of how the narcissist's behavior negatively impacts the children's emotional and physical well-being. By methodically collecting and organizing pertinent evidence, and presenting it effectively, you help the court see the real and detrimental effects of the narcissist's actions on the children. This approach not only supports your case but crucially centers it around what is most important – the health and happiness of the children.

Tips for Testifying: Demeanor, Clarity, and Honesty

Testifying in court can be a daunting experience, especially in high-stakes family law disputes where personal emotions and outcomes are deeply intertwined. The effectiveness of your testimony can significantly influence the judge's and jury's perception and ultimately, the case's outcome. Therefore, mastering the art of testifying is crucial. This section focuses on three fundamental aspects of effective testimony: demeanor, clarity, and honesty.

Maintaining a composed and respectful demeanor, ensuring your statements are clear and straightforward, and upholding honesty at all times are essential strategies. These elements not only convey credibility but also foster trust, making your testimony more persuasive. The following tips and guidelines will help you present yourself effectively, ensuring that your voice is heard accurately and respectfully in court.

Maintaining a Composed and Respectful Demeanor

Maintaining a calm demeanor in court is a crucial process that requires both mental and factual readiness. Understanding what to expect and how to prepare can significantly affect the effectiveness of your testimony and your comfort level during the proceedings.

Mental Preparation

Mentally preparing to testify involves familiarizing yourself with the courtroom environment and the nature of questioning you might face. If possible, attend a court session beforehand to observe how testimonies are given and how interactions between attorneys and witnesses unfold. This observation can demystify the process and reduce anxiety.

Practicing your testimony is also vital. Work with your attorney to conduct mock trials where you can rehearse your answers to potential questions, including challenging ones that may come from the opposing counsel. These practice sessions should also help you learn to manage your stress and maintain composure under pressure. Techniques like deep breathing, pausing before answering, and maintaining eye contact can be practiced during these sessions.

Factual Preparation

Factual preparation involves thoroughly understanding the facts of the case as they pertain to your testimony. Review all relevant documents, dates, and correspondences. Know the timeline of events like the back of your hand, and ensure that your recollection of facts is accurate and can be substantiated with evidence if challenged.

Your attorney (if you have one) should guide you through the discovery materials and help you align your testimony with the overall case strategy. It's important to stick to the truth and avoid exaggerations – precision in your statements will enhance your credibility and help prevent any potential pitfalls during cross-examination.

By combining mental readiness with a robust factual grounding, you ensure that your testimony is not only persuasive but also delivered with confidence, enhancing its impact on your case's outcome.

Best Practices for Maintaining a Calm Demeanor in Family Court

Maintaining composure while testifying in court, especially under the stress of cross-examination, is essential for ensuring that your testimony is clear, credible, and effectively communicated. Here are some strategic tips for staying calm and composed under pressure:

1. **Preparation is fundamental:** Being well-prepared is the most effective way to reduce anxiety. Familiarize yourself thoroughly with the details of your case, anticipate challenging questions, and rehearse your responses. Preparation also involves understanding the legal framework and potential strategies of the opposing counsel. When you know what to expect and have prepared your responses, you are less likely to be thrown off by tough questioning.

2. **Practice mindfulness techniques:** Techniques such as deep breathing, meditation, or even simple grounding exercises can help manage stress levels before and during your testimony. Practicing these techniques

regularly before the trial can make them more effective when you need them most.

3. **Maintain physical composure:** Your body language speaks volumes. Practice maintaining a calm demeanor by sitting up straight, keeping your hands still, and maintaining eye contact with the questioner. Avoid fidgeting, which can be interpreted as nervousness or dishonesty.

4. **Pause before responding:** Always take a moment to breathe and think before answering each question. This pause allows you to collect your thoughts, consider your response, and ensures that you do not react emotionally or hastily. It also gives you a moment to calm any immediate emotional reactions to provocative questions.

5. **Stay hydrated and rested:** Ensure you are well-rested and hydrated on the day you are to testify. Fatigue and dehydration can impair your ability to think clearly and maintain emotional control.

6. **Use 'grounding' techniques:** If you feel overwhelmed, focus on a physical sensation, such as your feet on the floor or the feeling of the chair against your back. These sensations can help anchor you in the present moment and push aside overwhelming emotions.

7. **Listen carefully:** Focus intently on the questions being asked. This concentration can help keep your mind from wandering to anxiety-producing thoughts and

ensures that your answers are directly relevant to the questions asked.

8. **Speak slowly and clearly:** Speaking at a controlled pace helps maintain a sense of calm and gives you more time to think as you speak. It also makes your testimony easier to understand and more authoritative.

By integrating these techniques into your preparation and testimony, you can significantly enhance your ability to remain composed under pressure, making your overall presentation in court more effective and persuasive.

Ensure Your Communications are Clear and Straightforward

Clear communication is crucial when testifying in court, as it ensures your points are understood and supports your case effectively. Achieving clarity requires both mental readiness and a strong grasp of the facts. By preparing in these areas, you can enhance your ability to communicate clearly and persuasively during your testimony.

Mental Preparation

Mentally preparing for your testimony involves equipping yourself with the skills to communicate clearly and effectively. Begin by familiarizing yourself with the courtroom setting and the nature of questioning you may encounter. Consider attending a court session to observe how testimonies are delivered and how questions are asked. This familiarity can alleviate anxiety and help you understand the communication dynamics at play.

Practicing your responses is vital for clarity. Work with your attorney to simulate questioning scenarios where you can rehearse answering questions directly and succinctly. During these mock sessions, focus on active listening to ensure you fully understand each question before responding. Techniques such as deep breathing can help calm nerves and keep your mind clear, allowing for more thoughtful responses.

Factual Preparation

Factual preparation is essential for ensuring that your responses are accurate and straightforward. Review all relevant documents, correspondence, and timelines related to your case. Having a solid grasp of the facts will enable you to articulate your points confidently and concisely.

Align your understanding of the facts with your attorney's guidance to ensure your testimony supports the overall case strategy. Being precise and truthful in your statements not only bolsters your credibility but also helps you avoid potential pitfalls during questioning. When you know the facts well, you can communicate them clearly, making your testimony more impactful.

By focusing on both mental and factual preparation, you will enhance your ability to communicate effectively during your testimony, ensuring your points are understood and your case is supported convincingly.

Best Practices for Communicating Clearly and Directly in Family Court

Clarity in communication is essential when testifying in court, as it ensures that your points are precisely understood and that your testimony supports your case effectively. To achieve clarity and make a compelling impact, here are some specific strategies:

1. **Listen carefully:** One of the most important aspects of clear communication is listening intently to the questions asked. This focus allows you to fully understand the query before you begin to answer, reducing the risk of giving irrelevant or off-topic responses. Listening closely also helps you pick up on the nuances of the question, which may influence how you should frame your answer.

2. **Answer directly:** Once you've understood the question, aim to answer it directly and concisely. Avoid the temptation to provide additional information that was not asked for, as this can lead to confusion and dilute the impact of your testimony. Direct answers help maintain the focus and flow of the examination.

3. **Use simple language:** Avoid jargon, technical terms, or overly complex language, unless it is relevant and you can explain it clearly. Using straightforward language makes your testimony more accessible and easier to follow for the judge, jury, and opposing counsel.

4. **Pause and think:** Before answering, take a brief pause to collect your thoughts. This not only helps you to formulate a clearer response but also signals to the court that you are considering the question seriously.

5. **Maintain eye contact:** While speaking, maintain eye contact with the questioner or the judge. This not only enhances the clarity of your communication by reinforcing your engagement but also builds credibility and trust.

By implementing these strategies, you ensure that your communication during testimony is clear, effective, and precisely targeted to the questions asked, greatly enhancing the effectiveness of your presentation in court.

Uphold Honesty at All Times

Honesty is not just a tactical choice in family court; it's a foundational principle that can shape the trajectory of your case and your long-term credibility. Upholding honesty establishes your reliability as a witness, which is vital in the eyes of judges and juries who are trained to detect inconsistencies and evasiveness. A commitment to truthfulness helps build trust, allowing your testimony to resonate more effectively with the court.

Moreover, being forthright about less favorable facts can enhance your standing. Admitting to difficult aspects of your case demonstrates maturity and integrity, qualities that judges often respect and reward. This transparency can lead to a more sympathetic response, especially in family law matters where the emotional stakes are high.

Lastly, honesty streamlines your legal strategy. When you focus on telling the truth, you eliminate the complexities that come with fabrication or manipulation. This straightforward approach minimizes the risk of contradictions during cross-examination, allowing you to maintain a strong, consistent narrative throughout the proceedings. By prioritizing honesty, you not only strengthen your case but also lay the groundwork for a more positive relationship with the court in the future.

Mental Preparation

Mentally preparing to testify with honesty involves fostering a strong ethical mindset. Begin by reflecting on the impact of your truthfulness on the case and everyone involved, especially children. Remind yourself that your integrity is crucial for building trust with the court.

Engage in self-reflection by journaling your thoughts and feelings about the case. This exercise can clarify your perspective and reinforce your commitment to honesty. Additionally, visualize yourself in the courtroom, confidently sharing your truthful account. This mental rehearsal can help reduce anxiety and affirm your dedication to being straightforward.

Consider discussing your values around honesty with a trusted friend or mentor. This conversation can strengthen your resolve and provide additional perspectives on the importance of truthfulness in your testimony.

Factual Preparation

Factual preparation requires a meticulous review of all relevant documents, timelines, and communications that pertain to your case. Create a detailed summary of key facts, emphasizing the elements you are confident about. This will help you articulate your truthful account without hesitation.

Instead of merely reviewing documents, engage in a fact-checking exercise with someone who understands your case. Discussing each point with a supportive person can ensure your recollections are accurate and complete, reinforcing your commitment to honesty.

Incorporate a strategy for addressing challenging questions that may test your honesty. Prepare to acknowledge any uncertainties openly. For instance, if you can't remember a specific detail, practice how to express that honestly, rather than attempting to fill the gaps with conjecture.

By embracing diverse strategies for mental and factual preparation focused on honesty, you enhance your ability to present credible and impactful testimony, contributing positively to the family court process.

Best Practices for Upholding Honesty in Family Court

Upholding honesty in family court is vital not only for the integrity of your case but also for the dignity of the judicial process itself. A commitment to truthfulness fosters fair outcomes and ensures that decisions are based on accurate, complete information. This benefits all parties involved and reinforces the integrity of the legal system.

1. **Focus on behaviors, not diagnoses:** In family court, the language you use carries significant weight. Avoid labeling the other parent with terms like "narcissist." Such accusations imply a formal psychological diagnosis, which most laypeople are not qualified to make. This approach can backfire, adversely affecting how the judge perceives you rather than the other party. Instead, concentrate on specific behaviors and facts that illustrate your concerns.

2. **Maintain professionalism and objectivity:** Judges expect a high level of professionalism and objectivity in the courtroom. Using charged terms like "narcissist" may be viewed as an attempt to pathologize the other parent, reflecting poorly on your credibility. This behavior can suggest emotional bias, making you appear vindictive rather than genuinely concerned for your children's well-being.

3. **Let the facts speak for themselves:** In family law, factual evidence should take precedence over labels. Present documented communications, third-party observations, and specific incidents that illustrate problematic behavior. This factual and direct approach allows the judge to recognize patterns without resorting to personal attacks, increasing the likelihood that the evidence will be taken seriously.

4. **Rely on expert testimony when necessary:** If mental health issues are genuinely relevant to the case, these should be addressed by qualified professionals. Licensed psychologists can conduct formal evaluations that hold weight in court. Such assessments are appropriate within the legal framework, unlike personal accusations made during testimony, which can undermine your case.

5. **Build a constructive case focused on the children's best interests:** Ultimately, the aim in any custody dispute should be to create the best possible environment for the children involved. Engaging in name-calling or making unsubstantiated diagnoses can distract from the critical issues at hand and hinder resolution. By focusing on behavior-based observations supported by evidence, you present yourself as reasonable and committed to your children's well-being, avoiding the pitfalls of personal conflicts or character attacks.

By following these best practices, you not only enhance your credibility but also contribute to a fair and just legal process, paving the way for decisions that truly reflect the best interests of your children.

Conclusion: Presenting Your Case

Presenting your case in family court can be a daunting experience, but maintaining a composed and respectful demeanor, ensuring your communications are clear and straightforward, and upholding honesty at all times can significantly impact the outcome of your case.

As you prepare to present your narrative, remember that building a compelling storyline is essential. A well-structured timeline of events, linked to concrete evidence, creates a logical framework that allows the judge and jury to grasp the progression of your case.

Emotional resonance also plays a vital role. By sharing your experiences and concerns in a relatable manner, you can engage the court's empathy while ensuring your narrative remains rooted in fact and focused on the best interests of your children. Addressing counter-narratives thoughtfully – anticipating opposing viewpoints and responding with factual evidence – can further strengthen your position and demonstrate your commitment to transparency and integrity.

As you move forward, keep these best practices in mind. They serve not only as a foundation for a successful court experience but also for fostering a healthier co-parenting relationship in the future. By prioritizing a composed demeanor, clear communication, and unwavering honesty, you lay the groundwork for a just outcome that supports your family's well-being. Embrace these strategies with confidence, knowing that your commitment to these values can lead to positive, lasting changes in your life and the lives of your children.

Key Takeaways:

- **Thorough Preparation**: Review all evidence, communications, and past behaviors related to the case. Understanding the patterns and key facts helps in structuring a compelling narrative and preparing for potential counterarguments.

- **Create a Detailed Timeline**: Organize events and key facts in a chronological framework. This helps in presenting a coherent narrative, reinforcing the story's structure, and addressing inconsistencies in opposing testimonies.

- **Consult Experts**: Work with experts to understand the emotional and psychological aspects relevant to the case. Their insights assist in crafting a narrative that effectively highlights the impacts of specific behaviors and supports your arguments.

- **Structured Narrative**: Develop a clear, logical storyline that integrates key facts and evidence. Use this structure to guide the presentation and make the case easier for the judge and jury to follow.

- **Link Evidence Effectively**: Align each piece of evidence with specific points in your narrative. Explicitly state how the evidence supports the storyline to reinforce the case's coherence and persuasiveness.

- **Demonstrate Emotional Impact**: Identify and highlight facts with emotional weight that naturally elicit responses. Present these facts clearly to enhance the emotional appeal of the narrative without straying into manipulation.

- **Address Counter-Narratives**: Prepare to counter opposing arguments by documenting their recurring themes and manipulative tactics. Use evidence to dismantle their narrative and maintain control over the case's storyline.

- **Maintain Testimonial Integrity**: Testify with composure, clarity, and honesty. These qualities build credibility and make your testimony more persuasive, significantly impacting the case's outcome.

- **Mental and Factual Readiness**: Mentally prepare by observing court proceedings and practicing testimony. Ensure factual accuracy by thoroughly reviewing relevant documents and details with your attorney.

- **Avoid Diagnostic Labels**: Focus on describing specific behaviors and their impacts rather than labeling the other party with psychological terms. This approach avoids potential bias and keeps the court focused on factual evidence.

- **Use Expert Testimony**: If relevant, present psychological evaluations or assessments conducted by licensed professionals. This provides credible, formal insights that support your case within the legal framework.

- **Maintain Professionalism**: Stay composed and professional throughout the proceedings. Avoid emotional reactions and focus on systematically presenting facts and addressing inconsistencies to maintain credibility and effectiveness.

6

MAINTAINING YOUR MENTAL HEALTH

The importance of maintaining mental health during and after legal disputes cannot be overstated. Legal disputes, particularly those involving personal matters such as divorce or custody, are inherently stressful and can take a significant toll on an individual's psychological well-being. The strain of navigating the legal system, the uncertainty of outcomes, and the potential changes to one's life and identity can lead to increased anxiety, stress, and, in some cases, depression.

During a legal dispute, individuals are often required to make critical decisions that can have long-lasting effects on their lives and the lives of others involved. The capacity to make these decisions in a clear-headed and informed manner is heavily dependent on one's mental health. Stress and anxiety can cloud judgment, impair decision-making, and lead to choices that may not be in the best interests of all parties involved.

Furthermore, the aftermath of legal disputes can also pose challenges for mental health. Regardless of the outcome, the adjustment to new circumstances or continued uncertainties can perpetuate stress and affect emotional stability. This is why it's crucial to prioritize mental health and seek appropriate support throughout the process.

Maintaining strong mental health provides a foundation for resilience, enabling individuals to better cope with the stresses of legal conflicts, recover more quickly from setbacks, and move forward more effectively once the dispute is resolved. It also supports better outcomes in the legal process itself, as well-prepared individuals are more likely to engage constructively in negotiations and advocate effectively for their interests. Ultimately, prioritizing mental health is not only essential for personal well-being but also a strategic aspect of navigating legal disputes successfully.

Understanding Stress and Its Impact

Stress is an inherent response to challenging or threatening situations, and legal battles can be significant sources of such stress due to their often unpredictable, extended, and personal nature. The impact of stress is not limited to one's emotional state; it affects both the mind and the body, leading to a range of symptoms and long-term consequences if not properly managed.

Impact on the Mind

In the context of legal disputes, stress can lead to decreased concentration, impaired judgment, and difficulty in making decisions. The pressure of ongoing legal proceedings can cause increased anxiety, feelings of overwhelm, and in some cases, depression. These mental effects can make it challenging for individuals to process information effectively, communicate their needs clearly, and make rational decisions – critical capabilities in legal settings.

Impact on the Body

Physically, the stress of legal conflicts can manifest in numerous ways. Common symptoms include headaches, fatigue, sleep disturbances, and changes in appetite. Stress can also exacerbate chronic health problems such as hypertension and heart disease. The prolonged release of stress hormones like cortisol and adrenaline, a typical response to chronic stress, can lead to more serious health issues, including a weakened immune system, increased risk of heart disease, and gastrointestinal problems.

Long-Term Consequences

If not addressed, the chronic stress from ongoing legal disputes can lead to long-term psychological and physical health issues. Psychologically, this might manifest as post-traumatic stress disorder (PTSD), long-term anxiety disorders, or chronic depression. Physically, prolonged stress can lead to serious conditions like heart disease, diabetes, and various autoimmune disorders.

Understanding these impacts is crucial for anyone involved in a legal battle. Recognizing the symptoms of stress and taking proactive steps to manage it can not only improve your immediate well-being but also enhance your ability to effectively navigate the legal process and mitigate the long-term health consequences associated with chronic stress.

Basics of Mental Health Care

Maintaining mental health during intense periods such as legal disputes requires basic yet essential care strategies that are often overlooked. Establishing a routine of fundamental mental health practices is critical for sustaining well-being and ensuring that one can handle the stresses of legal challenges effectively:

- **Sleep:** Adequate sleep is fundamental to mental health care. Sleep helps to repair and restore the brain, consolidating memories and processing the day's events. Lack of sleep can exacerbate stress, impair cognitive functions, and reduce one's ability to manage emotions effectively. Adults should aim for 7-9 hours of quality sleep per night, establishing a consistent bedtime and wake-up schedule even under stress.

- **Nutrition:** Good nutrition plays a crucial role in mental health. Foods that are high in vitamins, minerals, and antioxidants nourish the brain and protect it from oxidative stress – the waste (free radicals) produced when the body uses oxygen, which can damage cells. Reducing intake of processed foods and sugars while increasing consumption of whole grains, lean proteins, and a variety of fruits and vegetables can significantly impact one's mood and energy levels.

- **Physical activity:** Regular physical activity is highly effective in reducing symptoms of depression and anxiety. Exercise releases endorphins, often known as "feel-good" hormones, which act as natural painkillers and mood lifters. Activities need not be overly strenuous; even daily walks or light jogging can provide significant benefits.

- **Hydration:** Staying hydrated is often neglected in discussions about mental health. Dehydration can lead to fatigue, irritability, and difficulty concentrating. Drinking adequate amounts of water is vital for cognitive function and overall physical health.

- **Routine medical care:** Regular check-ups and discussions with healthcare providers about mental health are crucial, especially when dealing with ongoing stress. Healthcare professionals can offer guidance, support, and sometimes medication management that can help individuals manage their mental health effectively during challenging times.

By adhering to these basic mental health care principles, individuals facing legal disputes can better manage their stress and maintain their well-being throughout the process. This foundational care is essential not only for enduring the pressures of the legal environment but also for emerging from it with one's mental and physical health intact.

The Central Importance of Mental Health in Family Court Disputes Involving HCPs

Fighting an HCP ex in family court presents unique and significant challenges that can heavily strain one's mental health. The unpredictable, often manipulative behavior exhibited by HCPs can lead to increased stress, anxiety, and emotional turmoil. Maintaining robust mental health in such situations is not merely beneficial – it is essential for a number of reasons:

1. **Emotional resilience:** Engaging with a high-conflict or narcissistic individual in a legal setting requires a high degree of emotional resilience. HCPs often use psychological tactics such as gaslighting, emotional manipulation, and relentless criticism to unsettle their opponents. A strong mental state helps individuals recognize and effectively counter these tactics without being emotionally overwhelmed, enabling them to stay focused on their legal goals.

2. **Clear decision-making:** Family court decisions often have long-lasting impacts on personal and familial relationships. High mental health status ensures that decisions are made based on rational thought and thorough consideration, rather than being reactionary responses to the HCP's provocations. Mental clarity is crucial to evaluate the implications of legal choices and to strategize effectively.

3. **Effective communication:** Communicating effectively in court and with legal counsel is vital. Good mental health

supports clarity of expression, aids in articulating one's needs and arguments coherently, and helps maintain composure in the courtroom. This is particularly important when presenting oneself as a credible and reliable party in custody and other family-related disputes.

4. **Long-term well-being:** The strain of legal battles with a narcissistic individual can have enduring effects on one's mental and emotional well-being. Prioritizing mental health not only supports individuals through the duration of the court proceedings but also aids in the recovery process afterward, promoting healing and allowing for a healthier post-dispute life. It is imperative to remember that your mental health directly influences who you are and how you present yourself in court. Essentially, your psychological well-being is not just a shield that protects you – it is one of your strongest defenses and a compelling argument for your case.

5. **Your mental state as your defense:** Your ability to maintain composure, respond calmly to provocations, and display rational thinking under stress are key indicators of your capability and stability, especially in custody disputes. Judges often consider the emotional and psychological demeanor of the parties as a significant factor in their decisions. A well-maintained mental state demonstrates to the court your capability to handle stressful situations and make sound decisions, which are critical traits of a responsible caretaker.

6. **Demonstrating your capability:** Beyond merely defending against the HCP's tactics, your mental health reflects your overall capability to manage the responsibilities of life, including parenting and managing relationships. It shows that you are not just reacting to the immediate pressures of the court proceedings but are also preparing for the long-term welfare of your family. By prioritizing and demonstrating good mental health, you underscore your commitment to creating and maintaining a stable environment for your children.

7. **Credibility and reliability:** Parties who can manage their mental health effectively often appear more credible and reliable. This is particularly important in legal settings where the impressions and judgments of court officials can determine the outcome of the case. Your mental health can either bolster or undermine your credibility; therefore, showing that you are emotionally and mentally stable is paramount.

Your mental health is more than just a personal asset – it is a strategic element of your legal defense and advocacy. Mental health is not peripheral but central to successfully managing and emerging from family court disputes involving narcissistic individuals. It empowers resilience, fosters clear decision-making, enhances communication, and preserves long-term well-being, each of which is crucial in these challenging situations.

How you manage and maintain your mental health speaks volumes about your character and ability to handle parenting or other responsibilities. Thus, investing in your mental health is not only a means of personal preservation but also a critical strategy to ensure that you present the strongest possible case in court.

Advanced Coping Mechanisms

Managing the complexities of legal disputes, especially in family court, can be a major source of stress and anxiety. It's crucial to employ advanced coping mechanisms that go beyond basic self-care to effectively manage these feelings and maintain mental equilibrium. Consider the following techniques, which have been proven to help individuals handle stress and anxiety more effectively.

Mindfulness and Meditation: Mindfulness involves maintaining a moment-by-moment awareness of our thoughts, feelings, bodily sensations, and surrounding environment. Meditation, a practice often used to develop mindfulness, involves techniques such as focusing on breath or a mantra, which helps in reducing racing thoughts and bringing about a state of calm and focus. Regular meditation has been shown to decrease stress and anxiety levels by enhancing emotional flexibility and promoting a greater capacity for dealing with unpredictable and stressful situations.

Cognitive Behavioral Therapy (CBT): CBT is a form of psychotherapy that helps individuals manage their problems by changing the way they think and behave. It's particularly effective in treating anxiety, as it encourages a more balanced and less fearful outlook on life. CBT involves identifying negative or false beliefs and testing or restructuring them in a more realistic and positive manner. For individuals involved in family court disputes, CBT can be instrumental in challenging catastrophic thoughts about the proceedings and outcomes, thus reducing anxiety.

Progressive Muscle Relaxation (PMR): PMR is another technique useful in managing stress and anxiety. It involves tensing and then relaxing different muscle groups in the body. This practice promotes awareness of physical sensations and can develop a deep sense of relaxation throughout the body, which can counter the stress response that is often triggered in high-stakes environments like courtrooms.

Incorporating these advanced coping mechanisms into your daily routine can significantly bolster your ability to manage stress and anxiety, ensuring that you remain composed and resilient throughout your legal journey. These techniques not only aid in personal well-being but also empower you to handle legal challenges with a clearer mind and a more balanced perspective.

Polyvagal Theory and Its Implications

Polyvagal Theory, developed by Dr. Stephen Porges, offers a revolutionary perspective on how the autonomic nervous system mediates the body's response to stress and trauma.

This theory is particularly relevant in understanding the physiological underpinnings of reactions during high-conflict situations, such as those encountered in family court disputes involving narcissistic behaviors.

Understanding Polyvagal Theory

Polyvagal Theory introduces the concept of the vagus nerve being instrumental in controlling the heart rate and managing the fight, flight, or freeze responses. The theory posits that there are three distinct states of nervous system response:

- Social engagement system (ventral vagal state): A calm state where social communication and bonding occur.

- Sympathetic arousal system (fight or flight): Activated during stress or threats.

- Dorsal vagal state (freeze): A state of disassociation or shutdown experienced during overwhelming stress.

Relevance to High-Conflict Family Court Situations

In the high-stress environment of family court, particularly when battling an HCP, it's essential to understand the body's physiological responses to stress. High-conflict or narcissistic behavior can provoke defensive reactions such as fight-or-flight responses or even a dissociative state. Recognizing these reactions as normal can empower individuals to manage their stress more effectively and maintain composure during court proceedings.

Applying Polyvagal Theory in these situations involves activating the social engagement system to mitigate stress responses. This can be achieved through various techniques that promote relaxation and emotional regulation. For instance, engaging in deep, rhythmic breathing helps transition the body from a heightened state of arousal to a more relaxed state.

Practicing mindful awareness allows individuals to become attuned to their physical sensations, effectively reducing the intensity of stress reactions. Additionally, participating in brief, positive social interactions prior to court can further activate the social engagement system, fostering a sense of safety and calm. By employing these strategies, individuals can enhance their ability to navigate the challenges of family court with greater resilience.

By understanding and applying the insights from Polyvagal Theory, individuals can better prepare themselves to face an HCP in court. Techniques that stimulate the ventral vagal complex can help maintain a state of calm and assertiveness, enabling clearer thinking and more effective communication. This approach not only aids in personal stress management but also enhances one's ability to present a composed and focused argument in court.

Polyvagal Theory provides a valuable framework for understanding and managing the physical and emotional responses to the high stress of family court proceedings. This understanding is crucial for those involved in disputes with high-conflict or narcissistic individuals, offering strategies that support maintaining equilibrium and protecting one's mental health during such challenging times.

Dealing with Triggers and Flashbacks

Dealing with triggers and flashbacks is crucial for managing mental health, particularly in the high-stress context of family court disputes involving an HCP. Individuals often find that engagement with a high-conflict or narcissistic ex-partner, who may have been the source of past traumatic experiences, can intensively reignite emotional turmoil. The very nature of family court proceedings – discussing personal matters, revisiting past events, and confronting the narcissist – can bring these painful memories to the forefront. Identifying triggers (specific words, tones, or behaviors that provoke a deep emotional response) is the first step in managing this reaction.

Once triggers are identified, individuals can develop strategies to manage flashbacks or intense emotions effectively. Techniques like grounding exercises, mindfulness, and controlled breathing can help maintain emotional stability by anchoring the person in the present and mitigating the impact of past traumas re-emerging during court interactions. Such proactive management is essential for navigating the emotional challenges of legal disputes with resilience and composure.

Identifying Triggers:

Triggers are specific stimuli that elicit a strong emotional response, often because they subconsciously remind an individual of past trauma. In the context of family court disputes, triggers could be certain dates, places, phrases, or behaviors that are associated with unpleasant memories of the proceedings or the relationship with a high-conflict or narcissistic ex-partner. Seeing an email from a former spouse or hearing certain phrases that were used during your relationship can act as triggers.

Recognizing these triggers involves a heightened awareness of one's emotional responses and the circumstances that precede them. Keeping a journal can be a helpful way to document and identify patterns related to emotional upheavals. Over time, reviewing this journal can reveal patterns and specific triggers, making them easier to anticipate and manage.

Additionally, therapy sessions can provide a guided approach to uncovering these triggers, allowing for more targeted coping strategies to be developed in a supportive environment.

Recognizing and understanding your triggers is the first crucial step toward regaining control over your emotional reactions and maintaining your mental health during challenging times.

Managing Flashbacks:

Flashbacks are vivid, often intrusive, recollections of past traumatic events. They can be triggered by reminders of the event and may make an individual feel as though they are reliving the traumatic experience.

Managing flashbacks, particularly for those involved in stressful legal disputes like family court, requires effective strategies to mitigate their impact and regain emotional control. Flashbacks are intense, often vivid recollections of past trauma that feel as though they are happening in the present. They can be triggered by reminders of the trauma, which are common in settings that involve revisiting past conflicts, such as legal testimonies or interactions with an ex-partner.

To manage flashbacks effectively, grounding techniques are highly recommended. These methods help individuals detach from the flashback and return to the present moment. Techniques such as the "5-4-3-2-1" coping strategy involve focusing on immediate sensory experiences: naming five things you can see, four things you can touch, three things you can hear, two things you can smell, and one thing you can taste.

Additionally, deep, controlled breathing exercises can help calm the nervous system and reduce the physiological symptoms associated with flashbacks. Regular practice of mindfulness meditation can also strengthen an individual's ability to remain anchored in the present, reducing the frequency and intensity of flashbacks over time.

Techniques for Dealing with Triggers and Flashbacks

1. Grounding Techniques:

Grounding techniques are practical strategies that help individuals reconnect with the present moment, particularly during episodes of anxiety or distress, such as flashbacks. The purpose of these techniques is to anchor oneself in the here and now, diverting attention away from distressing thoughts or memories.

One effective method is the "5-4-3-2-1" technique, which engages the senses to bring awareness back to the current environment. Here's how it works:

- **Five things you can see**: Look around and identify five distinct objects. This could be anything from the color of the walls to specific items on a table. By focusing your eyes on your surroundings, you pull your attention away from your internal distress.

- **Four things you can touch**: Notice the sensation of physical objects around you. This could include feeling the texture of your clothing, the coolness of a metal chair, or the warmth of your hands. Engaging your sense of touch helps ground you in reality.

- **Three things you can hear**: Listen carefully to the sounds in your environment. This might include the rustling of papers, distant conversations, or the hum of a heater. Identifying sounds diverts your focus from intrusive thoughts.

- **Two things you can smell**: If you are in a place where you can smell something, focus on two distinct scents. If you can't identify any scents in your immediate area, consider the memory of two scents that you enjoy.

- **One thing you can taste**: This could be a sip of water or even the lingering taste of food. If you don't have anything to taste, reflect on a favorite food or drink that brings you comfort.

These grounding techniques not only help to diffuse immediate anxiety but also cultivate a habit of mindfulness, allowing individuals to strengthen their capacity to manage distressing situations over time.

2. Controlled Breathing:

Controlled breathing techniques are designed to help regulate the body's stress response by calming the nervous system. When faced with anxiety, the body often enters a heightened state of alertness, triggering the 'fight or flight' response. By practicing controlled breathing, individuals can mitigate these symptoms and regain a sense of calm.

One commonly used method is diaphragmatic breathing, which involves engaging the diaphragm for deeper breaths. Here's how to practice it:

- **Find a comfortable position**: Sit or lie down in a quiet space where you can focus without distractions.

- **Place one hand on your chest and the other on your abdomen**: This helps you monitor where your breath is coming from.

- **Inhale deeply through your nose**: Allow your abdomen (not your chest) to rise as you fill your lungs with air. Aim for a count of four while inhaling.

- **Pause for a moment**: Hold your breath for a count of two.

- **Exhale slowly through your mouth**: Let your abdomen fall as you breathe out. Aim for a count of six to eight during the exhale. This extended exhalation helps activate the body's relaxation response.

- **Repeat**: Continue this cycle for several minutes, focusing on the sensation of your breath and allowing any thoughts to drift away.

Practicing controlled breathing regularly can lower baseline stress levels and improve emotional regulation, making it easier to handle stressful situations like family court disputes.

3. Seeking Professional Help:

Seeking professional help is an essential step for anyone struggling with the emotional fallout of legal disputes, particularly when dealing with trauma or high-conflict individuals like narcissistic ex-partners. Mental health professionals can provide invaluable support through tailored strategies and therapeutic interventions.

Therapeutic approaches such as Eye Movement Desensitization and Reprocessing (EMDR) and trauma-focused cognitive behavioral therapy (TF-CBT) are particularly effective for individuals experiencing flashbacks or intense emotional distress.

- **EMDR**: This therapy is designed to help individuals process and integrate traumatic memories. During EMDR sessions, clients are guided through a series of eye movements while recalling distressing events. This process can help reduce the emotional charge associated with those memories, allowing individuals to reframe their experiences and lessen their impact.

- **Trauma-Focused Cognitive Behavioral Therapy (TF-CBT)**: TF-CBT combines traditional cognitive behavioral techniques with trauma-informed care. This approach helps individuals understand how their thoughts, feelings, and behaviors are interconnected, allowing them to challenge negative thought patterns and develop healthier coping mechanisms.

By engaging with a mental health professional, individuals can receive personalized strategies to manage their specific challenges, build resilience, and improve their overall mental health. Therapy can also offer a safe space for expressing feelings, processing trauma, and developing a deeper understanding of one's emotional responses.

Ultimately, seeking professional help reinforces the idea that maintaining mental health is not just about coping; it's about thriving despite the challenges presented by legal disputes and personal conflicts.

Preventing Intense Emotional Reactions

To prevent intense emotional reactions, it is important to establish a routine that includes regular self-care practices, setting boundaries in relationships, and possibly modifying environments to avoid known triggers. Techniques such as mindfulness meditation and regular physical activity can also help increase emotional resilience.

Setting clear boundaries in personal interactions, especially with individuals related to past traumas such as a contentious ex-partner, is also vital. This might involve specifying limited topics of conversation, using communication methods that provide emotional distance (like texts or emails), and having set times for interactions.

Additionally, modifying environments to avoid known triggers, such as changing routines that overlap with past traumatic experiences, can help in managing emotional responses. Integrating mindfulness techniques into daily routines enhances awareness of emotional states and facilitates a calmer response to potential triggers. These combined efforts help individuals avoid overwhelming emotional reactions and maintain composure, especially critical during legal disputes where emotional control can significantly impact outcomes.

Managing triggers and flashbacks is essential for individuals navigating high-stress environments like family court disputes. By employing these strategies, individuals can achieve a greater sense of control over their emotional responses, enhancing their overall well-being and ability to engage effectively in their legal and personal lives.

Planning for the Future

Planning for the future after a high-conflict family court case is essential for long-term well-being and success. As individuals transition out of litigation, they often find themselves at a pivotal moment, needing to redefine their lives beyond the legal battles.

Effective post-litigation planning encompasses strategies that promote healing and personal growth. Setting new personal and professional goals is crucial, as it helps shift focus from past conflicts to future opportunities, providing motivation and direction. Additionally, discovering a renewed sense of purpose through community involvement or volunteer work can enrich personal development and foster a supportive network.

Financial stability is another key consideration; creating a comprehensive financial plan with the help of an advisor ensures that individuals manage any economic impacts from the dispute and prioritize future security. Emotional recovery is equally important, involving continued therapy, reconnecting with loved ones, and building new supportive relationships.

By concentrating on these areas, individuals can transform a challenging period into a time for significant growth and new beginnings, paving the way for a fulfilling and stable future.

Bolstering Your Case with Parallel Parenting

In high-conflict family court cases, especially those involving a narcissistic ex-partner, traditional co-parenting can often be challenging, if not impossible. Parallel parenting emerges as a practical solution in these scenarios, offering a structured method of parenting that minimizes conflict and interaction between ex-partners while maintaining each parent's active involvement in their children's lives. This approach can not only provide a stable environment for the children but also help you build a strong case and defense in court by demonstrating a commitment to the child's welfare despite personal differences.

Parallel parenting is designed for situations where interpersonal conflict between the parents could potentially harm the child's well-being. It involves each parent taking on the responsibility of parenting the child during their designated times without interference from the other parent. This arrangement minimizes direct communication, with most interactions occurring through written means like emails or through legal or medical professionals when necessary. The key is each parent operates independently of the other, which significantly reduces opportunities for conflicts and stress.

Benefits of Parallel Parenting in a Legal Context

Parallel parenting offers a structured approach that minimizes conflict while supporting the independent roles of each parent. In the context of family court disputes, especially those involving complex emotional dynamics, it can be a strategic choice that supports your case and defense. By demonstrating a structured, child-focused approach to parenting, you not only protect your children from ongoing conflict but also present yourself as a responsible, proactive parent dedicated to the well-being of your children. This method underscores a commitment to stability and health in the parenting environment, qualities that are highly regarded in family court proceedings.

One of the notable advantages of parallel parenting is the clear delineation it provides between the environments in each parent's home. This separation can significantly aid in the presentation of your case and evidence, offering a straightforward comparison that can highlight the differences between a healthy, supportive home environment and one that may have issues.

Other primary benefits of Parallel Parenting include:

- **Reduces emotional volatility:** By limiting direct contact and communication, parallel parenting shields both the children and the parents from the emotional upheavals that often accompany interactions with a high-conflict ex-partner. This stability can be a critical point in your favor during court proceedings, as it shows a commitment to prioritizing the emotional and psychological health of the children.

- **Clear boundaries and rules:** Parallel parenting requires clear and detailed parenting plans. These plans typically outline decision-making protocols, schedules, and handling of extracurricular activities, which helps prevent disputes. Having such detailed agreements in place can demonstrate to the court that you are a proactive and organized parent who has thoughtfully considered the logistics of parenting post-separation.

- **Focus on child's welfare:** This parenting style keeps the focus squarely on the child's welfare, rather than the parental disagreements. Courts favor arrangements that safeguard the children's interests; showing that you can effectively manage your parental responsibilities independently of your personal feelings towards the other parent can greatly influence the court's perception of your suitability as a custodial parent.

- **Clarity in presentation:** Parallel parenting plans create distinct boundaries between the parental roles and responsibilities, which in turn, makes it easier to document and present specific instances or patterns that occur under each parent's care. For example, if one parent consistently maintains a nurturing and stable environment, while the other's home has regular instances of neglect or instability, these differences become stark and easier to document and demonstrate in court.

- **Evidence-based comparisons:** In legal settings, especially those involving custody disputes, judges rely heavily on evidence to make informed decisions. Parallel parenting arrangements facilitate the accumulation of evidence in segregated contexts. Each parent's ability to independently manage their time with the child means that the court can directly observe the outcomes of each environment on the child's well-being. For instance, school reports, medical records, or psychological evaluations can be specifically attributed to the time spent with each parent, making it easier to link the child's progress or challenges directly to specific parental influences.

- **Simplifying witness testimonies:** When third parties like teachers, doctors, or family friends testify, the structure provided by parallel parenting allows them to clearly associate their observations with specific contexts. For example, a teacher might note improvements in a child's behavior or academic performance correlating with time spent in one parent's care versus the other. This makes witness testimonies not only more impactful but also more straightforward for the court to interpret.

- **Objective assessment of parenting:** The segmented nature of parallel parenting inherently promotes an objective assessment of each parent's suitability and effectiveness. It diminishes the potential for conflicts or biases that might arise from overlapping responsibilities and interactions in more intertwined co-parenting setups. This clarity allows the court to assess which environment is more beneficial for the child's development, safety, and happiness.

The independent and separate structures inherent in parallel parenting not only simplify the management of day-to-day parenting tasks but also enhance the clarity and effectiveness of legal arguments in family court. By providing a framework that clearly delineates responsibilities and outcomes associated with each parent, parallel parenting setups enable a more straightforward presentation of evidence and a clearer narrative in court. This can be crucial in cases where demonstrating a stark contrast between the environments provided by each parent is essential to the well-being of the child.

Conclusion: Maintaining Your Mental Health in Family Court

Navigating legal disputes, especially family court matters such as custody or divorce, can profoundly impact one's mental health. The stress and anxiety associated with these conflicts can impair decision-making, affect physical health, and lead to long-term psychological issues if not managed effectively. Understanding the effects of stress on both mind and body, and implementing strategies for mental health care, is crucial for maintaining well-being throughout the legal process.

Prioritizing mental health is not only essential for personal resilience but also enhances one's ability to handle legal challenges constructively. By incorporating both basic self-care practices and advanced coping mechanisms, individuals can better manage stress and emotional responses. Additionally, planning for the future, including setting new goals and rebuilding social connections, is vital for long-term recovery and growth. Ultimately, a proactive approach to mental health supports not just survival through legal disputes but also fosters a healthier and more balanced life beyond them.

Key Takeaways:
- **Significant Stress Impact:** Legal disputes, particularly personal ones like divorce or custody cases, can cause substantial psychological stress, potentially leading to anxiety, depression, and other mental health issues.

- **Decision-Making Impairment:** High stress can impair judgment and decision-making, affecting the quality of critical decisions made during legal proceedings.

- **Post-Dispute Adjustment:** The aftermath of legal disputes can continue to affect mental health, with ongoing stress from adjusting to new circumstances or uncertainties.

- **Mental Health as a Foundation:** Maintaining strong mental health is essential for resilience, effective decision-making, and overall well-being during and after legal conflicts.

- **Stress Impact on Mind:** Stress from legal battles can reduce concentration, impair judgment, and lead to feelings of overwhelm and depression.

- **Stress Impact on Body:** Chronic stress can cause physical symptoms such as headaches, fatigue, sleep disturbances, and exacerbate existing health conditions.

- **Long-Term Health Risks:** Prolonged stress may lead to severe long-term health issues, including PTSD, chronic anxiety, depression, and serious physical conditions like heart disease and diabetes.

- **Basic Mental Health Care:** Fundamental mental health practices, such as establishing a routine, are crucial for managing stress and maintaining well-being during legal disputes.

- **Advanced Coping Mechanisms:** Techniques such as mindfulness, physical activity, and professional therapy are essential for managing intense stress and maintaining mental equilibrium.

- **Polyvagal Theory:** Understanding Polyvagal Theory helps explain physiological stress responses and aids in managing stress by engaging the social engagement system.

- **Managing Triggers and Flashbacks:** Identifying and managing emotional triggers and flashbacks is important for maintaining stability during high-stress legal situations.

- **Future Planning:** Post-dispute planning, including setting new goals, finding new purpose, creating a financial plan, and rebuilding social connections, is key for long-term recovery and growth.

- **Reduced Conflict and Stability:** Parallel parenting limits direct interaction between ex-partners, minimizing emotional volatility and providing a stable environment for children, which strengthens your case in court.

- **Clear Boundaries and Evidence:** The structure of parallel parenting creates distinct boundaries between each parent's role, aiding in clear evidence collection and comparison of the child's well-being across homes.

- **Simplified Legal Presentation:** Parallel parenting facilitates straightforward presentation of evidence and witness testimonies by clearly defining each parent's responsibilities and outcomes, enhancing objective court assessments.

CONCLUSION: OVERCOMING HIGH-CONFLICT SITUATIONS

As we conclude this exploration into managing and overcoming high-conflict situations in family court, particularly those involving narcissistic dynamics, it is crucial to reflect on the journey we've undertaken together through this project. Let's review the key strategies we discussed and underscore the importance of adhering to one's core values and integrity as you face these formidable challenges.

Recap of Key Strategies

Throughout this project, we have delved into a variety of strategies designed to manage the complexities and the often emotionally charged nature of high-conflict legal disputes:

Understanding High-Conflict Behaviors

Gaining insight into high-conflict and narcissistic traits is crucial for anyone navigating a high-conflict situation. By familiarizing yourself with the typical patterns of manipulation, gaslighting, and emotional volatility associated with HCPs, you can better anticipate and prepare for interactions. This knowledge serves as a protective shield, allowing you to respond thoughtfully rather than react impulsively. Remember, awareness is your ally; it equips you to maintain your composure and strategically navigate difficult encounters.

Recognizing and Countering Manipulative Tactics

Recognizing and countering manipulative tactics is crucial when dealing with high-conflict individuals, especially those with narcissistic behaviors. Start by identifying specific manipulative behaviors, such as gaslighting or blame-shifting, and trust your instincts if something feels off. Document these instances to establish a pattern and respond assertively by sticking to the facts rather than getting drawn into emotional arguments. Set firm boundaries to protect yourself and disengage from toxic conversations when necessary. Surround yourself with supportive people who can help validate your experiences. By understanding and addressing manipulation strategically, you can maintain control over your emotional well-being and navigate high-conflict situations more confidently.

Effective Communication and Documentation

Clear and precise communication is essential in high-stakes legal disputes. By articulating your thoughts and feelings in an assertive yet respectful manner, you can reduce misunderstandings and foster a more productive dialogue. Coupled with meticulous documentation – keeping records of all communications, agreements, and incidents – you create a robust foundation for your case. This practice not only helps counter any potential distortions or accusations but also reinforces your credibility in court. Each note, each email, and each recorded interaction adds strength to your position, empowering you to present your truth confidently.

Legal Preparedness and Integrity

Thorough preparation is key to success in any legal proceeding. Familiarize yourself with relevant laws, gather necessary documents, and develop a clear strategy with your legal counsel. However, it's equally important to maintain integrity throughout the process. Upholding your values and ethical standards not only enhances your credibility but also reflects positively on your character in the eyes of the court. When your actions are aligned with your principles, you present yourself as a reliable and trustworthy individual, which can significantly influence the outcome of your case.

Mental Health and Emotional Resilience

The emotional toll of prolonged legal disputes can be daunting, making it essential to prioritize your mental health. Incorporate stress management techniques such as mindfulness, meditation, and physical activity into your routine to build resilience against anxiety and emotional upheaval. Seeking support through therapy or connecting with a network of friends and family can provide additional strength. Remember, taking care of your emotional well-being is not a luxury; it's a necessity. A strong, centered mindset will empower you to approach challenges with clarity and confidence, both in and out of the courtroom.

Parallel Parenting

For those facing custodial challenges with a narcissistic ex-partner, parallel parenting emerges as a constructive approach. This strategy allows both parents to engage with their children without direct contact, minimizing opportunities for conflict and manipulation. By establishing clear boundaries and routines, you can create a stable environment for your children while protecting your emotional well-being. Emphasizing the children's needs over personal disputes cultivates a healthier co-parenting dynamic, enabling you to focus on what truly matters – the well-being of your kids.

Staying True to Your Values and Maintaining Integrity

In the heat of legal battles, especially those laden with manipulation and deceit, there is a real risk of straying from one's moral compass. It is essential to remain steadfast in your values and maintain integrity.

This commitment not only upholds your self-respect and ethical standards but also resonates with court officials and all who are involved in your case. Judges and legal professionals often look favorably upon parties who demonstrate honesty, responsibility, and fairness, regardless of the provocations they face. Your integrity becomes your shield and your advocate, speaking volumes about your character and your capability as a parent or a guardian.

o those of you facing the daunting challenge of navigating high-conflict family court scenarios, remember you are not alone. Many have walked this path and emerged stronger, more resilient, and successful. While the journey may be fraught with challenges, your commitment to maintaining your integrity, protecting your mental health, and employing strategic legal and interpersonal tactics will be the keys to your success.

To this end, I invite you to take the next powerful step in your journey by diving into the official Mastery Workbook, the companion guide to Family Court Solutions (available on Amazon). This incredible resource is designed to help you apply the principles and strategies we've discussed, providing you with structured exercises, tools, and actionable insights to build your case effectively in family court.

By working through the Mastery Workbook, you'll reinforce your knowledge, enhance your preparation, and gain confidence as you traverse the unique challenges of facing off against a high-conflict opponent. It's not just a workbook; it's a transformative tool that will empower you to advocate for yourself and your children with clarity and strength.

In addition, I encourage you to embrace the support systems available to you, whether they be professional counsel, therapeutic resources, or support groups – like the thriving online community I created on Instagram (@UnapologeticParenting). Allow yourself to lean on these supports as you navigate through this turbulent time.

Embrace the support systems available to you, whether they be professional counsel, therapeutic resources, or community support groups. Allow yourself to lean on these supports as you navigate through this turbulent time.

Furthermore, take each day at a time. High-conflict disputes can be marathons, not sprints. Pace yourself, care for your health, and keep your long-term well-being in sight. Above all, remember that by staying true to your principles and focusing on the best outcomes for yourself and your children, you are already advocating powerfully for your future.

As you continue on your path, carry forward the strategies and insights gained from this project. Use them as tools to fortify your resilience, guide your actions, and inspire your journey towards a resolution that honors your values and aspirations. With persistence, patience, and integrity, you can navigate through and ultimately rise above the challenges of high-conflict legal disputes.

ABOUT THE AUTHOR

 Carl Knickerbocker is an award-winning lawyer and litigation attorney, renowned for his expertise as a national case-strategy consultant, co-parenting coach, and best-selling author. As a father of six in a blended family, Carl brings both personal experience and professional insight to the challenges of co-parenting and family law. He is the owner of The Law Office of Carl Knickerbocker, established in 2012, where he has dedicated himself to helping families navigate the complexities of legal disputes.

His book, *The Parallel Parenting Solution*, has achieved best-seller status in the divorce and family law categories for over two years, empowering thousands of families to transform their co-parenting lives. Carl is also the host of the Unapologetic Parenting podcast, where he shares valuable advice and support for parents facing high-conflict custody arrangements. With over 225,000 followers on Instagram's @unapologeticparenting, he has created a vibrant community focused on resilience and effective parenting strategies.

For those seeking personalized guidance, Carl offers coaching and consulting services tailored to the unique needs of families dealing with high-conflict family court battles and the difficulties of co-parenting with narcissistic exes. Whether you're navigating the intricacies of co-parenting, preparing for court, or looking to build a healthier family dynamic, Carl's expertise can help you achieve your goals.

To learn more about Carl's coaching and consulting services, visit carlknickerbockerlaw.com and discover how you can take the next step toward a more positive and effective co-parenting experience.

Made in the USA
Las Vegas, NV
09 December 2024

13673636R30203